M000233780

THE ANATOMY
OF ZUR-EN-ARRH

UNDERSTANDING GRANT MORRISON'S BATMAN

THE ANATOMY
OF ZUR-EN-ARRH

UNDERSTANDING GRANT MORRISON'S BATMAN

CODY WALKER

SEQUART ORGANIZATION   EDWARDSVILLE, ILLINOIS

The Anatomy of Zur-en-Arrh: Understanding Grant Morrison's Batman
by Cody Walker

Copyright © 2014 by the author. Batman and related characters are trademarks of DC Comics © 2014.

First edition, June 2014, ISBN 978-1-9405-8904-6.

All rights reserved. Except for brief excerpts used for review or scholarly purposes, no part of this book may be reproduced in any manner whatsoever, including electronic, without express consent of the publisher.

Cover by David A. Frizell. Book design by Julian Darius. Interior art is © DC Comics; please visit dccomics.com.

Published by Sequart Organization. Edited by Samantha Atzeni, Scott Cederlund, Julian Darius, Glen Downey, Benjamin Hall, Mark J. Hayman, Tonio Hubilla, Steven King, Greg Matiasevich, Simon McDonald, Markisan Naso, Richard Pachter, Mike Phillips, and Patrick Wilson.

For more information about other titles in this series, visit sequart.org/books.

Contents

Introduction

Many fans have a definition of what Batman can and can't be. For some, Batman is the Dark Knight: a vengeance-seeking brawler who dwells in darkness. For others, Batman is the Caped Crusader – a bright, colorful super-hero. Batman can fit into any genre imaginable, so why do so many fans have a strict definition of what is and what isn't when it comes to Batman? Perhaps the problem is continuity.

Fans want comics that harken back to the comics they enjoyed because these ideas are familiar. Comic readers of the '60s believe that Batman is a bright and shining "Caped Crusader," while readers of the 80s' see him as a "Dark Knight" of vengeance. Different writers use references to continuity to touch that sweet spot of nostalgia so readers can connect with that idea they loved. Batman is a character that allows for detective stories, far-out super-hero tales, supernatural horror stories and much more. Yet some insist that Batman can only be used in one type of story, because a certain type of continuity worked for them and they believe it's the only one that matters. And when the paradigm shifts from one interpretation of what Batman can be to another, some continuity is deemed no longer necessary and is quietly forgotten.

But Grant Morrison did the impossible.

Over the course of his seven-year tenure with Batman, Morrison's modus operandi was that every Batman story ever told matters. Instead of ignoring the more bizarre parts of Batman's continuity, Morrison embraced them and created a whole new era for the character; an era defined by incorporating the absurd while still maintaining the character's integrity. Under Morrison's pen, Batman battled the Devil, traveled through time, and funded a corporation of international super-heroes. Each story was more bizarre than the next, but all of them illuminated some part of Batman's persona.

In Jim Beard's book, *Gotham City 14 Miles*, Beard uses characteristics of Michael L. Fleisher's *The Encyclopedia of Comic Book Heroes Vol. 1: Batman* (Collier, 1976) and Robert Greenberger's *The Essential Batman Encyclopedia* (Ballantine, 2008) to create a list of five criteria for what is essentially Batman. They are:

1. Batman is Bruce Wayne.
2. Bruce Wayne's parents were murdered when he was a boy, inspiring him to become a crimefighter.
3. Bruce Wayne dresses in a bat costume and calls himself Batman to fight crime.
4. Batman's mental and physical powers are at the peak of human capability.
5. Batman is an inventor who has created many devices and vehicles to aid him in his crimefighting.

Not only does Grant Morrison's Batman meet the criteria of Beard's list, he openly challenges the list in places and tests the limits of what can be a Batman story.

Batman is Bruce Wayne. Except when Dick Grayson is Batman. Or when Damian Wayne is Batman. Or when Terry McGinnis is Batman. Yes, Bruce Wayne is Batman, but Batman is more than just Bruce Wayne. Batman is an idea, a magic sigil that is so purely enmeshed with the concept of justice that the two cannot be separated.

Bruce Wayne's parents were murdered when he was a boy, inspiring him to become a crimefighter. Yes, but without an old, dying bat flying into his window, there would be no Batman. The bat is as essential as the deaths of Bruce Wayne's parents. And beyond the bat is the mythology surrounding the bat; by wearing the bat-symbol, Batman channels Barbatos, an aspect of the evil god Darkseid.

Bruce Wayne dresses in a bat costume and calls himself Batman to fight crime. This is somewhat redundant given the first point and the same arguments can be made. When Dick Grayson takes up the Batman mantle in the pages of *Batman and Robin*, it is no less of a Batman story. Bruce Wayne may be more comfortable as Batman, but Dick Grayson is no less of a Batman.

Furthermore, *anyone* who wears the sigil of the bat becomes Batman – as Commissioner Gordon finds out in *Batman, Inc.* Vol. 1 #6.

Batman's mental and physical powers are at the peak of human capability. Grant Morrison puts Batman through tests unlike any other writer. When Batman's identity has been stripped away, Bruce Wayne's mind falls into a backup personality known as "the Batman of Zur-En-Arrh." In *Batman: The Return of Bruce Wayne,* Morrison takes everything from Bruce Wayne and shows that Bruce's detective skills and survival instincts are at their peak to ensure victory.

Batman is an inventor who has created many devices and vehicles to aid him in his crimefighting. In *Batman, Inc.*, the hero uses his immense wealth to fund an international corporation of super-heroes to show off his gadgets.

Morrison's run shows how all five critera are usually true, but he also expands several of them. However, I would argue for two more criteria:

6. Batman is never alone.
7. Batman does the impossible.

Even in his darkest moments, *Batman is never alone*. When Bruce Wayne's parents were taken from him, he created a surrogate family, the numbers of which have fluctuated over the years.

Batman does the impossible. Super-villain deathtraps can't stop Batman and neither can the Devil, nor a trip through time.

No other writer in the history of Batman has tested his limits and found them to be so limitless. Grant Morrison has shown that Batman is everywhere and can be anything. So for readers used to a more down-to-earth approach to the World's Greatest Detective, Batman shooting a god of death with a cosmic bullet that is the blueprint for all bullets ever may seem bizarre, but Morrison makes it work.

Grant Morrison can do the impossible.

Grant Morrison is Batman.

Before *Batman*

Batman Vol. 1 #655 (Sept 2006) began Grant Morrison's extended run on the character, but it wasn't his first work with the character.[1] Morrison's previous encounters with Batman were sometimes of a very different tone than his later, extended statement about the character. One can, however, find remarkable consistency beneath the surface, as well as common themes.

Batman: Arkham Asylum

Grant Morrison's first work with Batman (published in 1989) may not seem to have a lot in common with his later tenure on the title *Batman*. After all, *Arkham Asylum* is self-contained, with little to no true references to past continuity save for the already-established villains, whereas *Batman* revels in referencing past events. *Batman* is an action-packed, super-hero title that begins with the more or less traditional art of Andy Kubert, whereas *Arkham Asylum*'s art by the incomparable Dave McKean is more experimental and cerebral. *Batman* is a monthly comic and had requirements to fulfill (like adhering to continuity and presenting Batman and his villains in a traditional manner) that a 128-page original graphic novel doesn't have to. According to Morrison (in the 15th anniversary edition of *Arkham Asylum*), "the intention was to create something that was more like a piece of music or an experimental film than a typical adventure comic book."

---

[1] Cover dates, like the one given here, will normally be excluded from this book. Instead, a quick reference has been provided in the form of an appendix, listing each comic of Morrison's run, along with cover dates and other information.

Although the two works are very different animals, *Arkham Asylum* is still essential to understanding Morrison's *Batman* because of the statements it makes on identity.

When reading *Arkham Asylum*, perhaps it's best to think of it in terms of what Morrison calls "the real page," on which Bruce wakes up and feels at peace. When the graphic novel is approached from the angle that it's a process of Bruce repairing his mind and discovering something new about himself, the narrative must be read as a highly symbolic experience where each character is a clue toward something important within Batman's mind. Timothy Callahan's *Grant Morrison: The Early Years* (Sequart, 2007) has already done an exemplary job in exploring the symbols present in the graphic novel, but there are some ideas worth revisiting when compared to Morrison's *Batman*.

Throughout Morrison's various Batman stories, Batman's speech bubbles change colors which are meant to reflect the state of Batman's identity. Normally, Batman's dialogue is colored like anyone else's, but in *Arkham Asylum* it has been reversed, with white text on a black background. In Morrison's *Batman,* during the "R.I.P." storyline (issues #676-681), Batman's text is white on blue when he assumes the identity of the Batman of Zur-en-Arrh, the savage persona of Bruce's subconscious that triggers when his mind is overwhelmed by psychological trauma (*Batman* #678). In *Arkham Asylum*, the Joker has red text without speech bubbles surrounding it, and the lettering looks scratchy in order to make it difficult to read at times. The Joker's insanity comes through even in the way the text *looks* not just in the words he says. In "R.I.P." the Joker's dialogue is white on a green background to emphasize the transformation he had undergone in *Batman* #663 to become the Clown at Midnight persona.

For Batman, the white-on-black text in *Arkham Asylum* evokes a much darker, far more frightening Batman. This is further emphasized by the fact that Bruce Wayne never makes an appearance in the book and even his flesh under his mask is rarely shown. The book focuses on Batman as a ghostly shadow who haunts his way through the asylum. If this is a story about Bruce Wayne's psyche trying to repair itself, then the damage needing repair is the darkness that is Batman. Later, when inmates suggest they want to see Batman's real face, the Joker insists that the Batman mask "*is* his real face." Here, Morrison uses the Joker to suggest that Batman has been written as a character with one identity and one face for too long.

Before Batman enters the asylum, he confides in Commissioner Gordon: "Sometimes I... question the rationality of my actions. And I'm afraid that when I walk into Arkham and those doors close behind me... it'll be just like coming home."

As Morrison states in an interview with io9 on 1 July 2009, "I never really subscribed to the idea that Bruce was insane or unhealthy. As I've said before, Bruce Wayne's physical and psychological training regimens (including advanced meditation techniques) would tend to encourage a fairly balanced and healthy personality."[2]

In *Arkham Asylum*, Batman may seem to doubt himself, but that's because the story is about the psychological repair of his mind. He has to go through these trials and the fear he has of entering the asylum in order to keep his mind grounded.

Before entering, Batman is taunted by the Joker who has threatened an asylum worker named "Pearl" – the name being an obvious play on the origin of Batman, in which Martha Wayne's pearls spilled on the street after she was killed. In nearly every origin story or film adaptation of Batman, the pearls are the image from the murders that reoccurs most often. Morrison later uses the pearl image in *The Return of Bruce Wayne* as one of the three last items to be archived at the end of the universe. But in *Arkham Asylum*, Batman's concern for Pearl is simply reflective of his concern for his mother and he seems relieved to learn that the Joker has not harmed her.

Once Batman enters the asylum, he sees a man hanging upside-down to represent the hanged man tarot card. The hanged man symbolizes an inward journey, and so this seemingly random act of madness is, in fact, a visual clue that Batman is on a journey to repair himself which will be a recurring motif throughout all of Morrison's tenure with the character.

Batman's villains have always been a reflection of the hero's personality. Harvey Dent (the Batman villain Two-Face) reflects the duality of Batman. In *Arkham Asylum*, the doctors have been rehabilitating Harvey Dent by replacing the coin that he uses to make decisions with a six-sided die. Later, they move on to cards. The process will eventually allow Harvey Dent to choose his own actions, rather than having them chosen by fate. However, Harvey's

---

[2] McMillan, Graeme. "Grant Morrison Tells All About Batman and Robin." 1 July 2009. Web. 23 July 2012. http://io9.com/5301435/grant-morrison-tells-all-about-batman-and-robin.

rehabilitation is flawed because he can't make simple decisions such as when to use the restroom without consulting chance. Batman argues with Dr. Ruth Adams that through their rehabilitation, they have destroyed Harvey's identity. Ruth replies, "Sometimes we have to pull down in order to rebuild, Batman."

Two-Face's rehabilitation in the graphic novel is meant to show that there is more to Batman than the simple duality of Bruce and Batman. His identity isn't a coin, or a die, or a pack of cards – Batman can be many different things at once. Batman can be campy, cool, gothic, dark, frightening, kind, inspirational, and many other things that go beyond simple duality; thus, it is ridiculous for him to be forced into one interpretation of the character. The very fact that Morrison and McKean can craft such a poetic, symbolism-heavy story as *Arkham Asylum* is proof of the character's diverse identity.

Batman paradoxically suggests that the seemingly insane identity of Two-Face is what keeps Harvey Dent sane, just as Morrison has argued that the Batman identity is what keeps has Bruce Wayne sane (which is also the reason why the identity of the Batman of Zur-en-Arrh will be constructed later). What others perceive as insanity is really just a coping mechanism that people develop when under trauma – or, as the Mad Hatter spells it out for the audience later in the graphic novel, "Order from chaos."

Of course, the Joker's insanity is far beyond both Two-Face and Batman. Dr. Adams explains that he is "more suited to urban life at the end of the twentieth century... unlike you and I, the Joker seems to have no control over the sensory information he's receiving from the outside world. He can only cope with that chaotic barrage of input by going with the flow."

Dr. Adams is arguing that the Joker's perceived insanity is in fact a coping mechanism that has made him super-sane. So while Batman and Harvey Dent struggle to cope with new identities, the Joker is so adept at adapting that it can almost be considered a superpower. Morrison is showing that the Joker can be anything he wants, but Batman has fallen into a routine of simply being the dark shadow of fear.

As Batman runs through the asylum, he's confronted with various members of his rogue's gallery. The Mad Hatter says, "Arkham is a looking glass and we are you," signaling that these encounters are deliberate and meant to reflect Batman in some way. Looking back over the entirety of Grant Morrison's time with the hero, however, we can see that these encounters are a blueprint of what is to come; the hero is deconstructed and rebuilt anew. From *Batman* to

Batman and Robin to *Batman: The Return of Bruce Wayne*, Morrison questions what the essential elements of Batman's identity are and it all starts in *Arkham Asylum*.

Dr. Destiny is next. In Tim Callahan's interview with Morrison, the writer states, "I seem to remember putting him in because I liked the idea of the visual: Batman kicking someone in a wheelchair."[3]

The interaction may not hold a lot of symbolic weight, but it's a perfect statement for Morrison's Batman philosophy. Batman has been typecast according to what people think he should be, and Morrison will later make it his mission to shatter those ideas – whether it is by having the hero shoot off into space as a shortcut to Gibraltar, by dressing him in reds and purples to show his madness, or by sending the hero hurtling back through time.

After the strange encounter with Dr. Destiny, Batman faces two god-like villains who will later reflect Batman's encounter with the New God Darkseid in *Final Crisis* and in *Batman* #701-702. Maxie Zeus was a mob boss who thought he was the reincarnation of the Greek god of the same name. The second godlike villain is Killer Croc, who represents the dragon of the monomyth that the hero must slay in order to become a whole person. Both characters are normally portrayed as Dick Tracy-esque thugs, but here, Morrison is elevating them to mythological status. Taken together, Maxie Zeus and Killer Croc are used in the same way that Morrison will use Darkseid in *Final Crisis*. In that story, Batman had to kill the evil god Darkseid in order to become a Bat-God.

Throughout the course of Batman's journey in *Arkham Asylum*, a parallel narrative is running about the life of Dr. Arkham. In the end, we learn that Arkham had constructed the asylum as a binding spell to contain an evil bat that had driven his own mother insane. Dr. Cavendish is the evil doctor at the asylum who has let all of the inmates out in order to lure Batman into a trap and capture him within the asylum. The origin story of the villain of "R.I.P.," Dr. Hurt, is similar in that he had created a binding spell to capture the Bat-God, Barbatos. Both Cavendish and Hurt were doctors who tried to bind the bat.

Finally, *Arkham Asylum* concludes with Two-Face flipping a coin to decide whether Batman can leave the asylum or not. Even though the coin tells him otherwise, Two-Face lets Batman go free symbolizing that Batman has allowed himself to move on.

---

[3] Callahan, Tim. *Grant Morrison: The Early Years*. Edwardsville, Illinois: Sequart Research & Literacy Organization, 2007. Print.

Arkham Asylum sets the thematic blueprint for all of Morrison's work on Batman. It's Morrison's *Batman* run in miniature, complete with Batman being deconstructed, meeting a god, slaying evil, and coming to terms with his identity. The story is essentially about Batman transforming into a better version of himself, which is *exactly* what will happen throughout the run and beyond.

"Gothic"

Arkham Asylum presented a Batman in turmoil, a figure who went through trials in order to become whole. 1990's "Gothic" features no such character.[4] Bruce Wayne is confident as Batman, and the first appearance of Bruce Wayne establishes exactly this.

Bruce has a nightmare in which he's a schoolboy. He enters a cathedral and is transformed into Batman. He says to an old teacher, "I'm a master now. Yes." The teacher replies, "I can tell by your cloak. Your father will be pleased."

Instantly, Batman is transformed into an adult Bruce Wayne. He sees a shadowy figure and he runs to it shouting, "Oh father, they told me you were dead!" In the next panel, he is a child again, and he says, "Father, I've missed you so much. Speak to me. Please. Please just say…" Before he can finish his sentence, his father turns and reveals his mouth has been sewn shut.

It's an enigmatic dream but one that shows the two aspects of Bruce Wayne's identity: the lonely son and the Batman. The lonely son is one who still regrets losing his father at such a young age. He seeks approval and searches for fulfillment. Rather than being a separate identity for Bruce, Batman is the identity created by Bruce in response to not being able to control the world around him at such a young age. The idea of harmony between identities is further solidified later in the story during another dream sequence in which the Batman uniform droops over a child version of Bruce, visually combining the two. The two identities are two parts of a whole, both necessary in order for the man to survive.

Batman is a survival identity who strives for complete control over his city, over his sidekicks, and even complete control over his own body. All of this stems from the one moment when the world spun out of control and he lost his parents. Even though Batman is symbolic of total control, a man who has

---

[4] The five-issue storyline was serialized in *Batman: Legends of the Dark Knight* #6-10 (Apr-Aug 1990) and first collected in 1992.

become both a "teacher" and a "master," he still feels inadequate. This inadequacy isn't relegated to one identity, but rather is part of both Bruce and Batman. He still can't make up for the fact that he lost his parents and can never get them back. He will always be that boy searching for his father's approval, no matter what identity he assumes.

Beyond the symbolism of the dream, after Bruce wakes from the first nightmare, he tells Alfred, "The same dream. My father, alive." It's a small but potentially significant moment that echoes one of the central premises of "R.I.P." (much later in Morrison's career) when Dr. Hurt suggests that he might be Thomas Wayne. In order for Batman to be born, Bruce *had* to lose his parents. Children rely on their parents to make sense of their world, and when Bruce lost his parents so suddenly, he had to make sense of it his own way by creating Batman. If Bruce Wayne's father had truly been alive after all of this time, then the rage that fueled Bruce's mission becomes unnecessary.

In the first full image of Batman we see in "Gothic" (other than the dream), our hero leaps from a gargoyle toward the sound of a scream, and Batman is framed upside-down. What would normally be a heroic Batman swinging into action is inverted and comes off as confusing, but connects visually to the inverted Bat-symbol that the crime bosses will use to summon Batman later. This is the first of many instances in which Batman is presented as a sort of Satanic figure.

The connection is made abundantly clear when Batman declares that "Gotham City is hell. We are all in hell. And I am the king of hell!"

It may seem strange for the Dark Knight to be comparing himself to Satan. But it's evidence of Morrison connecting Batman to larger ideas, especially to mythological ones such as gods. Batman's not simply a billionaire who dresses up in a costume to fight crime. He's an idea. And often, especially in Morrison's writing, a larger-than-life or even godlike figure.

He's also one who instills fear not only in criminals but in those he has sworn to protect, as evidenced by the innocent man in "Gothic" who begs "Don't hurt me" to Batman.

After the incident with the thugs, Batman returns to perching upon a gargoyle, and he sees an upside-down Batsignal in the sky. This inversion is meant to be blasphemous: the normal signal is used as a sigil of sorts to summon the Caped Crusader and defender of Gotham, but the reverse is being used by criminals to summon the lord of hell. These criminals try to strike a deal with Batman. They wish to find a man named Mr. Whisper, who is executing mobsters; in exchange for Batman's help, they will suspend all criminal activity. Strangely, Batman replies, "You and your kind have made Gotham hell, now rot in it." They have created the hell that Batman has declared himself ruler of.

Invoking hell is a common motif throughout the arc. In a flashback to his days in private school, Bruce is speaking to his childhood friend Robert who claims that the school is hell, the idea being that Bruce cannot escape it. Later, as Bruce is being punished by headmaster Winchester, he sees Robert's decapitated head in a waste basket. Before Bruce can be the next sacrifice, his father rescues him from Winchester's clutches. When they return home, Thomas suggests the family go out for a movie to celebrate Bruce's return – the suggestion being that Winchester had inadvertently caused Thomas and Martha Wayne's deaths.

After a rather tenuous clue about Austria from a recording of Thomas Wayne, Batman is off to Lake Dess to investigate Mr. Whisper. While it may seem like a misstep in logic for Batman to leave Gotham to investigate a killer in the city, it's a first step to show that Batman is an international hero who shouldn't be confined to his home city. If he needs to leave for a quick investigation half a world away, then by all means, Batman should do so. To keep the idea of a Batman relegated to Gotham City would be a disservice to the idea of a billionaire playboy spending money on fighting crime. Morrison was so preoccupied in *Arkham Asylum* with Batman's psyche and personal growth that he never had the chance to explore the billionaire aspect of the character, and "Gothic" begins those ideas which will be essential in his *Batman* run.

Of course, Winchester and Mr. Whisper the mobster-killer are one and the same. He's also known as Mr. Wicker. Before these identities, however, he was a monk known as Manfred. It's worth noting that "Manfred" is also the title of a dramatic poem written by Lord Byron in 1816-1817; the poem features a tortured protagonist who has fled to the Bernese Alps. There is a certain sense of duality between Byron's Manfred and Morrison's. Byron's Manfred is trying to forget the past by conjuring spirits and committing suicide, while Morrison's Manfred is trying to live on as an immortal. The invocation of Lord Byron is quite deliberate, and Batman's persona falls into the brooding character archetype that Byron formulated.

In a monastery near Lake Dess, Batman learns from an abbot that Manfred had been corrupted by a young man named Conrad, who made him believe the only way to reach God and truly be redeemed was to give in to every sin. The image of the upside-down cross is a visual cue meant to reflect the blasphemy of Batman's signal being reversed by the mobsters; Batman and the cross are now connected visually and are meant to suggest similar ideas.

After turning the rest of his monastery into a castle of sin, Manfred sold his soul to the Devil in exchange for 300 years of life. When Batman returns to Gotham, he is captured by Mr. Whisper, who explains he had known Batman and Bruce Wayne were one and the same. Returning to the Batman's connection to hell, Mr. Whisper says, "You're still little more than a brutalized child for whom the world is all shadows and fear. I pity you. I suppose it's a kind of hell." With this, Morrison has made the ultimate statement on how miserable it must be to be Batman: a damned monk *pities* Batman.

Not only did young Bruce Wayne attend a school that was like hell, not only did Batman declare himself to be the lord of hell, but the villain of the story – a monk who was 26 hours away from being eternally damned to hell and was planning to murder hundreds of people in the hopes of not being damned – actually *pities* him. Whisper is suggesting that to even *be* Batman is "a kind of hell." Throughout "Gothic," Batman uses variety of cool gadgets, speeds off to Austria in his Batplane, and generally looks cool in everything he does. Readers might want to be Batman because of such advantages, but deep down, being Batman is hell. It's an odd philosophical statement from Morrison, given how far he goes to emphasize the coolness of Batman in later work, such as *JLA* and *Batman*.

Despite being the voice for Morrison's statement on the hell that it would be to be Batman, Mr. Whisper also represents a different kind of Batman villain. While most of Batman's rogue's gallery consists of colorful criminals with catchy codenames, Mr. Whisper is an occult villain more suited to the old pulps (and early *Detective Comics*) rather than the modern *Batman* comic. In a way, it's Morrison's first attempt at modernizing some of the more irreconcilable parts of Batman's past. Way back in *Detective Comics* #31 (Sept 1939), Batman traveled to France and Hungary to battle a villain known as the Monk. Mr. Whisper and the Monk aren't terribly similar, but the idea of Batman leaving the safety of Gotham to travel to battle an occult villain in Europe, rather than a colorful gangster, is an old idea that Morrison is channeling and reusing here. If

Mr. Whisper is a modernized template for the occult villain of Batman's past, then this same template is the one Morrison uses later when crafting Dr. Hurt.

While not *exactly* like Dr. Hurt, he and Mr. Whisper have many striking similarities. Both go by many different names: Whisper is Winchester, Wicker, and Manfred, while Dr. Hurt is also known as Thomas Wayne, the Black Glove, Mangrove Pierce, the Hole in Things, and El Penitente. Both are linked to Batman's origin in some way: Whisper was Bruce's headmaster, while Hurt is an ancestor to Bruce Wayne and also experimented on Batman. Both use their moniker as a title (doctor / mister) and an evocative but general word (hurt / whisper), rather than using a name like the Joker or the Penguin. Both sold their souls to the Devil in exchange for longer life: Whisper had done so in the 17th century, while Hurt had done so in the 18th.

The comparisons don't end there, but other similarities are simply the conventions of an archetypal Batman villain (such as crafting an overly-elaborate plot to destroy Gotham, setting a deathtrap for Batman, using a serum to enact a plan, etc). Dr. Hurt is a far more complex and interesting villain than Mr. Whisper, but the villain of "Gothic" may be read as a rough blueprint for what comes later when Morrison takes the reins of *Batman*.

JLA

In Grant Morrison's philosophical treatise on mythology and super-heroes, *Supergods*, he discusses the "conventional wisdom" that has plagued Batman, writing: "Convention has it that Batman's adventures work best when they're rooted in a basically realistic world of gritty crime violence and back-street reprisals, but from the very start of his career, he was drawn into demented episodes of the supernatural, uncanny and inexplicable" (22).[5]

Arkham Asylum was a very different take on Batman because it was a psychological adventure, but it was still relatively grounded by featuring familiar villains as symbols for Batman's psychological journey. "Gothic" was Morrison's first experiment with placing Batman out of his comfort zone of Gotham and ground-level villains, but the haunting, gothic themes that pervade the story still feel like Batman's element. It wasn't until *JLA* that Morrison's take on Batman would be truly tested.

---

[5] Morrison, Grant. *Supergods: What Masked Vigilantes, Miraculous Mutants, and a Sun God from Smallville Can Teach Us About Being Human*. New York: Spiegel & Grau, 2011. Print.

Batman had been a founding member of the Justice League in the team's first appearance in *The Brave and the Bold* #28, and although he had appeared in various incarnations of the League over the years, there were still those that questioned the necessity of Batman on a team that featured heavy hitters like Superman, Wonder Woman, and Green Lantern. Including Batman in Justice League stories poses a bit of a narrative problem because when the story centers on threats that distract all of the super-powered heroes with only Batman left to save the day, it makes him look weak. The '70s cartoon *Super Friends* played this narrative device to its death and is perhaps where the stereotype that Batman shouldn't be on the Justice League came from. The alternative to the "Batman as a last resort" story is the "Batman as drill instructor" story where Batman rallies his team together and acts as their unimpressed leader. The Keith Giffen and J.M. DeMatteis era of *Justice League* began with this sort of Batman.

For years, writers had stuck to writing Batman as a normal human who worked alongside a group of amazing super-humans. What these writers failed to realize is that Batman isn't just a normal human — he's the most perfect human on the planet. He is able to fight alongside Superman because he is Superman's equal. Grant Morrison realized this and according to *Supergods*, he and *JLA* editor Ruben Diaz had to convince Batman editor Denny O'Neil to let them use the Dark Knight as O'Neil was "determined to make the Dark Knight's adventures as real and convincing as possible" (291-292). Fortunately, they were successful and a historical era with the Justice League began.

JLA marks a different era for Grant Morrison as a writer because it was his first time writing a more traditional comic book. Given that his mission was to write stories about "unadulterated, gee-whiz, unadorned sci-fi myths in comic form, giving back to the superheroes the respect and dignity a decade of 'realism' and harsh critique had stripped away," (292) it's amazing that he was allowed to use Batman in such a context. But Morrison doesn't use Batman in that way at the start nor does he use Batman in every story. *JLA* is an ensemble book with each of the seven core members getting a chance to shine. Batman's role is even further diminished after the Justice League doubles their membership to 14 members. However, the moments where Batman is the focus are incredibly important in order to understand Morrison's run on *Batman* later.

The first four-issue story arc revolves around a group of aliens called the Hyperclan who come to Earth and begin executing criminals. These "heroes" are meant to represent the realistic mentality that had plagued super-heroes for years at that time; like the Punisher, Wolverine, or other "grim-and-gritty" super-heroes, the Hyperclan killed villains so that crime wouldn't come back. Morrison is using them to show that the 80's era of grimness was over by emphasizing the heroic, god-like qualities of the Justice League. In the first issue of *JLA*, Batman doesn't even appear until the final two pages when it has been revealed that he has been stalking his new teammates. When Superman wonders, "Strange. I didn't hear your heartbeat" Batman replies, "Hh! Gadget worked" showing a small sense of paranoia in the hero, but also establishing his genius and ability to stand next to Superman on a team.

In the second issue, the League employs their old divide-and-conquer tactics by breaking up into teams to investigate the Hyperclan. Batman pairs off with Superman and the Man of Tomorrow asks his friend, "You don't like working with... with superpeople." Batman responds with a statement that reflects the logic that had been applied to the character and his relationship with the League for years, "I don't have superspeed or invulnerability. I can't risk wearing a bright costume that makes me a target and I can't afford to trust poorly-trained people who do." Batman's dialogue casts the hero as more vulnerable than the others, but his actions will prove otherwise later.

After the League is captured by the Hyperclan, it's revealed that Batman had evaded capture and it's up to him to save the day. Unlike episodes of *Super Friends* when the more powerful characters were distracted by solving challenges with their powers and Batman is left to save the day, *JLA* features a completely defeated Justice League with Batman as their only hope. The Leaguers had rushed into battle only to be beaten in combat by the Hyperclan, who mistakenly left Batman for dead in the wreckage of his bat plane. Still very much alive, his brilliant mind deduces they are Martians in disguise and quickly takes down four Hyperclan members on his own. Even though Batman may not have the powers of his teammates, his intellect has surpassed them all and he saves the day.

After defeating Superman-level threats, Batman informs Superman in issue #5, "I promised the league I'd be prepared to function in an advisory capacity." And so, he disappears for issues #6 and 7.

In issues #8 and #9, the Key has captured the JLA and has placed them in a machine where each individual experiences a powerful hallucination. Once the team breaks out of the hallucination, the resulting "psycho-electric surge" will allow the Key to attain ultimate power. In Batman's hallucination, he is much older and married to Selina Kyle. It's during an exchange between the former Batman and Catwoman that Morrison establishes a significant phrase that will echo throughout his *Batman* run.

A reluctant Bruce Wayne fears for the new Dynamic Duo and Selina reassures him by saying, "It's too late to stop it now. You and Tim have been training Bruce Jr. almost since the day he was born. Don't tell me you didn't want this. You said it yourself. As long as Gotham needs them, Batman and Robin can never die." Nearly ten years later, the first sentence in Morrison's *Batman* story "R.I.P." comes from a darkened Batman shouting "Batman and Robin will never die!" and the idea is further repeated in the closing pages of *Batman* #700 as the reader is shown future versions of Batman lasting on into the year one million.

"Rock of Ages"

Arguably the best of Morrison's entire *JLA* run, the "Rock of Ages" storyline took place in issues #10-15, beginning with a rather standard battle in the streets of Star City and following the League to the end of Earth at the hands of Darkseid. In these issues Morrison experiments with Batman's identity in some very interesting ways.

In the story, Lex Luthor has assembled a new Injustice Gang in opposition to the new Justice League. Luthor's plan is methodical; he explains, "We don't fight them in the streets like brawlers. We apply the principles of the boardroom and we plan. We observe."

In short, he tells his team to "Prepare for the corporate takeover of the Justice League." Instead of fighting the heroes head-on, Luthor orchestrates deathtraps, reveals that he has been financing the Justice League member Aztek (whom Morrison co-created a year earlier for the short-lived *Aztek: The Ultimate Man*) all along, and uses Wonder Woman villain Circe to manipulate Green Arrow into a lethargic state in order to gain an advantage over his foes. But despite all of his planning, what Luthor hadn't planned for was an opposing businessman.

At the end of *JLA* #11, Batman sits in the Batcave with his mask off and talks to Robin. He says, "Luthor still has no idea he's dealing with someone who's as familiar with corporate takeover techniques as he is. Someone who plays the game much better than he does… Bruce Wayne. Let's take him out."

Here, Morrison is showing that Batman and Bruce Wayne aren't two different identities, but are one in the same. The Bruce Wayne identity is just as important as the Batman identity.

Not content with just exploring the Bruce Wayne / Batman dynamic in a different way, Morrison goes a step further and presents a more light-hearted Batman as well. The exchange between Tim Drake and Bruce Wayne at the end of the issue is reminiscent of the old Adam West and Burt Ward television series days. Tim reports, "The surgeon case is all wrapped up. Me and Nightwing took out his crime consultants and closed down the clinic. Anything new on the Joker case?" and Batman replies, "It's 'Nightwing and I,' Robin. Grammar." Even amidst the destruction of the Justice League, Batman makes good grammar a priority.

In issue #11, Mirror Master says, "I work strictly for the highest bidder, ya know? No questions asked," which allows for Batman to recruit the villain by donating money to his old orphanage. Batman continues to show his humorous side by telling Superman, "Never underestimate the sentimentality of a Scotsman, Clark." It isn't the fear tactics of Batman that allows for Mirror Master to act as a spy on Luthor's team; it's the power of Bruce Wayne's money.

This isn't the only character that Batman will recruit, however. Dressed in his Matches Malone persona, Batman also recruits Plastic Man at a club. Batman demonstrates the fluidity of his identities by going from traditional super-hero in issue #10 as the team saves Star City, to Matches Malone when he is undercover, to Bruce Wayne when he has to deal with a hostile takeover. His identity is truly put to the test in the coming issues.

Issue #13 takes place 15 years into a possible future in which Darkseid has enslaved Earth. A rag-tag group of heroes leads an assault on the evil god and they learn that Batman has survived all these years by defeating Desaad and assuming his identity. Although Superman and Martian Manhunter had died along with dozens of other heroes, Batman was able to survive because of his intelligence and his ability to adapt to any identity.

Issue #14 serves as a sampling of what will later occur in *Final Crisis* as Batman leads the assault on Darkseid. To change the past, Batman outsmarts the New God Metron by having him become human and promptly punching him out so that others can use his Mobius Chair to travel back in time. But as Batman faces off against Darkseid himself, the dark god uses the Omega Effect on him. The Black Racer, the New God who embodies death, comments, "Then he is gone, out of time, out of space. Beyond what even gods know." Later, in *Final Crisis*, Darkseid will use the Omega Sanction to send Batman hurtling through time.

The final issue of the story is a fairly standard brawl between the Justice League and the Injustice Gang, where Batman leads an attack on Lex Luthor. The conclusion may be rather straightforward, but the lead up is an absolutely incredible exploration into the role that identity plays in Batman. His identity shifts and changes to match the situation and allows him to survive – a theme that will pervade Morrison's tenure on *Batman* and be explored in much more depth during "R.I.P."

Prometheus

What would happen if everything you knew about Batman was the opposite? This is the basis for Prometheus. His parents were hippie criminals who were gunned down by police, and so, he used the wealth they acquired to travel the world and become the ultimate human. Taking place over issues #16-17, Prometheus invades the Watchtower by posing as a hero who won a contest to meet the JLA. He reprograms Steel's suit, turns Martian Manhunter into a puddle of slime, sends Zauriel to an alternate dimension, knocks out Huntress, shoots Green Lantern and the Flash, holds the press hostage, nearly forces Superman to commit suicide and (most blasphemously) defeats Batman in combat.

The title of "Prometheus Unbound" is a reference to the lyrical drama by Percy Bysshe Shelley (who appears in Morrison's comic *The Invisibles*) about the mythical Titan Prometheus being tortured by Zeus. This invocation of a mythological play reflects the idea that the Justice League are modern analogues for Greek gods. Ironically, it is the Batman villain Catwoman who defeats the Anti-Batman.

While Batman remains on the team after this point, his role is somewhat diminished after the JLA doubles in size and Morrison decides to focus on larger, more bombastic stories. Batman's final act with the team during Morrison's run is to do little more than play the role of cheerleader as Superman absorbs the energy of the anti-god Mageddon. Yet throughout his run, Morrison was able to do what seemed to be impossible. Even though some would try to dismiss Batman's membership in the Justice League as absurd, Morrison proved that the Dark Knight is no mere human and could believably participate in larger-than-life stories. This is an important concept for readers to be able to accept in order to connect with Morrison's *Batman* run, in which Batman appears even more godlike.

JLA: Classified

In late 2004, after years of working on the X-Men franchise at Marvel, Grant Morrison returned to the Justice League in the pages of *JLA: Classified* for a three-issue story (#1-3, Jan-Mar 2005) with artist Ed McGuinness that would see the return of the Ultramarines and also serve as a prologue to his massive *Seven Soldiers of Victory*. Throughout his career at DC, Morrison has a history of creating wild and fantastic concepts that are rarely utilized outside of his own work. The Chinese super-heroes known as the Great Ten from the DC series *52* didn't receive a mini-series until years after the year-long series had wrapped. The Japan-based Super Young Team from *Final Crisis* starred in their own mini-series written by Joe Casey titled *Final Crisis Aftermath: Dance* (the *Final Crisis* branding was used to help sell the series due to a lack of faith in its ability to stand on its own). But before these teams, there were the Ultramarines from the pages of *JLA*. By the end of their introductory arc, Morrison had positioned the team to be a group of heroes that were different enough to support their own brand. Years later, it was evident that DC had no intentions for these characters, and so, his *JLA: Classified* begins with their destruction.

To provide context for those who hadn't read their first appearance in *JLA*, the trade has a short background where it explains that "the Ultramarine Corps operates independent of any nation. Upon founding Superbia, a sovereign 'city of tomorrow' floating high above the ruins of what was once Montevideo, it has recruited heroes such as Vixen, the Knight, Jack O'Lantern, Goraiko, and the Squire to support its cause as a first-strike global peacekeeping force. And if keeping the peace means eliminating those who would make war, that's okay with them."

The idea of international heroes from different nations operating outside of governments is thematically similar to that of *The Authority* – the WildStorm comic that, in 1999, made the idea of paramilitary heroes who executed criminals the go-to motif for super-team books.

The inclusion of Knight and Squire on the team is Morrison's first official acknowledgment of a secret history of their story coming through in his work.

Batman gets into his sci-fi closet. From *JLA: Classified* #1 (Jan 2005). Art by Ed McGuinness and Dexter Vines. Copyright © DC Comics.

In the bonus material for the second hardcover of *Batman and Robin*, Morrison discusses Knight and Squire, saying, "I introduced the new Squire and Knight in the pages of *JLA* back in 1998 and I've been slipping them into stories like *JLA Classified* #1-3 and *Batman* #667-669 ever since. For some reason I'll never be able to explain, this pair have developed a complex, intricate backstory and web of relationships that so far exists solely in my head and is only hinted at in these brief appearances."

As Squire tries to contact the League in Qwewq, she mentions some of the villains she has faced including the Metaleks, Old King Coal, and Springheeled Jack – characters that would later appear in Morrison's *Batman and Robin* run and are part of this secret backstory that only exists in Morrison's head.

After Gorilla Grodd has destroyed Superbia, things get wild. Batman takes a phone call from Squire in the Batcave on his red emergency phone via the 60s *Batman* series, and then he goes to his "sci-fi closet" which features Thanagarian hawk wings, a ray gun, a robotic claw, what appears to be the head of the robot from *Iron Giant*, and a Dalek from *Doctor Who*. Morrison punctuates the absurd scene with Batman asking Alfred, "Did my flying saucer arrive from the factory?"

While Batman was shown as being more than a simple detective in Morrison's *JLA*, he was never shown as a sci-fi weapon hoarder. Some may decry this scene as absurd and unbelievable for Batman to be cast in this role, but Morrison handles the scene with such deftness that it isn't outside of the realm of possibility that Batman could be put into the role of Science Fiction super-hero like this.

Batman saves Squire in his flying saucer from jetpack-wearing gorillas and the two use a boom-tube generating gauntlet to teleport to Pluto (a subtle reference to Morrison's *DC One Million* story where the Batman of the 853rd century turned the dwarf planet Pluto into a prison-world) where Batman just happens to keep a robot Justice League. The second issue reveals that the Justice League are trapped in the infant universe called "Qwewq" – a world without heroes that is shaped like a cube made of stars. The first appearance of this cube universe is in the *JLA* story, "Rock of Ages" when Green Lantern, Flash, and Aquaman visit Wonderworld. It will later be revealed in *Seven Soldiers of Victory* that this is the larval state of the villain Neh-buh-loh who is working with Grodd in this arc. It also shares a connection to Earth-Q from *All-Star*

Superman – the universe that Superman created to see what a world without Superman would be like.

Just as it looks like the Ultramarines have been defeated, Batman arrives with his robotic league. Unfortunately, Batman and his team are outclassed by the mind-controlled forces of Neh-buh-loh and Grodd. Among their ranks is Black Death – the villain that the Justice League has been hunting in Qwewq. As Grodd threatens to eat Batman, Squire contacts the League and they return to defeat Grodd's forces.

The final issue features Batman being roasted like a pig, only to escape and punch Gorilla Grodd in the crotch. While Batman is still in the issue, more page time is given to the rest of the League. Each member of the team has a moment to shine and save the day. The arc concludes with Superman angrily preaching to the Ultramarines about how heroes don't execute criminals. Here, Morrison is placing Superman in a similar position to Joe Kelly's *Action Comics* #775 (Mar 2001) story, "What's so funny about Truth, Justice, and the American way?" where Superman criticized the idea that traditional definitions of "super-hero" are outdated.

52

Spinning out of the mega-event *Infinite Crisis, 52* was a weekly series written by Geoff Johns, Grant Morrison, Greg Rucka, and Mark Waid, which ran in real time and told the story of a year in which the DC Universe had to go without Superman, Batman, and Wonder Woman. However, unable to completely stay out of the series, Batman makes his first appearance in issue #30, titled "Dark Knight Down." The story revolves around Bruce Wayne trying to atone for his sins. In the commentary at the end of the issue in the trade, Rucka explains that the story was "long, long, *long* overdue" and goes on to explain that he had advocated to change Batman "from the dour-faced humorless vigilante and [bring] some light back into his life." While the story might be light, and Batman's role in *52* is incredibly minor, it's still an essential transition piece thematically because it shifts Batman's personality from dark, brooding hero to one who can tackle the most bizarre cases.

The issue begins with an image of a much younger, inexperienced Batman battling hooded monks with the narration, "Everything started out so well..." On the next page, Batman and Robin are fighting thugs and it becomes clear that the narration is Dick Grayson's as he says, "but Alfred always used to say

Bruce would have self-destructed if he hadn't met me and learned some responsibility."

Even though most Batman stories feature narration that gives insight into the thoughts of the hero, we never really know what Batman is thinking. He isn't necessarily emotionally guarded so much as he uses those emotions to fuel his mission and therefore rarely reflects upon them.

A panel features the Joker waving a white flag while Grayson explains, "The Joker gave up being a murderer for a while and there was just this crazy, brilliant clown running around."

This sentence reflects the philosophy Morrison first established in *Arkham Asylum* and that he will return to again in his *Batman* run – the Joker is a transformative figure who consistently changes his identity. At one time, he wasn't a murderer at all, but rather, just a nuisance.

A barrage of panels then reflect Batman's worst mistakes. The first is of Dick Grayson leaving. Next, Jason Todd stealing a wheel off of the Batmobile followed by a panel of Batman holding Jason's dead body. The credits page has the Joker shooting Barbara Gordon, Bane breaking Batman's back, the Batsignal being destroyed, Jason Todd returning as the Red Hood, Batman holding Tim Drake in the aftermath of *Identity Crisis*, and Batman holding a gun to Alexander Luthor's head in the climax of *Infinite Crisis*. Grayson says, "When you think about everything that happened – it's too much for any man. Even the strongest."

Grayson's words echo a problem that had plagued Batman stories for far too long; it seemed that each new story was constructed to bring Batman down to his lowest point. If Batman is the most human hero of the DC Universe, then writers had fallen into the trap of always forcing Batman to deal with loss the way real people do. Barbara Gordon, Jason Todd, and Jack Drake were harmed because of Batman's choices and the guilt of those deaths have haunted him along with every other failure over the years. This guilt and atonement is an idea that will resurface later during Morrison's *Batman*.

Dick Grayson reveals that they have been traveling the same path that Bruce went on years ago in order to become Batman and Tim suggests that Bruce "wants us to be the new Batman and Robin, right? It's obvious." While the idea probably seemed ridiculous at the time of the issue's release (29 Nov 2006), the line plants the seed for Grant Morrison's *Batman and Robin*, except starring Bruce Wayne's son Damian as Robin rather than Tim Drake.

Bruce is walking through the desert when he is attacked by an updated version of hokey Batman villain, the Ten-Eyed Man. In the notes for the issue, Mark Waid describes the character as "Bat-foe from the 1970s whose optic nerves were in his fingertips." Sure, the idea of a villain whose only notable quality is that his eyes are in his fingers is a ridiculous notion, but reimagined as a tribe of desert nomads who claimed to have trained Bruce Wayne to "fight as ghosts fight," makes the concept work.

It seems that Bruce has been seeking the Ten-Eyed Tribe so that he may find peace after many years of suffering. He tells them, "My soul feels black and I feel sick. I've lost my resolve." In order to absolve him of his sins, the Ten-Eyed Tribe surround Bruce with swords raised. They explain, "If you flinch. If you shudder. You will not survive." The scene does not offer much context for what is happening. It's really just a transition scene to thematically transform Batman into the character Morrison was already writing, but the red and black color scheme serves as a visual cue for Batman's inner-turmoil.

During "R.I.P.," we learn that when the Joker imagines himself killing people, he sees the world in black, white, and red. Similarly, Batman sees the world in red and black. In 52, Bruce's battle with the Ten-Eyed Tribe is punctuated with red and black to emphasize Bruce's transformation just as it will emphasize his transformation during "R.I.P."

Of course, Bruce survives the Ten-Eyed Tribe and he tells Tim, "The Ten-Eyed Men kill demons, Tim. I asked them to kill mine. I asked them to cut out all the dark, fearful, paranoid urges I've allowed to corrupt my life... and they did. It's over. Batman is gone."

This statement is both literal in that Bruce Wayne doesn't return for the rest of 52, and figurative as it refers to the change that Batman has undergone. While Grant Morrison have his share of darker tales that delve deep into Batman's psyche, the encounter with the Ten-Eyed Tribe has eviscerated the brooding Batman who fears his own failure. Now, a new age of Batman is ready to begin.

Bruce Wayne and Batman: The Duo Dynamic

To better understand Grant Morrison's take on Batman, one has to look no further than *Supergods*, in which he writes (on page 17) that "Batman was clearly the product of applied craft, cleverly but rapidly assembled from an assortment of pop culture debris that together transcended the sum of their parts." From "Batman and Son" all the way through to "R.I.P.," Morrison precisely examines this "pop culture debris," adds new depth to the character by comparing Batman to literary traditions, and then uses all of this to play with the idea of identity. The result is not only a great analysis of Batman, but it also reconciles past iterations into a new, all-encompassing definition of what he is and what he can be.

In *Arkham Asylum*, Dr. Ruth Adams says in reference to Harvey Dent's rehabilitation, "Sometimes we have to pull down in order to rebuild, Batman." Remove the comma of this sentence, and the mission statement for all of Morrison's Batman stories is clear.

"Batman and Son"

In the beginning, there was Batman and the Joker. Even though Batman's colorful counterpart of catastrophe wouldn't appear until years after the creation of the Dark Knight, they complement one another so perfectly that it's hard to believe there was ever a Batman without a Joker. Conscious of this,

Grant Morrison began his legendary *Batman* run in issue #655 with a familiar conceit: the Joker believes he has conquered his foe after hatching a bizarre, ridiculous plot in an attempt to make Batman look foolish. As straightforward as the conflict may be, it is also the most heavily symbolic of any scene in Morrison's run.

The first page shows Commissioner Gordon falling from a building and laughing like a maniac. As he is caught in a net held by police officers, someone shouts, "The Commissioner's been poisoned by the Joker!" Gordon has been a staple of the Batman franchise since the very first Batman story in *Detective Comics* #27 (May 1939). The Joker's poison itself is a staple of the Batman franchise as it is one of the most commonly used plot devices for the character.

Next is a two-page spread of children roped together and tied to a helicopter with the Joker's face on it, while the Joker holds a bloody crowbar and declares, "I did it! I finally killed Batman! In front of a bunch of vulnerable, disabled kids!!!!"

While this image actually sets the reader up for an obvious bait-and-switch, it also illustrates that the traditional Batman story we once knew is dead and gone. Everything the reader knows about what a Batman story should be is dead with this image.

As the Joker gleefully calls for Santa Claus's execution, "Batman" pulls a gun from his utility belt. The Joker speaks directly for Grant Morrison as he looks directly at the reader and says, "I love messing with your head. Ever taken an acid trip? Hydrochloric, that is."

Here, Morrison is drawing upon the classic Shakespearean motif of placing the words of truth in the mouth of the fool. The writer relates to the changing nature of the Joker and therefore uses him as Morrison's own tongue to tell the reader that this will be unlike any Batman story they've ever read. And then "Batman" raises his gun and shoots the Joker in the head.

While it's a shock to see Batman shoot the Joker in the face, readers should remember that in his earliest appearances in *Detective Comics*, Batman used a gun. Of course, this isn't the real Batman, but an imposter. However, the idea is still there and it offers a very small hint of the central conceit that fuels Morrison's *Batman*: every Batman story exists, matters, and can still be used.

As Batman throws the Joker's body into the dumpster, the words "Zur-en-Arrh" act as a kind of magic graffiti nearby. Though they are hardly noticeable upon the first read through, subsequent reads make the words stand out like vivid neon. "Zur-en-Arrh" doesn't just act as an early narrative device that will be returned to later, but it also symbolically connects *Batman* with Morrison's *The Invisibles*.[1] In the first issue of *The Invisibles*, teenage anarchist, Dane McGown wreaks havoc upon London with his friends, but along the way, the words "King Mob" are graffiti that follow and haunt them. This idea of graffiti acting as magic words to lead the hero toward some end is the first of many connections that Morrison makes between *Batman* and *The Invisibles*.

As the opening scene concludes, the message is made clear: the identities of our hero and villain, the tone and scope of the series, and the readers' perceptions of what a Batman story can all be changed very quickly. Morrison immediately contrasts the darkness of the Joker's "death" with Jim Gordon who (under the influence of the Joker's toxin and is therefore able to speak for Morrison) looks to the reader and says, "Everybody needs to lighten up." It's a call for Batman readers to calm down and remember that Batman can be so much more than just a grizzled detective solving "realistic" mysteries.

Batman visits Jim Gordon in the hospital. After the commissioner remarks that the hero looks ridiculous in his costume, Gordon reveals that the fake Batman was an ex-cop who had snapped and decided to "clean up the city" – the implication being that only a crazy person would do what Batman does. Then, Gordon points out that Batman's crime blitz has cleaned up the city and he asks, "What do you do now, Batman?"

It's a logical question. If Batman is driven by protecting Gotham City, then what is his purpose when Gotham is at peace? Batman as an idea is so much more than just Gotham City. Although the gothic spires and dark alleyways are essential to the character's identity, Morrison is establishing his argument that Batman can't be confined to a single location – a point that will be explored in its full depth during *Batman, Inc.*

So, Bruce and Alfred agree to go to London for a charity event and Alfred notes a disturbing change in Bruce, "that growl in your voice – the one you used to have to practice before you went out as Batman... you're doing it all the time, sir."

Again, it's a subtle commentary that Batman has become completely indistinguishable from Bruce Wayne, as if the two identities have molded into

---

[1] *The Invisibles*, often regarded as Grant Morrison's masterpiece, was published by DC Comics / Vertigo from 1994 to 2000. For more information, see Patrick Meaney's *Our Sentence is Up* (Sequart, 2010).

one. Morrison rejects the notion that Batman is the dominant identity for Bruce Wayne in his (previously mentioned) interview with io9:

> Bruce Wayne would have gone mad if he *hadn't* dressed as a bat and found a startling way to channel the grief, guilt and helplessness he felt after the death of his parents. Without Batman, Bruce would be truly screwed-up but with Batman he becomes mythic, more than human and genuinely useful to his community. I believe he began to slay his demons the moment he became a demon.

Just in time to remind Bruce that he is more than just a Dark Knight, Robin (Tim Drake) slides down what appears to be a Bat-Pole in all his colorful glory. While Tim's arrival is a reminder that Batman isn't a lonely, insane man on the path to self-destruction, it's his entrance that is the true reminder. Sliding down the pole is a subtle connection to the '60s Batman TV series and a time where the two would crack puns and fight crime. It seems that Bruce's influence is rubbing off on Tim Drake, however, as Alfred has to remind Tim to take off his Robin mask before he goes racing off on a motorcycle. Even though Morrison is a writer who loves to emphasize the "super" parts of super-heroes, this issue has many moments that humanize the characters, with Alfred reminding them that they have civilian identities.

Once in London, Alfred retrains Bruce on how to be a billionaire playboy. After commenting on Bruce's posture and voice, Alfred notes that Bruce has to get back into celebrity gossip columns, and he mentions Bruce's ex-girlfriends Kathy Kane, Julie Madison, Vicki Vale, and Silver St. Cloud, reminding the reader that all of Bruce's past romantic relationships matter and are being taken into account as part of Morrison's vision. Bruce takes Alfred's advice as he flirts with women at the Action for Africa charity event.

While most of the event seems to be a showcase for Roy Lichtenstein-like paintings, the upside-down dinosaur in a green glass case at the center of the event seems a little out of place. One could argue, however, that it is a visual connection to the dinosaur in the Batcave. Yet because it is upside-down, it is implying the inverse. If the dinosaur is in the Batcave where Bruce Wayne learns to be Batman, then the inverse dinosaur is where Batman is learning how to be Bruce Wayne. Despite the progress Bruce Wayne has made, as he approaches Alfred, the butler remarks that he still needs to "lose the growl."

By the end of Grant Morrison's first issue, he has established all of the essential elements of Batman and subverted them to new ends. Batman interacts with all of the most important elements of his life – the Joker,

Commissioner Gordon, Alfred, and Robin (nemesis, friend, father, and son) – in order for the reader to understand some fundamental truths about Batman – every story from the past matters; Batman and Bruce Wayne are two identities that are becoming inseparable; only a crazy person would be Batman; while Gotham City needs Batman, the character is so much more than one city – he is an idea that one city cannot contain.

Meanwhile, in-between these fantastic moments of showcasing the elements of Batman, we learn that Francine Langstrom (wife of former Man-Bat, Kirk Langstrom) has been kidnapped by Talia Al-Ghul. Kirk is to deliver the Man-Bat formula to Talia in exchange for his wife's life. Perhaps the best moment during this sequence is when Kirk gets into a car driven by two men in full ninja gear. This is a scene that could only be seen as plausible in a Grant Morrison comic. It's humorous in a way, but completely in accord with the rest of Morrison's idea that Batman can be whimsical at times.

And so, after all of the essential elements of Batman are presented to the reader, there could be no more perfect threat than a swarm of ninja man-bats created by a serum. If Batman is unique because of all of the elements that Morrison has meticulously established throughout the issue, then the serum is his commentary on the remedial take on the character over the years. It's as if writers used this magic serum to craft generic Batman story after generic Batman story to the point where nothing feels special any longer and now the newly born Morrison Batman has come to kick their asses.

The big reveal at the end of the first issue is that Bruce Wayne has fathered an illegitimate child with Talia Al-Ghul. In the coming issues, Damian Wayne would become one of the most hated characters in comics, only to be ultimately redeemed later. Even though his part is very small in this issue, Damian comes off as innocent and a bit timid. He is, after all, a boy who has never met his father, so there is an element of sadness to the character. But whatever empathy the reader may have for Damian will be shattered in the coming issues.

Batman #656

Most of Morrison's second issue takes place at the Action for Africa charity event. Pop art lines the walls and is used for some of the exceptionally inventive humor. Jezebel Jet makes her first appearance on the first panel of the first page and a pop art painting hangs in the background with the word "Wow!" on it to emphasize her sensuality. She and Bruce walk about the fundraiser when, and Bruce comments, "All this comic book stuff is way too highbrow for me," which is perhaps a commentary on the meticulous construction of the previous issue. Bruce goes on to say that he collects, "tribal art" and the works of "schizophrenic painters." Though it seems like a small, almost forgettable throwaway detail, it is actually an exceptionally insightful look into the character and the themes established throughout Morrison's entire run.

The "schizophrenic painters" foreshadows the "R.I.P." storyline where Batman falls into a hallucinatory madness. Yet that madness is constructed and organized by Bruce's brain in order to keep him alive and well.

The "tribal art," on the other hand, strikes at much larger themes. The Bat-Symbol is a magic sigil, meaning that it is a symbolic representation of everything that encompasses Batman. It not only represents heroism, but also deep suffering. Furthermore, it is the sigil of the ultimate human being; a man who is so much more than a man in a mask. In *Batman: The Return of Bruce Wayne*, the first issue finds Bruce leading the Migani tribe which later becomes a tribe of Batmen. In *Batman, Inc.*, the Bat-Symbol becomes a corporate sigil for heroes around the world to rally behind (after all, what are corporations if not tribes of people working toward a common goal?).

In the next panel, Bruce looks at a sculpture of a paint can and says, "There's a message here somewhere. I know if I just stare hard enough..." For some modern art, the message is what the piece represents aesthetically. So, in some cases, the art has no message beyond the pleasure one gains simply by looking at the art in question. Bruce Wayne doesn't think this way, however. To his naturally analytical mind, everything has a purpose and a reason. The yellow paint could be joy, happiness, fear, intellect, decay, sickness, jealousy, or have any number of symbolic meanings. Even the paint can itself could be symbolic. Yet, if the artist intended the sculpture to be devoid of meaning, and to exist for its aesthetic beauty, then Bruce could be wasting his time. Strangely, this one panel of a paint can perfectly summarizes the conflict between Batman and the Joker in "R.I.P." Batman is always looking for hidden meanings, and the Joker has none.

Jezebel Jet and Bruce Wayne flirt more and we learn that she is not just a model, but also the leader of a small African nation. After Bruce asks if he can call her, she replies, "Don't worry. I know where you live." At first, it seems like a harmless comment, but after reading "R.I.P.," Jezebel's insistence that she knows where Bruce lives actually comes off as sinister and somewhat frightening.

Outside, Kirk and Francine Langstrom frantically approach Alfred. They try to warn him about the man-bats, but it's too late – the ninja man-bats have attacked the Action for Africa charity event. Bruce changes into Batman and proceeds to beat them mercilessly for the next 11 pages. As Batman pulls a ninja man-bat to the ground, he thinks, "Six hundred pounds of meat, gristle, and hide. What does that remind me of?" The next panel, we are shown Bruce and Dick sitting at a dinner table as Bruce's aunt Agatha brings them a turkey. Aunt Agatha was introduced in *Batman* #89 (Feb 1955) and for the most part has been forgotten, but in this one panel, she lives again and remains in continuity. In the midst of the conflict, this one panel reminds the reader that every Batman story has occurred.

At the end of their conflict, Batman is knocked unconscious and awakens in a cave where he faces Talia. The man-bats hold Batman down and a few more seem almost intimate with Talia as they surround her. It is here that Talia most clearly represents the demon mother, Lilith.

In Jewish folklore, during the creation of the world, Adam was made from the earth itself along with his first wife, Lilith. During sex, she insisted that they lie side by side because they were equals. After her husband refused her, Lilith left to the Red Sea where she gave birth to over a hundred baby demons a day. Prior to her role in the Talmud, Lilith was a storm demon who ravaged men in their sleep and ruined their satisfaction with mortal women. She also caused women to be barren and murdered babies in their sleep.

Morrison's portrayal of Talia al Ghul (whose last name means "Demon's Head") follows similar ideas in the Lilith myth. Batman states that he was drugged and forced to have sex with her which can be interpreted as a sort of magic spell that Lilith would place upon her victims. It is worth noting that in the original 1987 *Son of the Demon* graphic novel, Batman had consensual sex with Talia; but if the sex were consensual, then she wouldn't really be representing Lilith. Furthermore, the man-bats swarm around Talia in a way that makes them seem demonic and as if she were motherly to them – another important detail that solidifies her role as a mother of demons.

Talia explains that the result of coupling with Bruce was the birth of their son whom Batman will have to take care of. She concludes by saying that she intends to "hold the world hostage to a new kind of terror" – a promise she

Batman and Damian meet for the first time. The final page of *Batman* Vol. 1 #656 (Oct 2006). Art by Andy Kubert and Jesse Delperdang. Copyright © DC Comics.

doesn't act on until *Batman, Inc.* a full six years later. The issue ends with the first meeting of Bruce Wayne and his son, Damian, as the boy holds a sword to Batman's throat and says, "Father. I imagined you taller." This first full appearance of Damian is powerful and establishes his personality as being strong, defiant, and unafraid of his father.

Batman #657

The reader is fully introduced to Damian as Bruce takes him to the Batcave and it isn't any wonder why the character was so hated from the start. After asserting his intelligence through condescending questions about the methane gas byproduct of bats, unveiling the new Batmobile before it is finished, and then challenging his father to a fight, Damian comes off as completely unsympathetic and downright rude. He's the equivalent to an unwanted character introduced in the final seasons of a sitcom – an annoying ploy to attract a certain type of audience.

The first issue of Morrison's run was titled "Building a Better Batmobile." Every element of what makes Batman unique is distilled into one issue in order to establish the basics of the character and move toward a new kind of narrative. In a way, the Batmobile is a metaphor for the changing nature of Batman himself. Each new writer and artist team brings in a new Batmobile with altered looks and weapons. The metaphor can even be extended to the film franchise as well: the Adam West Batmobile had a classic look complete with goofy gadgets, the Michael Keaton Batmobile made Batman sleek and cool, and the Christian Bale Batmobile was designed to look like a tank and grounded the character in a more "real-world" sensibility.

Damian's unveiling of the unfinished Batmobile teases the audience and uses the Batmobile as a metaphor for the frame of his overall Batman run. The unfinished Batmobile is a signal to the reader to realize that the story of Batman and his son is not the main narrative Morrison will tell. Hidden beneath this story is the real skeleton for all Morrison's Batman stories which is that every Batman story matters. Even though years before, DC swore that "Son of the Demon" was not in continuity, here is Morrison asserting that it is, along with every insane story from the '60s.

Tim Drake returns from his trip to the mountains and tries to make friends with Damian. The son of Batman responds with rude comments, mentions that his mother lets him do what he wants, and then he storms off and swears at Alfred. In James Robinson's "Face the Face" arc which preceded Morrison's first story arc, Bruce had adopted Tim, so Tim's question of "What about us?" reads with a tone of worry as he wonders if he's going to be replaced by Bruce's biological son after just being adopted.

Bruce reassures him by saying, "This doesn't change anything," but it did. Even though Tim Drake had his own title and a starring role in *Teen Titans*, the introduction of Damian would be the beginning of the end of Tim Drake's tenure as Robin. It would be a few years, but the change would happen nonetheless.

Despite Damian's attitude, Bruce does his best to stick up for his son. He tries reasoning with Tim by explaining, "He was raised by international terrorists in his grandfather's league of assassins. Brutalized, indoctrinated, then used as a weapon in his mother's insane war against me. If he is my son – even if he's not – he deserves some love and my respect."

If raising a child is part nature and nurture, then Damian was doomed from the start. By nature, his father is obsessive, and his mother is insane and he was raised by assassins, so it isn't any wonder that Damian is as bad as he is.

Tim isn't as sympathetic, replying, "So let him earn it, like everybody else."

This reply stabs at the core of Bruce's biggest flaw as a human being; he has never been a nurturing person. If Dick Grayson and Tim Drake are Bruce's surrogate children, he has been a terrible father, because he has imprinted upon them that they must "earn" his love and respect rather than being bestowed these praises unconditionally. Bruce isn't all bad, however, as he feels responsible for Damian and therefore doesn't apply these same conditional affections that Dick and Tim were bound to.

In Wayne manor, Damian acts like an insolent child as he asks question after question. "Why can't I get a laptop?" "What have you done with my sword? Where are we?" Bruce responds with patience, but Damian screams, "I hate it here!" and "I've been sent here against my will! You can't make me do anything I don't want to do!"

Finally, Batman has had enough and shouts, "Enough! You dishonor your sensei with this loss of composure! Your rage is born of fear and is unbefitting in a student of the martial arts! You'll be given opportunities to prove yourself to me. Until then, boy – patience is a virtue!"

What Batman doesn't realize is that Damian's warped sense of honor would take this as a challenge rather than as an admonition.

In the Gotham sewers, a villain called the Spook has kidnapped the mayor. Batman comes from out of nowhere to save an undercover cop and then he discovers that the Spook has somehow been beheaded. Back at the Batcave, Tim finds Damian training with a sword. Damian reveals that he had escaped and murdered the Spook saying, "I fought crime tonight. Crime lost." Of course, it would seem as if Damian is evil for committing murder, but one has to remember that he was raised to believe his enemies deserved no mercy. He killed because he was raised to believe that killing was the only way. In his mind, he believes that he has risen to the challenge his father set before him and that he has restored his honor after behaving childishly before. Finally, Damian defeats Tim Drake in battle thinking that beating Batman's sidekick will allow himself to assume the role of Robin.

Batman #658

The final issue of the "Batman and Son" story begins with Damian justifying his attack on Tim Drake, "He was my rival. He's not your real son, I am! It's my right to replace him. That's how it works in the assassin's league." This bit of dialogue furthers Morrison's defense for Damian that the character can't help how he was raised and if he continued with this repetitive defensive rhetoric without some act of redemption, then the character would be one note and irredeemable. However, Damian insists that he isn't simply there to disrupt Batman's work, and he reveals that Talia wants to capture the garrison at Gibraltar. Taking Damian with him so the boy won't get into further trouble, Batman commands his son to obey orders. With a newfound resolve, Damian replies, "I won't fail you, father" and the two race off in the Batmobile.

Of course, the Batmobile was revealed as unfinished in the previous issue, but looking closely, it is apparent that this vehicle is an older design. In fact, it has an older style bat-shield on the front that resembles the very first Batmobile. On the surface, it reestablishes that even those Batman stories from the '40s exist, but metaphorically speaking, Morrison is channeling this older design in order to evoke old feelings of Batman and Robin racing to save the day. Prior to Morrison's run, Batman had been relegated to the role of hardened detective of Gotham City, but this Batmobile emphasizes the "super" part of the "super-hero" Batman. It is explicitly unrealistic and goofy from the giant fins to the bat-shield and right down to the fact that the wheels aren't touching the road. More specifically, however, it sets up the most absurd Batman moment yet.

After visiting Kirk and Francine Langstrom, Damian asks his father how they will get to Gibraltar so quickly and Batman reveals that he owns a rocket. It may be bizarre for Batman and Damian to be in a rocket to Gibraltar, but it is an important moment because it establishes the fun and absurd nature of Morrison's Batman. If Batman is one of the richest men in the world and has all sorts of other fun toys, then why *wouldn't* he have a rocket? It is so far beyond the idea of what is necessary for a detective and quite literally launches Batman into the role of super-hero.

As they launch off into space, there is a short, but poignant moment as Damian asks what Bruce's father was like. It's only a page, but it is evidence that as tough as Damian is, he ultimately wants to know his father. He wants to be part of Batman's life. More importantly, it puts Batman into a role that he has never quite been in before. Of course, he has acted as a father to Dick and Tim, but never in this way. If Batman is the perfect human being as Morrison and other writers have asserted in the past, then this is Batman completely and totally out of his element. This is Batman at his most vulnerable. It didn't take a brilliant villain to put him there, it took the uncomfortable notion of Batman trying to understand and bond with the son he never knew he had.

At Gibraltar, Batman and Damian battle the ninja man-bats and afterward, Damian excitedly says, "Mother. I've ruined your plans!" It's a subtle reminder that Damian is still a child, a boy with the perception that the world is just one giant game.

Talia explains that it was all part of her plan for them to become a family. She asks for Batman to reform her and says, "If you do, I'll combine my vast resources with yours to fight crime at your side and together we can raise our son to be the master of the Earth." She goes on to say, "What I want is you. I want us to fulfill my father's wishes and be a family. Who else in this world is like us, Bruce Wayne? The century's greatest crimefighter, the daughter of its greatest crimelord. And their genetically perfect child. Join me and I promise I'll never threaten civilization ever again."

While Talia is an insane terrorist and her word can't be trusted, Batman doesn't even weigh the option of peace. When one considers the advantages of a reformed league of assassins being guided by Batman into an organization dedicated to the protection of the world, marriage to Talia al Ghul shouldn't even be a question; Batman absolutely should reform her and establish an empire with her. Of course, when Talia continues to use the verb "rule" instead of "protect," then maybe her motives aren't as altruistic as she seems to believe. Batman rejects her proposal and Talia responds, "Then it's war. And you're responsible." She swears revenge, but she won't enact it until *Batman, Inc.*

In a sense, Batman is to blame for the coming conflict with Talia because of his unwillingness to be with her, but we could further interpret his decision as unwillingness to be anything beyond Gotham City's protector. At the beginning of Grant Morrison's extended run with Batman, the character's worldview is narrow and he can't see how essential it is to expand his role. Even though Batman is the perfect human being, he is still ultimately flawed and Morrison will tear the character apart and rebuild him into something new and something much larger than just one man.

Batman #664

Due to his overwhelming schedule of working on the weekly comic *52,* Morrison had stepped away from *Batman* during issues #659-662 and was replaced by the team of John Ostrander and Tom Mandrake. Morrison's first issue back was the mostly prose issue titled, "The Clown at Midnight" (#663) and it is mostly an issue that explores the Joker's changing personality rather than a strict commentary on Batman himself. This issue is discussed in depth in the Joker and Dr. Hurt chapter of this book. The first issue that Morrison *truly* returns to full form is in the first part of "Three Ghosts of Batman" (#664).

It had been six months since the conclusion of the "Batman and Son" story, and so Morrison quickly reminds the reader of everything that had occurred on the first page with a single image of Bruce Wayne standing in Gibraltar with piles of defeated man-bats in the streets. Every theme is present within this image: Batman is trying to act more like Bruce Wayne; the ninja man-bats are a fun and wild idea that stretch Batman beyond being a detective; Batman has been operating in Gibraltar rather than being relegated to Gotham City.

It's a provocative image as well. We don't know how Batman has managed to defeat the ninja man-bats, but it excites the imagination and allows for the reader to fill in the blanks. And because the image is of Bruce Wayne dressed in a suit with an undone tie rather than as a battle-worn Batman, it leads the reader to believe that the encounter was relatively easy for our hero because he seems relaxed and casual.

Bruce is on his cell phone and a voice tells him to be at La Flegere at 10:30 the next day. On the next page, we learn that it was Jezebel Jet who had summoned Bruce to go skiing with her. At one minute early, Bruce parachutes onto the mountain. "I've always wanted to do that," he says upon landing. Of course, the irony is that he had performed a HALO jump out of his rocket at the end of "Batman and Son" and that parachuting on the mountain is tame by comparison. The parallel parachuting adventures are indicative of the Bruce Wayne and Batman personas becoming increasingly more aligned. Bruce Wayne no longer makes himself appear to be an aloof playboy who lazes about his bedroom. Now, the adventurous Batman persona is bleeding into Bruce Wayne and making him more dangerous.

After giving Jezebel Jet a blue rose (a breed known as a "Pennyworth Blue," created by Alfred, that has a sort of tangential connection to Alan Moore's Superman story, "For the Man Who has Everything," where Batman's butler had bred a "Krypton" rose), one of Jet's bodyguards comments that he is cool like James Bond to which Bruce replies, "Oh, I'm *much* cooler than he is."

The Bruce Wayne / Batman identity bleed continues further as a paranoid Bruce launches a ski pole into a paparazzo's helicopter blades — clearly not a standard reaction from a billionaire playboy. At dinner, Bruce laments that he can't save his reputation with the tabloids and that they have labeled him as "Mad, bad, and reckless." It's here that Morrison is deliberately connecting Bruce Wayne to the poet, Lord Byron, who was called "Mad, bad, and dangerous to know" by Lady Caroline Lamb. Morrison had previously used Lord Byron's *Manfred* in creating the villain of Mr. Whisper for "Gothic," but Morrison had also invoked Lord Byron and his friend Percy Bysshe Shelley in his seminal work, *The Invisibles*. The two poets were revealed to have been members of an Invisibles cell (a group of anarchists seeking to overthrow the oppressive, evil alien overlords who rule the world) during the 19th century. Morrison has a fascination with Lord Byron and though the connection between Batman and Byron may be a seemingly small reference, it is an absolutely perfect connection given that Batman exemplifies the characteristics of the Byronic Hero archetype.

Originally defined in Lord Byron's *Childe Harold's Pilgrimage,* a Byronic Hero is a dark, brooding, attractive character with a troubled past who rejects society. The influence of this type of character can be seen in Heathcliff from Emily Bronte's *Wuthering Heights*, and Alexandre Dumas's *The Count of Monte Cristo*, but also extends to films like *Donnie Darko*, *Brick*, and the James Bond movies. Make no mistake, this archetype can be seen in literature far before

Byron's definition as well with the character of Satan in John Milton's *Paradise Lost* and even further before that with William Shakespeare's *Hamlet*, but the clear definition of the archetype is attributed to Lord Byron.

Batman has been built within the Byronic hero archetype and by invoking Lord Byron himself in the description of Bruce Wayne, Morrison is connecting the character to a rich history of a similar archetype. A deliberate connection between Batman and Byron creates the argument that the character can be as complex as Satan in *Paradise Lost* or Heathcliff in *Wuthering Heights*. Though it may not be necessary to legitimize *Batman* as literature, this is exactly what Morrison has done by tying the character to a literary tradition.

Jezebel seems to try and comfort Bruce by saying, "I read about your parents. I'm so sorry, Bruce, you were so young. It must have been terrible. My own father was assassinated because of what he believed in. I want you to know I understand." Of course, knowing the ending of "R.I.P." we understand that Jet's father was murdered because he was part of the Black Glove criminal organization and that she is using the death of Bruce's parents to worm her way into his heart.

With eyes closed and seemingly peaceful, Bruce replies, "Jezebel, it was... it was a long time ago." Then, the final panel is a close-up shot of Bruce's frightening eyes that contradict his assertion of, "I got over it." On the next page, Batman stands on a rooftop in the rain emphasizing the point that Bruce has never gotten over the deaths of his parents. In the alley below, a pimp makes a deal with some policemen and after Batman breaks up their meeting, he learns that the pimp has been supplying girls to a cop who looks like a monster.

Before he goes to investigate, Batman hands a Waynetech business card to a very young prostitute and tells her to get a job. This shows that even though the Batman persona seems to be bleeding into the life of Bruce Wayne, the interaction isn't one way. He is still Bruce Wayne under the mask and he will use his resources outside of being a super-hero in order to help people in need. This interaction is even more important than Bruce's attack on the paparazzo because it shows that Batman needs the Bruce Wayne identity in order to maintain sanity – a point that will really be important during "R.I.P." when the Bruce Wayne identity is completely stripped away and all that is left is the Batman of Zur-en-Arrh.

As Batman investigates the lair of the monster cop, he finds the dead bodies of prostitutes and piles of old pizza boxes. Perhaps in order to keep his sanity and process what he is seeing, he thinks, "The *locker room* smells so thick in here it's like *weather.* Makes me think of board meetings. The *stock exchange*. Executive washrooms. It's *testosterone*. Alpha male hormone." Here, Batman is falling back on Bruce Wayne's persona in order to understand and process what is going on around him into something that makes sense.

The monster cop has the appearance of Bane, the man who broke Batman's back, but dressed in Batman's cape and cowl. Batman tries to evade the monster and he mentions something called "the black casebook." The issue ends with the monster cop smashing Batman to the ground and leaving a giant footprint in his back.

Batman #665

A group of unsympathetic prostitutes watches as Batman struggles to get to his feet. Passing back out, Batman mentions "bells ringing" for the first time. The bell is a symbol that will reoccur throughout Morrison's run and this is the first instance of it.

After a prostitute named Roxy dumps him in an escape tunnel on Finger and Fourth (Finger being a reference to artist Bill Finger, the creator of the Joker), and Alfred is called to the penthouse, Batman hallucinates and sees the three ghosts of Batman. These three former cops who have been transformed into Batmen haunt him in his sleep along with Damian who claims "the third ghost is the worst of them all" – perhaps a reference to the Ghost of Christmas Yet to Come from Charles Dickens's *A Christmas Carol.*

As Bruce recovers, he explains that the Black Casebook was a collection of all of the unexplained encounters he had faced as Batman including "vampires, flying saucers, time travel..." and that these three ghosts were in that casebook. Bruce says, "I was sure they were hallucinations, cautionary tales, visions of what I might have become in other lives. But this... this is real."

Given that Morrison's run on *Batman* is steeped in Satanic images to foreshadow the coming of Dr. Hurt (the villain who may or may not be the Devil), these Three Ghosts of Batman are meant to represent an unholy trinity of sorts. In a sense, they represent the worst aspects of Batman and serve as reminders of Bruce's failings.

The first was the Gun Batman who shot the Joker in the head in Morrison's first issue. He represents Batman's hidden desire to kill his enemies, but more specifically, he reflects Batman in his original creation when he carried a gun. Though he really doesn't have much of a role in the story, the ghost with a gun serves as a subtle reminder of what Batman once was.

Meanwhile, the second ghost had "dosed himself with Hugo Strange's Monster serum and daily venom shots" and so, he is a reminder of the man who broke Batman: Bane. But the character is also a reminder that Batman once experimented with Venom himself. After his encounter with Bane, Batman had used Venom and found that it made him overly aggressive, so he had to quit the drug. The Monster Batman is not only a symbol of fear for when Batman lost, but he is also a symbol of addiction.

Finally, the third ghost will be revealed to be the Anti-Christ in *Batman* #666 in a story where Damian is the Batman of the future. In a strange way, these Three Ghosts of Batman are almost like the three ghosts in "A Christmas Carol" with Bruce Wayne as an unconventional Ebenezer Scrooge. The ghost with a gun is of the past, the monstrous ghost is the present, and the third ghost is the future and they are the start of Bruce Wayne becoming a better Batman.

Horrified that Tim would face the monstrous ghost on his own, Batman prepares to go out. Alfred asks why Batman is toweling himself off with Bruce Wayne's unlaundered shirts (note that Alfred doesn't say "your shirts" and thereby implies a stronger disconnect of the dual-identities) and Bruce explains, "The man I faced tonight has been transformed into a testosterone-driven hulk. But I come from generations of old money. I've beaten up Superman... I wore this shirt when I was chewing out the shareholders in the Waynetech boardroom yesterday. What's the one thing an alpha male is programmed to respect? Alpha male plus."

Fiction is littered with stories where the hero loses to the villain in the first encounter and prepares for the next encounter by using a secret weapon. Morrison has subverted this formula by making Bruce Wayne's testosterone the secret weapon to Batman's success. No bat-gadget is necessary here – it is the natural odors and secretions of Bruce Wayne that are potent enough to defeat the monstrous ghost of Batman. This is the idea that Bruce Wayne is used to controlling Batman made manifest and it will later be explored in "R.I.P."

Robin encounters the monstrous ghost first and after Batman shows up and the two defeat the villain, the police arrive to take the ghost of Batman into custody. Afterward, Batman meets with Commissioner Gordon who reveals that the monster Batman had "vanished, like he was never there." Batman is facing something far more powerful than himself, or as Gordon puts it, "Why did you have to choose an enemy that's as old as time and bigger than all of us, Batman?" In this one line of dialogue, Morrison has tipped his hand as to the identity of the overarching villain – the Devil himself.

Batman #666

Bruce Wayne doesn't appear in this issue except in two flashback panels to explain Damian's origin story. In a panel where Damian kneels over the dead body of Batman, we learn that Damian is "driven by guilt and haunted by his legacy" and that he "walks a lonely path between good and evil as Batman." The reason for this jump in time (besides the fact that Damian is utterly, undeniably cool as Batman) is to show that Batman is more than just Bruce Wayne. Batman transcends one person; it's more than just a job as well. Batman is an idea.

No hero seems to be more preoccupied by his own mortality than Batman. Maybe it's the character's humanity or perhaps it is connected to the loss of his parents, but a common motif in Batman stories is that no matter how hard Bruce Wayne tries, his mission will end in failure. *Batman* #666 is no exception. While the idea of legacy is meant to be comforting because it reminds us that Batman will live on after Bruce Wayne, the story is heavy with melancholy. The legacy may continue, but no matter how much good he does, Bruce Wayne is long dead and Damian Wayne continues on in his stead. The idea that "Batman and Robin will never die" is first shown in this issue, but it's a rather somber one.

Bruce Wayne was never a man at peace, but he surrounded himself with others to keep himself grounded. The tragedy of Bruce Wayne isn't that he lost his parents, but rather that he uses that rage to blind himself from the fact that he has created a surrogate family that loves him. Alfred, Commissioner Gordon, Dick Grayson, Barbara Gordon, Tim Drake... the list of people within his family goes on, but he will never find peace because of the tragedy of his childhood.

Future Damian, however, is in far more difficult position than Bruce ever imagined. The Anti-Christ, dressed in a Batman costume, wages war on the criminal underworld to signal the coming of the beast. Damian is shown to be living alone, popping pills, with only a cat named Alfred for company. While Bruce may have felt alone in his mission, he always had a support network around him. Even the police are against Damian, but he still defends the city because he promised his father.

At the end of the issue, Damian battles the Anti-Christ and reveals that he has sold his soul to the Devil in exchange to keep Gotham City safe. It's in this moment that we realize the depths of Damian's commitment. He's so dedicated that he literally commits himself in ways that were only figurative for Bruce Wayne.

Batman #667

If "Batman and Son" was Morrison's statement on who Batman is, and "The Three Ghosts of Batman" were what Batman could have been if he were evil, then the "Island of Mister Mayhew" is about Batman as an idea that can be replicated. As Bruce and Tim fly toward their island destination of Mayhew Island, and Tim asks why Bruce would go, Batman replies, "What do eccentric men who have everything do when they get bored?"

The implication is that Batman is neither eccentric nor bored. After all, Batman calls his war on crime "the mission" not "the hobby."

Tim laments that his choices are to stay home and avoid Alfred's construction work on Wayne Manor or to "hang out with a bunch of weird c-list crime fighters." We are to understand that this International Club of Heroes is far from the efficient, fearsome heroes that we all know and love. American super-heroes are to be viewed as "normal" and heroic while others are considered "weird." Tim's ethnocentrism is acting as the voice of the reader in this statement. To some, the International Club of Heroes may be considered a ridiculous idea because they were characters conceived during the '50s and '60s – an era in Batman's history known for its absurdity. When Tim scoffs at the idea of the heroes, he is really voicing the skepticism of the audience, but Morrison's mission is to turn the audience's expectations around.

With the story of the International Club of Heroes, Morrison is establishing ideas that will come into full fruition during his *Batman, Inc.* run, but they are not without precedent. In *Batman* #56 (Dec 1949 - Jan 1950), Batman trained a hero named Bat-Hombre. The heroes Knight and Squire first appeared in *Batman* #62 (Dec 1950 - Jan 1951). Wingman was trained in *Batman* #65 (June-July 1951). Sioux Indian super-hero Man-of-Bats and his sidekick Little Raven met Batman in issue #86 (Sept 1954). In *Detective Comics* #215 (Jan 1955), Batman brings together Ranger, Legionary, Knight and Squire, Gaucho, and the Musketeer, and they form the "Batmen of All Nations." Finally, in *World's Finest*

#89 (July-Aug 1957), John Mayhew brings the heroes together to form "the International Club of Heroes."

The characters were mostly forgotten until Morrison brought back Knight and Squire for a single, non-speaking appearance as they joined the Ultramarines in his *JLA* run, and then again in *JLA Classified* as the Ultramarines were under attack.

For this arc, Morrison has not only brought these characters back, but has also given them a sense of progression. The former Squire is now the current Knight, Ranger has now become "Dark Ranger," Musketeer accidentally murdered a man and went to an insane asylum, Wingman is in denial that Batman had ever trained him, Legionary has retired and reflects upon his glory days, and Little Raven has now become Red Raven and his relationship with Man-of-Bats is strained. Not only has Morrison continued to establish that every Batman story is in continuity, but by giving these characters stories of their own, he has established that they have personalities and a world beyond their few appearances in the DCU.

Billionaire John Mayhew is their host, but it is revealed that Mayhew has been murdered and skinned. We will later learn that the man in the Mayhew skin is Dr. William Hurt (also known as the Black Glove) but for the time being he is just a rich mastermind who has trapped the heroes on an island and taken bets on whether good or evil will win the day. The first issue ends with Legionary being stabbed 23 times.

The second issue begins with a flashback to a meeting of The International Club of Heroes where the former Knight attacked Legionary as Knight's son, Cyril watched. Now that Cyril is the current Knight, he is considered the prime suspect in Legionary's murder by some of the heroes. The atmosphere Morrison has created is similar to the Agatha Christie story *And Then There Were None*, in which a group of strangers is stranded in the mountains and one by one, they are murdered. Paranoid, the stranded begin accusing one another.

Once again, Tim returns to ridiculing the rest of the International Club of Heroes, calling them the "League of Losers" and "Batman Impersonators of All Nations." Batman corrects him, by first calling Tim "unfair" and then explaining, "El Gaucho's a well-respected crime fighter in Argentina. Even the Legionary was great once." Batman is speaking for Morrison here and meant to answer Tim's voice of the audience. Just because the heroes aren't American doesn't make them "losers" and just because they were introduced as different variations on Batman doesn't make them "impersonators." The argument seems to be that these characters are no different than any other characters introduced in a Batman comic; it's just that no one has done anything with them to make them great.

Dick Grayson, Tim Drake, and Damian Wayne are supporting characters with their own successful and forgettable stories. They are characters with their own share of fans and detractors. Characters like Knight and Squire or Man-of-Bats may not have been original in their conception, but with the correct writer and the right story, they could be great characters. Morrison shows this by giving each hero something more than just their name and costume. The Musketeer isn't just a guy in a costume from France who fights crime – he is an emotionally tortured individual who accidentally murdered someone and became a sensation after his story was made into a movie. Knight isn't the Batman of England; he is a legacy hero that inherited his identity from his father. Morrison is using these characters to argue that with proper context no idea is ridiculous, and any character can be interesting when enough of an effort is made.

Batman investigates Legionary's death and notes that the hero left them a series of clues to decipher. Afterward, they find Knight beaten and forced to swallow a bomb. Chief Man-of-Bats is also a doctor and stays to help Knight while the others are attacked by robotic knights. Wingman has apparently been burned to death. Finally, Robin and Squire are captured after they find a secret passage behind a bookcase. Even though no villains have appeared, the heroes note the calling cards of their respective foes which sets up their introductions during "R.I.P."

The final issue of the storyline – *Batman* #667 – begins with the flashback to eight years ago. Knight attacks John Mayhew and accuses the billionaire of orchestrating the death of Knight's wife. As Cyril reminisces, Chief Man-of-Bats says, "The papers called us 'the Batmen of Many Nations' but we were really just a bunch of tough guys who'd heard about this new kind of man in Gotham City."

Here, Man-of-Bats tells us that the idea of Batman is inspirational. As Man-of-Bats explains, "We were all inspired in different ways – some saw a chance for redemption, some were thrill-seekers, some were rich and bored..." and while he is specifically referring to The International Club of Heroes, his words are applicable to readers as well. Batman appeals to the world because he can be anything. He is hope, camp, cool, vengeful, dark, evil, magic, and any other number of words people want to use to describe him.

The arc concludes with the revelation that Wingman has murdered Dark Ranger and switched places with him, and that Wingman hates Batman for ruining his chances of becoming a famous hero when Batman refused to work with The International Club of Heroes. "It's not fair! Recognition came easy for you! Respect came easy! I've been running in place for years! I should have been an international hero, but you turned me into a villain!"

The story also concludes with the revelation that John Mayhew had been alive the entire time and has been masquerading as El Sombrero. He also blames Batman as he says, "it was your disdain that killed the enthusiasm of the Club of Heroes."

Casting blame on Batman for Wingman and John Mayhew's turn to villainy, is a plot point that directly connects with the conclusion of "Batman and Son." Batman's stubbornness caused Talia al Ghul to create the terrorist organization Leviathan just as it caused Wingman and Mayhew to switch sides.

While "the Black Glove" story might not be Morrison's strongest, it lays the foundation for a number of plot points that will come up again later. The most obvious is that it introduces the Black Glove as the overarching villain. Morrison also establishes that the international reach of Batman can be replicated. Most importantly, but perhaps more elusive, is that Batman's narrow worldview continues to create problems.

"The Resurrection of Ra's al Ghul"

There was a time when all of the Bat-titles routinely crossed over into one another as part of large, editorially mandated, overarching storylines that typically required readers to purchase most, if not all, of the Batman family's comics in order to keep a grasp on continuity. The earliest and most successful of these mega-crossovers was "Knightfall," in which the villain Bane broke Batman's back. After DC realized the commercial success of the mega-crossover, it seemed as if each crossover would beget another.

A lethal disease spreads through Gotham City in the 11-part series "Contagion," followed by the 18-part follow-up mega-crossover "Legacy." A year later, an earthquake struck Gotham City in the 18-issue arc "Cataclysm" which was immediately followed by "No Man's Land," a story that spanned a massive 77 issues. While there were crossovers after this, none were on par with the mega-crossovers of the past.

In an effort to revive the crossover format, Grant Morrison's *Batman* was united with Paul Dini's *Detective Comics*, Peter Milligan's *Robin*, and Fabian Nicieza's *Nightwing* under a single story revolving around the return of eco-terrorist villain, Ra's al Ghul. The result was a convoluted mess that lacked any semblance of coherent storytelling. Essentially, Ra's al Ghul wants to possess Damian's body, but he also wants to go to Nanda Parabat to attain eternal life. However, a villain named "Sensei" wishes to stop Ra's al Ghul. Batman chases after Ra's to stop him, but ends up helping him, only to stop him later in the story.

Characters travel to various locations without any established motivation. Action scenes erupt out of nowhere and accomplish nothing. Action scenes that *should occur* happen off-panel and are explained through exposition. Sexy assassins provide distractions for no reason whatsoever. Batman wears armor with no explanation. Also, the classic DC character named "I-Ching," rarely seen since the'70s, seems to only exist in order to hang out and appear to look cool.

Even though Damian and Talia are involved in this crossover, there is literally no reason to read it. It provides no further understanding into the relationship between Bruce, Damian, and Talia, it provides no insight into Batman at all, and it is the only tarnish within Grant Morrison's otherwise flawless run on *Batman*.

In short, it's best left forgotten.

Batman #672

After six issues, the third ghost of Batman (the Anti-Christ) returns in his mad glory to attack the G.C.P.D. He demands to speak to Commissioner Vane which is a clue to how long this former cop has been out of action given that Vane was a rather obscure character from *Detective Comics* #121 (Mar 1947), when Gordon was demoted. When Gordon confronts him, the third ghost says, "I walked all the way from hell. With a secret to tell. About Batman and me" which is a dead giveaway that the third ghost serves the Devil and the Devil is Dr. Hurt.

Meanwhile, the latest gossip is that Bruce and Jezebel Jet have been rather involved with one another which seems to upset talk show host (and former Bruce Wayne girlfriend) Vicki Vale. This appearance by Vale is another instance of Morrison acknowledging the vast Batman continuity and how it all still exists now. Alfred seems upset that Bruce and Jet have been seeing so much of one another and calls their relationship a "far cry from the parade of superficial liaisons" that Alfred had suggested.

Bruce describes the connection he shares with Jezebel, by saying "she understands how it feels to lose someone you love to violence." By the end of "R.I.P." it's unclear if Bruce really loved her or if it's just all an act, but the very fact that he was attracted to her ability to relate to his loss is a rather dark statement on the identity of Bruce Wayne. Even his new relationships are defined by the death of his parents.

The third ghost has captured Commissioner Gordon and brought him to the roof of the G.C.P.D. It's there that he turns on the Batsignal and informs Gordon that he was responsible for releasing the monstrous Batman (where he let him out from, we don't know, but it wasn't prison considering the conclusion of that arc revealed that the monster cop had disappeared). Once Batman appears, the two fight and after Batman is shot in the chest. The third ghost says, "This police department... this city betrayed me... sent me to hell to learn from the Devil."

When Gordon is shot, Batman looks to the third ghost and his face appears to be an absurd purple cartoon mask. It's unclear what this means, but it will return later.

Then, as Batman has a heart attack, he envisions a bat shattering a window like the night that he was born and the words "Zur-en-Arrh" appear written in green. Finally, the last page is a single image of the magical 5th-dimensional imp, Bat-Mite who says, "Now you're in trouble, Bruce."

These final images are symbols that will recur whenever Batman feels out of his depth, but for now, they are strange, ominous omens of the future.

Batman #673

Issue #673 is titled "Joe Chill in Hell" and features a fractured narrative meant to symbolize Batman's shifting consciousness as he suffers through a heart attack. In the original continuity, the man who murdered Thomas and Martha Wayne was never caught. Later, in *Batman* #47 (June-July 1948), the murderer was identified as "Joe Chill." Eventually, Batman got his revenge upon Chill in the three-issue mini-series *The Untold Legend of Batman* (1989) when Chill is murdered by other criminals for creating Batman. Over the years, Joe Chill has come and gone in continuity with some retellings of Batman's origin stating that the identity of the killer of the Waynes was unknown. Since

Morrison decided that every Batman story told was now in continuity, this issue is designed to update Joe Chill and give him a new purpose.

To this point in Morrison's run, the writer had explored the different aspects of Batman's personality, but he had left the origin untouched. In some ways, re-exploring the origin was unnecessary because it was so engrained in the American psyche that most knew it already: Bruce Wayne's parents were murdered, and then he became Batman. Before this point, it wasn't necessary to revisit the origin because even though they were the beginning of Batman, the truly essential elements were addressed in Morrison's first issue.

The first panel shows a nervous-looking Joe Chill taking medication with alcohol. The next panel takes place years later during the series *52* when Batman underwent the Thogal Ritual of meditation – a seven-week process where "the practitioner undergoes an experience designed to simulate death and after-death. And rebirth, too." Batman's meditation through the Thogal ritual is important because it connects him to the Joker's own death and rebirth in "The Clown at Midnight" during #663. The two are intrinsically linked through their rituals of reshaping their identities.

Our third narrative shift occurs on the next page as a black panel features narration where Batman wonders, "Where am I?" with the realization afterward, "I'm having a heart attack. Some kind of flash forward. Déjà vu." But it's when Batman states, "I have to get out. How long have I been in this cave?" that the message becomes ambiguous. Does Batman mean the Thogal ritual? Does he mean his heart attack? Does he mean literally the Batcave itself? Or does he mean all of the above? It's when Batman asks, "How long have I been in this darkness?" that we realize he is no longer referring to Thogal specifically, but the darkness that has pervaded his life – the darkness that defines his identity.

When we finally see Batman, he is patrolling the city on a whirly-bat – a single person, mini-helicopter that Batman used during the silver age. The whole idea of the whirly-bat may seem ridiculous, but absurdity doesn't exclude something from Morrison's Batman canon. To reemphasize the idea that whirly-bats were common at one time, Batman says in his narration, "All of this is normal" because at one time, it *was* normal for him. For the character, however, the idea of "All of this is normal" also acts as a mantra to keep his sanity. He is, afer all, a man who dresses up as a bat and fights crime.

Batman explains his methodology and how he fights crime every night: "I record the details in a black A4 spiral-bound notebook as if it's procedure and not just madness. I practice that self-conscious, hard-boiled style Alfred loves to read. Anything to keep it interesting. Alfred insists I have to maintain a record of everything."

This takes the narrative down a new, meta-textual path that not only references and reconciles some of Batman's strange past stories, but also offers a reason for why Batman's narration is written in that hard-boiled, detective style.

For one panel, the narrative shifts to *52* continuity where Bruce Wayne battles the Ten Eyed Tribe. He says, "There's nothing left but a deep, black well where my heart should be. These last few years I've seen too many deaths, made too many mistakes." It's an admission of his inability to atone for his mistakes – a confession of the flaw in himself where he will always put himself through trials to help him cope with loss. Bruce Wayne developed Batman to cope with the loss of his parents, and he experienced Thogal to cope with his losses as Batman.

The narrative returns to Batman at the start of his career as he haunted Joe Chill. But rather than portraying Joe Chill as a remorseless killer, Morrison gives the character a certain degree of sympathy as the criminal explains that crime "wasn't a lifestyle choice," and that, "My mother was a prostitute. I had to fight and kill my way to the top of the food chain." While Chill can be remonstrated for his lack of remorse over the lives he had taken, and perhaps he is foolish for not accepting some responsibility for his actions, we have to understand that in his mind, he is a victim of circumstance. He didn't *want* to be a criminal, but because that was the life he was born into, he had to live it.

Joe Chill's most damning line, however, is when he says, "If it ain't the rich preying on the poor like vampires, you tell me what else it is?" There is a degree of humor and irony to this line, because it describes Batman perfectly: – a rich man who preys upon the poor like a vampire. This isn't an isolated instance of Morrison's philosophy of class either. In an interview with *Playboy*, Morrison says, "He's a rich man who beats up poor people. It's quite a bizarre mission to go out at night dressed as a bat and punch the hell out of junkies. And then he goes home and lives in this mansion."[2] Morrison doesn't normally explore the

---

[2] Edwards, Gavin. "The Super Psyche." *Playboy*. 18 Apr 2012. Web. 28 Apr 2012.

issues of class with Batman, but the conflict with Joe Chill is a notable exception.

Since his creation, Batman's quest for vengeance has been fueled by his rage towards Joe Chill and the reader has always been meant to just accept that Chill is irredeemably evil. Morrison is challenging the notion that Joe Chill is simply a cold-blooded killer with no motivation. Chill may have killed the Waynes, but it's because Chill has been born and raised within a cycle of poverty that he can't break away from. His killing of the Waynes may be deplorable, but perhaps Batman is just as deplorable for being a wealthy man beating criminals who have no other choice but to continue living the lives they were born into.

Chill continues his rant of how tortured he feels and while he had built a certain amount of sympathy for himself with his commentary on economic class, all credibility is lost as he says, "I shoulda shot the kid right there – I shoulda done him first. Three for three. But he was like my own boy. The son I lost."

The sympathy isn't enough for Batman who is revealed to have been in disguise as one of Chill's men the entire time. The lights in the room go out, Batman beats the thugs, and then simply laughs at Chill. It's cruel, but necessary for Bruce to cope with his own pain.

The flashback returns to the 23rd day of Thogal and Bruce remembers when he was five and first encountered the bats that lived in the caves underneath Wayne Manor – his first encounter with his own mortality. Young Bruce looks away to see Clark Kent, Hal Jordan, Dick Grayson, and Oliver Queen carrying his casket as Alfred and Barbara Gordon follow. Bat-Mite acts as a coping mechanism for Bruce to confront death. The imp says, "The dark ain't so bad when you learn how to make friends with it." Whether this actually occurred when Bruce was a boy or whether Bat-Mite is helping to repair Bruce's subconscious now that he is suffering from a heart attack is unclear.

On the next page, four different times in Batman's life are represented in five panels. The first is when Bruce was five and confronting death for the first time. Next is Dr. Hurt explaining that Batman had imagined Robin's death during the isolation chamber experiments (a reference to *Batman* #156). The third time period reveals when Batman felt as if he had kept Tim Drake at arm's length. These three moments when Batman ponders mortality lead to the last panel set in the desert during *52* as Bruce Wayne tries to heal the darkness in his soul. Just as *Batman* #666 ponders Batman's mortality, this issue shows that his fear of death is pathological or perhaps engrained within his DNA. Death and tragedy are essential elements of Batman's narrative and identity. Without that fear of death that was born in the murder of his parents, there would be no motivation for Batman.

Relief comes to Batman when he sees Robin (Dick Grayson) is alive and well after the hallucinations of the isolation chamber had made him believe otherwise. A voice says, "Batman's a hardy specimen with an above-average mind. But even a Batman can succumb to stress and shock. I just hope there won't be any after-effects." Though we aren't sure who says these words, we can reasonably assume they come from Dr. Hurt who is foreshadowing the events of "R.I.P."

A general compliments Batman for being part of the experiment because it contributed to "space medicine," but Batman explains to Robin that he agreed to the experiments because he "wanted a glimpse of how the Joker's mind worked." It's a powerful moment when Batman admits that he had undergone the experiment to better understand his nemesis. The characters are more intrinsically linked than perhaps we were ready to believe.

The narrative returns to Joe Chill as Batman holds a gun to the criminal's face. After torturing Joe Chill for over a month, Batman basically admits to being Bruce Wayne. Joe Chill realizes, to his horror, that he created Batman and that if anyone else knew, Chill would die. And so, in order to avoid being tortured by other criminals, Joe Chill takes his own life.

This climax of the story is problematic. Batman, the hero who refuses to kill, isn't above haunting Joe Chill to the point of Chill committing suicide. This torture that Batman inflicts upon Chill is never considered to be unfair or unnecessary. Batman never seems proud of it either, but the quest for vengeance is so driving that the moral implications of the torture Batman is inflicting are never considered by the hero.

A further problem is the nature of Batman's mission. When the identity of Thomas and Martha Wayne's killer was unresolved, it gave Batman an unidentifiable target – a shadowy figure he could never catch. As a result, the hero resorted to battling crime in general. With Joe Chill, the killer has a face, and once that problem is taken care of, Batman *should* be at peace. Yet, even after Batman gets his revenge, his mission continues. Time passes and Batman finds more reasons to be haunted, to search for revenge, and to search for completion. Without Joe Chill to obsess over, Batman obsesses over the Joker, torturing himself in order to understand his enemy. Because he lost his parents, Batman fears he will lose Robin as well.

More than any other issue of Morrison's run, "Joe Chill in Hell" shows us that Batman will never be at peace. As the issue visits different times in Batman's life and we see Bruce Wayne confront mortality at different times in his life (as a boy, when he is first Batman, when he confronts Robin's mortality, his own "death" in the desert), we begin to realize that Batman's condition isn't born of one event, but is pathological. He will never be able to get over the deaths of his parents, because he will always have to confront death in some way, which opens those old wounds anew. Like a serial killer, he has an obsession with a certain target. His target just so happens to be criminals, and because of this, he will always fall back into his circle of loss and forgiveness. Death and rebirth.

Finally, Batman awakens and finds himself at the mercy of the Anti-Christ Batman.

Batman #673 is a masterpiece in the way that it revisits Batman's origin to uncover new layers of depth, and the way it makes a fractured narrative work so well. What makes it so fascinating is how closely it mirrors Lord Fanny's own journey in "Apocalipstick" (*The Invisibles* #15, Dec 1995).

Lord Fanny is the transgender member of King Mob's Invisibles cell, and one night, he experiences multiple moments of his life at one time while he is in the bathroom of a club. The narrative shifts from London to an 11-year-old Lord Fanny in Rio and then again as he is inducted into the Invisibles by an agent named John-A-Dreams. Just as Batman meditates during the Thogal Ritual to later be reborn a whole person, Fanny travels to the dead lands to become a sorcerer. At one point during "Apocalipstick," there is even a 16-panel page featuring a news story that strongly resembles the breakdown of Frank Miller's *Dark Knight Returns*.

These may seem like tenuous connections, but during the interview with *Playboy*, Morrison seems to deepen the Batman / Lord Fanny connection further, saying that Batman is "very plutonian in the sense that he's wealthy and also in the sense that he's sexually deviant. Gayness is built into Batman. I'm not using gay in the pejorative sense, but Batman is very, very gay. There's just no denying it. Obviously as a fictional character he's intended to be heterosexual, but the basis of the whole concept is utterly gay."

So in a sense, Batman has undergone magical trials that are similar to Lord Fanny's and can be considered to be reborn as a new kind of Batman that has stronger ties to the magical world of *The Invisibles* than ever before.

Batman #674

As the issue begins, Morrison emphasizes that Batman is a constant detective, but especially whenever he is threatened or vulnerable. As the third ghost speaks, Batman thinks, "The accent is east side Gotham. Scholarship boy. Breathes like an athlete." He is trying to discern the fake Batman's identity and he knows that "everything is a clue." In addition to his detective mind, Batman will also rely on his subconscious (in the form of Bat-Mite) to help him cope with his mental anguish.

The third ghost explains that he had been one of the three cops who were experimented upon by Dr. Hurt because "somebody wondered what we'd all do if Batman died" – the idea being that Batman is a normal man and is vulnerable, but the idea of Batman is something that can be replicated. Morrison is arguing through the three ghosts that as an idea, Batman can't be replicated with the same results. Yet over the years there have been many different characters created to be in the same vein as Batman, but none have had the enduring success the Dark Knight has had.

Batman blacks out and flashes back to a night of crime fighting with Dick Grayson and then to a conversation between the two in the Batcave. Ever since the isolation chamber experiment, Batman has been experiencing blackouts. Fearing that he is putting Dick's life in danger, Bruce says, "I must put away my Batman costume and retire from crime fighting" but Bat-Mite questions Bruce by saying, "Wonder who hid *that* command in your head" the implication being that Dr. Hurt had planted hypnotic suggestions in Bruce's brain during his time in the isolation chamber.

First appearing in *Detective Comics* #267 (May 1959), Bat-Mite was an imp from another dimension who worshipped Batman. An absurd character that was definitely a product of the time in which he was created, Bat-Mite would plague Superman and Batman in the pages of *World's Finest* and at times team up with Mr. Mxyzptlk (another imp character from the 5th dimension who typically plagued Superman). In 1964, when editor Julius Schwartz decided to reduce the members of the Batman family, Bat-Mite was removed. Since that time, the character has made just a few appearances, but given that all of

Batman continuity is fair game for Grant Morrison, the character makes his triumphant return in this issue in a manner that actually makes some sense.

Rather than being an imp who is a fan of Batman, Bat-Mite acts as part of Bruce's subconscious. Later, during "R.I.P.," the Batman of Zur-en-Arrh will ask Bat-Mite, "Are you really an alien hyper-imp from the 5th dimension... or just a figment of my imagination?" to which Bat-Mite simply replies, "Imagination *is* the 5th dimension. Some world's greatest detective you are." With this, Morrison has perfectly reconciled both the original interpretation of Bat-Mite and his own modernized interpretation of being part of Batman's subconscious. Of course, if Bat-Mite has always been part of Batman's subconscious, then it's a little telling that Bruce needed to create his own biggest fan from another dimension.

After piecing some of the clues together, Batman realizes that he is in the same room where Dr. Hurt had experimented on him years ago. Bat-Mite cheers him on and it's here that we see a rather large, parasitic creature is attached to the back of Bat-Mite. The creature had been hinted at earlier, but this is the first time we receive visual proof. It's never explained as to why there is a creature on Bat-Mite, but given that he is part of Batman's subconscious and that Dr. Hurt has damaged Batman's mind, the parasite could be interpreted as a side-effect of Hurt's influence.

The Anti-Christ Batman burns a file that contains all of Dr. Hurt's research, including "the post-hypnotic keywords he planted in all of us," which foreshadows the reveal about "Zur-en-Arrh" that Morrison has been subtly teasing since his first issue. The Anti-Christ Batman goes on to reveal the names of the other two ghosts as Batman relives his first encounter with them as he hallucinated in Dr. Hurt's isolation chamber. To this point, the mystery behind the Batmen has been an intriguing plot point, but it unfortunately doesn't play out in a meaningful way. While the three ghosts of Batman are interesting figures who could be interpreted as alternate versions of Batman had he made different choices, the revelation that they are Josef Muller (Gun Batman) and Branca (Monster Batman) shows that there really is only one Batman. All other imitations are merely names with no significance.

In another flashback, Dr. Hurt reveals he has discovered that trauma is what fuels Batman's rage. So, Hurt has Officer Michael Lane's family murdered by Satanists to cause the trauma that will make him a superior Batman to the other two officers. After his family is killed Lane leaves the force but remains an agent for Dr. Hurt. He gives away Dr. Hurt's true identity as he says to Batman, "Doctor Hurt was the Devil. Sometimes he visits this world to destroy the good and make slaves of men like me." Lane isn't being hyperbolic in his description; he is being literal.

Back in the first issue of Morrison's run, he had established the standard elements in a Batman story (Robin, the Joker, Commissioner Gordon, Gotham City) and with the three ghosts of Batman, he is starting to explore what really makes up the character. Training and trauma aren't the only elements that make up Batman. As Morrison describes in *Supergods,* "Batman, then, may have been a construct, but he was an immaculate construct, precision engineered to endure" (25).

Batman is the sum total of all his parts; from the costume, to the gadgets, and the origin, the training, the coolness, the rage, the supporting cast, the villains – all work in concert with one another to make Batman special. There are dozens of vigilantes that are similar to Batman in some way, but none of them can equal. He's madder and badder than Lord Byron. Cooler than James Bond.

Lane attempts to cut off Batman's hand, but of course, our hero has planned for this eventuality. He explains, "Every day I run through a thousand different scenarios. I work out ways to defeat villains with M.O.'s and pathologies that haven't been thought of yet. I imagine a thousand potential death traps and plot my escapes."

This forward thinking not only shows Batman's brilliance, but also how volatile his mind must be. As he continues to pummel Lane, doubt begins to set in as Batman wonders what would happen if he faced something he couldn't imagine.

A popular topic of conversations around comic shops is the inevitable "who would win" battle where two characters who wouldn't normally do battle face off against one another and fans debate the outcome. One of the more commonly held beliefs is that if Batman had the proper time to prepare, then he could defeat any adversary. Here, Morrison is having Batman question his own ability to plan for any eventuality. In essence, Batman is only as good as the plan he imagines, but if he faces the unimaginable, then he cannot win.

Monster Batman makes an appearance and then is promptly shot and killed by a police officer. Batman chases down Michael Lane who disappears in a cloud of smoke, leaving Batman holding his glove and thinking, "If the king of crime is real... is he telling me his real name?" The connection between the adversary with the Black Glove is blatant, but functions as a red herring to throw readers away from the suggestion that Dr. Hurt is the Devil.

Finally, the issue ends with Bruce Wayne putting his parachuting clothes back on and crawling into a dumpster. He has Alfred make an excuse to Jezebel Jet and the press that he had overshot his landing and had significantly hurt himself. It's a much-needed comedic scene meant to remind readers that despite having a heart attack and technically dying for four minutes, Batman must maintain his Bruce Wayne identity.

Batman #675

Even though the business with the three ghosts of Batman was concluded in the previous issue, *Batman* #674 ended with a "to be continued." However, the following issue titled, "The Fiend with Nine Eyes," acts as a prologue to "R.I.P." It is a strange issue that centers on a dinner date between Bruce Wayne and Jezebel Jet. Batman never makes an appearance.

The issue begins with Nightwing and Robin standing over defeated thugs in dog masks. Robin says, "Dog bandits? We can do so much better than this, Nightwing," but Nightwing respond with, "*I* had a great time." It's a visual cue that is meant to remind the reader of *52* #30, when Tim Drake suggested that Bruce wanted Dick and Tim to be the new Batman and Robin. It foreshadows the new dynamic that will form after "R.I.P.," but that will be with Damian Wayne instead of Tim Drake.

Bruce and Jezebel are on a date in an empty restaurant, save for some bodyguards and waiters. Jezebel reveals that a week has passed since the parachute incident and she is unhappy that their relationship feels so superficial. Her line, "Why do I feel as though all I ever see is... is the mask of a man, Bruce?" echoes the sentiments that some fans have had about Bruce Wayne — insisting that he is a mask and Batman is the true identity. Jezebel's line is perfect for this prologue because it sets up the central conflict of identity that pervades "R.I.P."

All of the clues for Jezebel's eventual betrayal are here in her dialogue. She suggests that there is something "deep, dark, and terrible" underneath the surface of Bruce Wayne and also that he may be "cruel." The moment she really tips her hand, however, is when she suggests the secret he is hiding is that he is into "S&M," a blatant admission that she knows he is Batman.

Their dinner is interrupted by the Nine-Eyed Man, a member of the Ten-Eyed Tribe (the tribe who cut out the darkness in Bruce's soul back in *52*), but he is missing the middle finger on his left hand so he only has nine eyes instead. He is there to kidnap Jezebel Jet for reasons that are never quite explained. We only learn that he has been hired by the enemies of her father. Mostly, he is there to remind readers of Bruce's experience from *52* #30, but just in case anyone missed that, the narrative shifts back to Robin and Nightwing who summarize the events from that story.

The narrative shifts once more to Talia watching as Damian trains with the archer Merlyn. She hates that Bruce is dating Jezebel, and both she and Damian fear for Bruce's life. The scenes with Talia are reminders that she and Damian still exist and that their roles will be important in the future.

Rather than changing into Batman, Bruce takes down the Nine-Eyed Man himself but gives off an icy laugh to suggest that he is using a Batman voice as he stalks the villain from the shadows. The speech bubble is a light blue which suggests he is slowly transforming into the Batman of Zur-en-Arrh whose speech bubbles are dark blue. Bruce's identity is in flux. As Jezebel watches Bruce pummel the Nine-Eyed Man, Bruce shouts to her, "Bruce Wayne is a shallow, selfish, reckless mask of a man who never grew up!" The rage in Bruce's face suggests that he is shouting in a Batman voice and it appears that he has been so caught up in the events that he doesn't even realize that he has been battling the Nine-Eyed Man out of costume.

The issue ends with Jezebel Jet holding up her hands next to Bruce's head to make a silhouette of Batman as she "realizes" they are one in the same. Finally, all of the pieces are in place for "R.I.P."

"R.I.P."

The most controversial storyline in Morrison's *Batman* run, "R.I.P." (#676-681) is the psychological destruction of the Dark Knight. Cryptic, bizarre, and at times genuinely frightening, "R.I.P." features the much-awaited confrontation between Batman and Dr. Hurt, the mysterious villain who has remained in the shadows up until this point. Symbolism is packed into every panel as the red and black motif explodes into a full frenzy to reflect Batman's fractured psyche.

But of course, this isn't *just* about Batman; it also establishes the conflict between the Joker and Dr. Hurt that will haunt the pages of *Batman and Robin*. However, for the purposes of this chapter, I will be focusing more on the effect "R.I.P." has on Bruce Wayne.

After a prologue in *DC Universe* #0, "R.I.P." proper begins in issue #676. The first page features Batman and Robin bathed in black and red as lightning strikes behind them and Batman declares, "Batman and Robin will never die!" This statement emphasizes that even though the title suggests the death of Batman, the idea and concept behind the character is immortal. We won't know that this is Dick Grayson and Damian Wayne until the end of the third issue of *Batman and Robin*, but the implication is clear that this isn't the traditional dynamic duo.

The opening image is meant to be a symbol of comfort for the reader as Bruce Wayne's life spirals out of control. The statement "Batman and Robin will never die" is one of defiance in the face of the conventional logic that Bruce Wayne is Batman and if Bruce Wayne dies, then Batman does as well. Morrison is suggesting, however, that should Bruce Wayne die, Batman will still live on. Bruce Wayne and Batman are not so intrinsically linked that the identity of Batman dies with Bruce. Then, one has to consider what exactly the identity means. If no one person is Batman, then anyone and everyone can be Batman. Truly, Batman and Robin can never die because these masks and identities can be assumed. Batman may be an identity that Bruce Wayne assumes when he fights crime, but Batman is an idea that isn't tied just to Bruce Wayne and ideas can live on.

"R.I.P." isn't about the death of Bruce Wayne, either. The story is a culmination of the themes first established in *Arkham Asylum*, "Gothic," and *JLA*. Batman is going through a transformative experience (*Arkham Asylum*) brought on by a Satanic figure ("Gothic") to prove that he is the ultimate human who can survive even the strangest and most outlandish encounters (*JLA*). And while Dr. Hurt is an excellent villain worthy of Batman, the real conflict is between the identities of Bruce Wayne and Batman.

Batman and Robin arrive on the scene in a brand new Batmobile that sports red headlights and red-tinted windows. After Tim compliments Bruce on the new car, Bruce replies, "I don't know... it's not how I saw it when I first had the idea." Morrison's first issue on *Batman* was titled, "Building a Better Batmobile" and the intention was rebuilding Batman into a new and better franchise. Bruce's comments on the Batmobile could reflect upon Morrison's own evolution of the series itself or it could simply be a reflection of how much Dr. Hurt's psychological warfare has affected Wayne's psyche.

Tim Drake shows concern for Bruce's sanity during a conversation with Alfred, which suggests that Bruce's mind might not be well after being technically dead for a few minutes and then brought back to life during the encounter with the Third Ghost. Alfred acts as the voice of reason by believing in Batman's training. "The absolute physical mastery of the top martial artists, gymnasts or yogins... the logical and deductive skills of master philosophers, forensic scientists and detectives... the understanding, discrimination and moral clarity of ultimate Zen adepts... need I continue?"

Alfred's evidence shows us that while the audience should fear for Bruce, it's worth remembering that he *is* the ultimate human being. Bruce Wayne is prepared for anything. He's the guy who has gone toe-to-toe with Superman, after all.

Tim then reveals that Damian is really on his mind and asks Alfred whether Bruce took a paternity test. Alfred never states one way or another emphatically, but Tim comes to the conclusion on his own, stating, "The son of Satan is my brother? That's it. Time out."

While the label of "son of Satan" is perhaps fitting for Damian, it implies that Batman is Satan – an interesting connection especially given Batman's declaration that he is the Devil during "Gothic." And of course, Damian sells his soul to the Devil to protect Gotham in *Batman* #666, and Morrison has been hinting that Dr. Hurt is the Devil himself.

Jezebel Jet makes an appearance and she continues the red and black motif not only with her appearance, but also with her name. "Jet" is an obvious reference to something being "jet black" and "Jezebel" slang for a "painted woman" or a prostitute. And with the name Jezebel deriving from the Biblical character who caused many Jewish priests to be slaughtered, it should come as no surprise that she would betray Bruce Wayne to the Devil. Her invitation to the Black Glove's "Danse Macabre" is further telegraphing that she will betray Batman.

It's the end of the issue, however, that really ties the red and black motif all together. As the Joker goes through a Rorschach test, he envisions himself killing Robin, Nightwing, and Commissioner Gordon and the scene is colored in black, white, and red. Notice that Batman is nowhere to be found in the hallucination because the Joker doesn't want his death – he wants Batman to break. More importantly, it's this scene that explains the significance of the black and red.

The Joker sees his world in black and red. Through the use of black and red imagery, Dr. Hurt is transforming Batman's mind so he can break the hero and transform his mind into a psychotic mess much like the Joker.

Batman #677

Batman's obsession with the Black Glove causes him to push his loved ones out of his life. In the first scene, after a battle with one of Le Bossu's gargoyles, Batman insists the Black Glove is backing the gargoyles. Commissioner Gordon doubts the existence of the Black Glove which seems to create a distance between the two. Later, after Alfred reveals that Tim has been gone for two days due to Bruce distancing himself emotionally, Batman dismisses his butler to the theater to watch *The Black Glove* movie. Morrison had established the importance of Batman's supporting cast in his first issue and now he is showing how Bruce's obsession has led to his own alienation.

Bruce then brings Jezebel Jet to the Batcave where he continues his mission of alienation by instructing her to stay away. Their conversation strikes at the heart of the dual identity motif as Jezebel says, "When we met, you were charming, witty Bruce Wayne. But now... I've fallen in love with Batman, a dangerous vigilante... this person people say might be mad."

We know that Jezebel is part of the Black Glove, so we can understand that she is trying to convince Bruce that his true identity is actually Batman. But it's interesting to consider that she could have given birth to the idea of *Batman, Inc.* when she says in reference to the Batcave, "You could erase my country's national debt with what it costs to maintain this place." Her comment underlines Batman's main problem, which is that his mission is too narrow.

The scene between Jezebel and Bruce holds meaning on its own with Jezebel acting as a voice for an audience convinced Batman is going crazy. Bruce's comments seemingly provide further evidence for her assertions. However, rereading the scene after the revelation that Jezebel is part of the Black Glove and that Bruce was aware of this the entire time gives the scene an extra layer of cat-and-mouse, cloak-and-dagger, spy versus spy fun to it. Jezebel thinks she is attacking Bruce's subconscious when she suggests he isn't well and Bruce plays along by saying that the Black Glove would use everything to his advantage, including using her.

Still, despite Bruce's knowledge of Jezebel's betrayal, he is still vulnerable to subconscious attack by means of the "Zur-en-Arrh" code word that appears on his Bat-computer screens. Instead of seeing the words, Bruce seems to see a purple bat head that looks like a tribal mask. The face, previously seen in the story of the Third Ghost just before Batman had "died" from a heart-attack, is a signal of an oncoming change within Bruce. It is somewhat reminiscent of the moments in *The Invisibles* when Dane's Jack Frost persona appears during moments of great stress. The purple mask is a magic persona programmed by Bruce's mind that appears to save Batman when he is faced with something incomprehensible.

Also, in the midst of the conversation between Bruce and Jezebel, there is one short, two-page scene between Jim Gordon and the Mayor of Gotham that highlights how far Dr. Hurt will go to not just ruin Batman, but also Bruce Wayne. It is revealed that Thomas Wayne (Bruce's father) has been alive and well all of these years. So, not only has Hurt orchestrated an all-out attack on the reputation of Batman through the use of the Three Ghosts, but he has also ruined the name of Wayne by claiming to be Bruce's dead father. These attacks on the identities of Bruce Wayne and Batman reflect what a member of the Black Glove will say in *Batman: The Return of Bruce Wayne* #5, "Destroy a reputation. Destroy a soul." By ruining the names of Bruce Wayne and Batman, Dr. Hurt has effectively destroyed both identities which will leave Bruce no other choice but to reinvent himself into the Batman of Zur-en-Arrh.

Batman #678

In a cabin in the woods, Tim Drake reads Bruce's mad ramblings from the Black Casebook which reveals why Bruce created the Batman of Zur-en-Arrh identity. When Bruce writes, "I don't *want* to know what goes on in the Joker's head. I *have* to know," he is referring to the isolation experiments that he underwent with Dr. Hurt. The isolation drove him to madness which helped him see through the Joker's eyes. He describes that experience as a "snake with a broken back, flipping and tracing intricate, agonized arabesques in the dust." The image of the snake emphasizes the Joker's changing personality by connecting personality with the shedding of a snake's skin. Later, the Joker will continue this image when he cuts his own tongue into a fork with a razor blade.

Bruce's writing continues with, "Five years into the mission and it feels like a ghost train ride." Trains are a continuing motif in many of Grant Morrison's stories and are often used as a symbol for a transformative experience. Here, Batman declares his mission to be a "ghost train ride" which ties his years as Batman to a state of constant transformation. This goes along with Morrison's assertion that Batman's identity has changed over time. Bruce attributes his continued sanity to "Robin's humor and forthrightness," which contrast with an identity that is most often characterized by darkness.

This issue chronicles Bruce Wayne's transformation into the Batman of Zur-en-Arrh. Bruce is kicked awake by a blind, homeless man named "Honor Jackson" who calls Bruce a "cockroach." Sharp-eyed readers should recognize Honor Jackson as the homeless man that Batman almost runs over in his black and red Batmobile in issue #676. Here, Bruce's transient identity is connected with the Joker's from "the Clown at Midnight" (in *Batman* #663), as both are called "cockroaches." Of course, the image of a cockroach once again is inherently connected to Kafka's *Metamorphosis* and the transformation of Gregor Samsa.

In order to remember how he came to be in a dirty alley, his flashback is depicted in black, white, and red — the colors that indicate how the Joker sees the world around him as seen at the end of issue #676. It isn't any wonder that Bruce is going insane; the flashback reveals he had been injected with "weapons grade crystal meth" and "street heroin." Fortunately for Bruce, one-eyed Honor Jackson is there to help Bruce on what Jackson refers to as an "odyssey." Drugged out of his mind and without his Bat-gadgets or partners to help him, Bruce Wayne has been stripped of everything that made him Batman. Still, even without the traditional items that define the Dark Knight, Bruce can always fall back on his naturally inquisitive mind to piece his memory back together.

Near the end of the issue, we learn that Honor Jackson died the night previous after he spent all of his money on drugs (money that Batman had given him for almost running him over with his Batmobile). Therefore, the interactions between Bruce and Jackson hold a special significance as Jackson is part of Bruce's fragile psyche.

First, the name "Honor Jackson" itself is could be a clue and a connection to the Joker. Most regard the Joker's real name to be "Jack" and if Bruce Wayne is going through a similar cycle of mental repair that the Joker went through, then one could surmise that his personality is the "son" of this mental preparation. Also, since Bruce Wayne is building a personality that won't be based upon murder, it stands to reason that it would be based upon "honor."

Honor and Bruce travel through Gotham and end up in Giordano Park where Jackson explains to Bruce, "You gotta understand somethin' about this world... even the brightest angel can fall."

If Honor Jackson is part of Bruce Wayne's psyche, Jackson's advice shows that Bruce has already pieced together that Hurt is the Devil.

Jackson then gives Bruce the Bat-Radia which just so happens to be wrapped in a red and black checkered handkerchief. The park is named after legendary artist Dick Giordano who is responsible for some of the most iconic images of the Joker ever to be produced. Of course, Bruce Wayne would have no knowledge of this, but this is a clue from Morrison to his readers about the process our hero is going through. Between the Joker vision, Honor Jackson, and Giordano Park, Morrison is deliberately connecting Bruce Wayne's experience with madness to the Joker's own connecting the identities of the hero and villain.

Finally, Bruce ends up in Crime Alley where Batman was born. His dialogue begins with standard black lettering on white background and as soon as he puts on the purple cowl, his dialogue transforms to white on blue to symbolize his rebirth into the Batman of Zur-en-Arrh.

Batman #679

Once the transformation into the Batman of Zur-en-Arrh is complete, the comparisons to the Joker are apparent and numerous. First, Batman's costume has gone from the traditional dark tones to a gaudy, ridiculous, and comical red, purple, and yellow – in the next issue, Batman says that "the colors demonstrate total confidence. Robin dressed this way for years and survived" to explain their significance. Next, Batman's dialogue balloons are in white lettering over a blue background and while the Joker's text is written in green, they remain the only two characters with different colors for their lettering. Finally, the first image of the Batman of Zur-en-Arrh features the hero crashing through a door with a baseball bat. The bat is a pun as Bruce has become a literal "bat" man – a hint that the character has embraced a more absurd persona.

Batman's first line in the issue is a "Hsss" that seems to echo the snake imagery associated with the Joker. Batman's first victim is a tailor who has been supplying Le Bossu's men with gargoyle costumes, ironic given that Batman's new costume is so hideous. Also, now that Batman has completely snapped, Bat-Mite has returned to act as Bruce's conscience and to keep him sane. He seems to take some glee in Batman's rampage.

Batman's Zur-En-Arrh costume is revealed. The final page of *Batman* Vol. 1 #678 (Aug 2008). Art by Tony Daniel and Sandu Florea. Copyright © DC Comics.

Atop a roof, stone gargoyles start talking to Batman. They ask, "You ever see the grids? Takes slow-vision to see the grids... hang around for years, you get to see the layout. People make the city and the city makes the people."

Batman begins to see the city as a pattern of grids and he describes the city as "a checkerboard, a blueprint, a machine designed to make Batman." Notice that Bruce doesn't say "to make me" but rather "to make Batman" indicating that the identity itself can be replicated again and again because of the nature of this city factory.

Morrison has explored the magic of cities in *The Invisibles*, but there, he called them a virus that only had the goal of spreading. In that series, Dane was taught to see patterns and magic words in the world around him. Here, Gotham is being presented as a mechanism to create Batman and that Batman is an idea that spreads like a virus. Gotham City is characterized by the crime that created Batman, who built his frightening costume to echo Gotham's gothic architecture. Therefore, even though Bruce Wayne is Batman, you could say that the Batman identity was manufactured by Gotham. In this too, the Batman identity goes beyond just Bruce Wayne – a point that's reemphasized with the International Club of Heroes. Without Batman, the other heroes in the club would not have been inspired to become vigilantes, so the idea of Batman is completely without borders.

Bat-Mite, as always, brings Batman back to reality by reminding him that the Black Glove's men are still tracking him. After Batman rips a tooth out of his mouth and defeats the human gargoyle henchmen, he sets up a new base of operations in an abandoned movie theater. This is the same theater where Bruce saw *Mask of Zorro* with his parents; this is where Batman was truly born and where he has gone to be reborn. Without his mask, Bruce's dialogue is normal as he tells Bat-Mite that his mind "seems so much... faster now. Clearer. Simpler. Like a streamlined engine, a silver bullet..."

In case anyone forgot who is responsible for Batman's transformation into a more Joker-like character, Bat-Mite kindly reminds Bruce:

> All this stuff came out during the trauma of the space isolation experiment you took part in for the army, remember? Which is when Doc Hurt got the idea to use "Zur-en-Arrh" as a hypnotic trigger phrase that would give him the power to switch off Batman any time he wanted.

Dr. Hurt did what the Joker could never do; he destroyed Batman's mind. However, Hurt didn't understand how empowering identity can be, because Hurt has used different identities to obscure who he is. While Batman and the

Joker embrace identities to empower themselves, Hurt hides behind them, never adopting one long enough to truly know who he really is.

Bat-Mite then spells it all out for the reader, saying, "Batman thinks of everything. Batman even prepared for psychological attack with a backup identity, remember? He made a secret self to save him. The Batman of Zur-en-Arrh."

Even though it looks like Dr. Hurt had won by breaking Batman, this identity was developed by Bruce a long time ago just in case. It may seem crazy, but really, it's all part of the plan.

Later, Batman battles Charlie Caligula and criticizes the villain's identity, "You like people to think you're some brilliant, unpredictable criminal mastermind like the Joker, don't you? Funny, all I see is a set of uninspired tics – a played-out act you can't escape even if you wanted to."

Batman seems to admire the Joker in his criticisms of Charlie Caligula. He argues that Charlie will never be anyone because his identity is a charade of the Joker's, a cheap imitation that won't grow, shift, or transform with the times. One could almost make the same argument for The International Club of Heroes except that their identities actually have changed; the growth of Knight and Squire is evidence of this.

Batman's torture of Charlie Caligula ends with the hero saying that the Batman of Zur-en-Arrh is "what you get when you take Bruce out of the equation." He is the purest form of Batman because he is devoid of Bruce Wayne's humanity.

Batman #680

The Black Glove meets at Arkham Asylum for their final confrontation with Batman. Considering that Morrison began his Batman career with the graphic novel *Arkham Asylum,* the setting for the explosive finale could be nowhere else. The Batman of Zur-en-Arrh is an identity devoid of Bruce Wayne, but Bat-Mite warns that "The Batman of Zur-en-Arrh was only a short-term fix to get you out of trouble in the event of an attack on your mind. You can't run at this speed all night." So, no matter how powerful Batman is in this identity, Bruce Wayne is essential to balance his mind. Being Batman is difficult, but sustaining the purest form of the Batman of Zur-en-Arrh just isn't possible.

As Batman stands in the entrance of Arkham Asylum, Bat-Mite refuses to enter. "I'm the last fading echo of the voice of reason, Batman. And reason won't fit through this door." Just as before in *Arkham Asylum*, Batman must cast aside his fears and his reason so that he can confront evil. Before he does, Batman turns to ask the burning question that surrounds Bat-Mite's appearance, "Are you really an alien hyper-imp from the 5th dimension... or just a figment of my imagination?" Bat-Mite perfectly answers the question by replying, "Imagination *is* the 5th dimension. Some world's greatest detective you are," which is vague enough to reconcile that he is a figment of Batman's imagination *and* that he is real as well. This moment proves that Grant Morrison is a writer who can do the impossible because he incorporated Bat-Mite back into Batman's mythology in a way that was interesting and essential to understanding his identity.

Finally, Batman fights his way through Arkham to face off against the Joker. The story reaches a feverish climax as Batman tries to piece together all of the obscure symbols that have plagued him thus far. "Diamonds, clubs, rich people! Hearts and spades, love and death, the joke and the punchline, the Harlequin's motley, red and black! Cupid and the Devil! You gave it all away in the dead man's hand!"

But the Joker says, "The real joke is your stubborn, bone deep conviction that somehow, somewhere *all of this* makes *sense*! That's what cracks me up every time!"

Just as Bruce Wayne tried to make sense of the pop art back in the second issue of "Batman and Son," he has been trying to make sense of the patterns here.

Batman leaps down a spiraling staircase to the lowest level of Arkham symbolizing the inner-most part of his mind. On a black and red checkered floor, Batman and the Joker finally meet. The Joker calls back to Morrison's first issue when he says, "You and I, we had a special arrangement. A yin / yang thing. Holmes and Moriarty, Tweety and Sylvester, hats and gloves, but you... you shot me in the face."

Batman tries reasoning with the Joker by explaining that the Black Glove is responsible for the shooting, but the Joker merely cuts his own tongue to resemble the forked tongue of a snake – more satanic imagery, but this time indicating the Joker's penchant for lies.

The dynamic between Batman and the Joker has always been about opposites. Batman is the dark, grim hero and the Joker is the bright, colorful villain. More importantly, Batman thrives upon order and methodology and the Joker is an agent of chaos. Therefore, Batman can never truly understand the

Joker because his mind deals in symbols and clues. The Joker doesn't need to operate on that level, but oftentimes does use orderly clues to create his chaos.

In their confrontation, the Joker goes on to say that there is no order to the chaos he inflicts on the world and that Batman can never truly understand him. The forked tongue, however, is a dead giveaway that he is a liar. Of course there is some sort of order, because the Joker had been diagnosed in *Arkham Asylum* as a sort of "superpersonality" which means his personality must be able to recognize patterns and have some sort of order so that he can adapt. Perhaps the Joker is simply upset that Batman has succumbed to madness and that the Joker himself wasn't responsible for it.

Jezebel Jet sits tied to a chair, crying for Bruce to save her, and as he removes his mask, he declares, "I'm the Batman of Zur-en-Arrh" but it's as if his identity is finally returning. Bruce crashes through the glass only to pass out as it is revealed that Jezebel Jet had been working for the Black Glove the entire time.

Batman #681

The final issue of "R.I.P." begins with four black panels divided by a green line that indicates that Batman's heart has flatlined. When Batman's eyes finally open, his narration returns as if it were written in a notebook. It reads, "But that's the thing about *Batman*. Batman thinks of *everything*." Once Batman is fully revealed, we see him confined by a straightjacket inside a coffin.

The narrative then flashes back to when Bruce Wayne went through the Thogal ritual. Once again, Bruce's memories are colored in black, white, and red to symbolize the Joker's vision and to emphasize an important moment in Bruce's life connected to the Batman of Zur-en-Arrh identity. Bruce explains to a monk that he had found "a scar on my consciousness" as he went through Thogal. He goes on to describe it as "a hole in my mind waiting to open up and swallow me whole." This hole in Bruce's mind is a reference to Dr. Hurt who will describe himself as the "hole in things."

Bruce explains that he has "read how traumatized children sometimes develop cover personalities to protect themselves from painful repressed memories," a point that is punctuated by the letters "Zur en a" written backwards in the panel. He then wonders if it is possible to create a "back-up human operating system." What he doesn't realize is that he had already created that system long ago and only through Thogal (and Dr. Hurt's isolation experiment before) that Bruce was able to experience the identity.

After the monk reveals he had poisoned Bruce's tea, Bruce reveals he had switched cups when the monk blinked, and then explains that he experienced Thogal because he "wanted to taste the flavor of death" and that "in the cave, in Nanda Parbat, I hunted down and killed and ate the last traces of fear and doubt in my mind."

Batman had been prepared for Dr. Hurt even back in *52* in which he had fortified his own mind as he adopted a new identity.

In the coffin, Batman continues his narration. "Obvious variations aside, there's only *one* human body..." While this is meant to transition into a speech about the amount of physical preparation he had gone through in order to become Batman, it is also fascinating when compared to the many different identities Bruce has assumed. There may be only one human body for Bruce, but he is so many different people at once: Batman, Matches Malone, Zur-en-Arrh, Bruce the orphan, Bruce the philanthropist, Bruce the businessman. Since Batman is an idea, he is more than just one person as well; he's also Dick Grayson, Damian Wayne, Terry McGinnis, the genesis for the International Club of Heroes, and the basis for dozens and dozens of knock-off heroes created by other companies.

Escaping the grave, Batman launches his assault on Dr. Hurt and the Black Glove in Arkham. Finally, Bruce is alone with Dr. Hurt. The villain continues to claim he is Bruce's father, Thomas Wayne, and that he faked his death. Hurt's identity is further muddied as Bruce accuses him of being the actor Mangrove Pierce. Then, Hurt says, "I am the hole in things, Bruce, the enemy, the piece that can never fit, there since the beginning."

Their conversation emphasizes Hurt's Satanic role, and once the truth is revealed far later, in the pages of *Batman: The Return of Bruce Wayne*, the scene holds new significance. For now, Hurt merely offers to save the Wayne family name as long as Bruce swears allegiance to him. Our hero refuses and as Hurt tries to escape via helicopter piloted by the Third Ghost, Bruce attacks and punches through the windshield of the helicopter as Hurt says, "The Black Glove always wins." The helicopter crashes in Gotham bay and it is left ambiguous as to whether Bruce dies or not.

This is the second time in the series that Batman has been tempted by a villain to join forces. At the conclusion of "Batman and Son," Talia had invited Bruce to join forces with her and create a new world order and now Dr. Hurt has offered Batman a place in his army. Refusing Talia results in the creation of the terrorist organization Leviathan, and one could argue that his refusal of Hurt leads to Batman's destruction at the hands of Darkseid in *Final Crisis*.

The last four pages of the issue tie up all of the loose ends with Dick Grayson holding Batman's cape and cowl to signify that he will take on the role in *Batman and Robin*. On the next page, Jezebel Jet is shown on her private plane when it is attacked by Talia's ninja man-bats. And finally, the narrative jumps six months ahead to when Le Bossu is attacked by the new Batman and Robin (which will also be the conclusion to *Batman and Robin* #3).

On the last page is the epilogue to the story in the Zur-en-Arrh colors of black, white, and red. A young Bruce looks happy one last time as he and his family are leaving the *Mask of Zorro*. Bruce tells them, "Imagine if Zorro came riding down the street right now on his horse!" His father laughs and says, "The sad thing is they'd probably throw someone like Zorro in Arkham." And Bruce responds with, "What?" as Joe Chill looks on.

It's an obscure scene and of course, we know what will happen next, but it's important because it shows that the origin of "Zur-en-Arrh" is from Bruce mishearing his father saying, "Zorro in Arkham." A magic word is born from a boy's overactive imagination being applied to misheard words just before a traumatic event. Amidst this magical and horrific event, an identity of the purest form of Batman is born, but it will be years of training before Bruce Wayne can learn to tame the identity and use it for the benefit of others.

"Last Rites"

Issues #682-683 of *Batman* act as a coda of sorts to Morrison's entire run to this point and serve as a much-needed connection to the mega-event, *Final Crisis*. These two issues are incredibly dense and cover almost the entire history of Batman, and it would be exceptionally tedious and unnecessary to document each reference that Morrison packs into these issues, so I will simply focus on the relevant details to the overall themes that are present in Morrison's overarching narrative.

Bruce sits in his study with the same bell in his hand that summoned Alfred to save his life after his first night out fighting crime in Frank Miller's *Batman: Year One*. This is a scene that will be returned to at the conclusion of *Batman: The Return of Bruce Wayne*. However, the scene here is reset as Alfred points out that the details weren't right. "The window was open, not broken." Something is messing with Bruce's memory and pretending to be Alfred while doing so.

Two panels show what could have been if circumstances were different with Bruce wearing a moth costume and dressed as a snake as he approaches a car called the "Side-winder." These panels are reminders of Morrison's philosophy from *Supergods* that Batman "may have been a construct, but he was an immaculate construct, precision engineered to endure" (page 25). No other animal or symbol could have worked the way the bat does. The bat is essential in the identity of Batman.

After the origin scene from *Year One*, the narrative moves on through the different eras in his career. From the dark, obsessed knight of vengeance to the caped crusader who is far more relaxed with his partner, Robin, these two issues are the final word; Batman's entire history has occurred and is intact. Amidst the history lesson, however, Morrison still has some things to say about Batman's identity as Robin ponders what *Hamlet* would have been like if the titular hero had become a masked avenger. The connection between Batman and Hamlet is yet another reference meant to expand the Dark Knight's persona just as references to Lord Byron and James Bond had done before.

Batman's preoccupation with the Joker is another recurring motif in these issues. The Joker loses in a laughing contest with Robin. He later uses obscure clues for Batman and Robin to decipher and after he is caught, he ponders using "practical jokes next time around."

After Batwoman Katy Kane (she is usually "Kathy Kane," but Robin calls her "Katy" in this issue) breaks Bruce's heart, Robin wonders how Bruce will survive and Alfred says, "He learns. He perseveres. He begins again." We see Batman going into Dr. Hurt's isolation chamber in order to better understand the Joker. While we knew that Batman had undergone isolation in order to understand the Joker, the Katy Kane information gives us new context. So, rather than just an obsession with the Joker as it appeared back in *Batman* #673, Batman had to reinvent himself because his heart had been broken.

Eventually, we learn that these memories are occurring because Darkseid's torturers, Mokkari and Mister Simyan, have imprisoned Batman and are sifting through his memories in order to duplicate them to make the perfect soldiers. Mokkari says that they will "build a production line *army* of mindless 'batmen' to fight and pillage and die in the name of our dark empire. That will be his legacy." This destruction of Batman's legacy is similar to the way that Dr. Hurt planned on destroying the hero.

Mokkari and Simyan are meant to be metaphors for the writers over the years who have mined the details of Batman but left out the soul. They are the ones who have created relentless knock-offs of the hero that had no lasting power. The Batman production line is a frightening thought because of how easily it distills what makes the character great into something so worthless. Morrison will later return to this theme in much greater detail in the pages of *Action Comics* where a corporation believes they can build a perfect Superman.

Issue #683 begins with Bruce and Talia just before they conceive Damian and then the narrative shifts to a world where Batman never existed. Mokkari and Simyan have created these false memories out of Bruce's worst fears in order to steal the real ones for their army. It's these fears that are particularly telling of Batman's identity. First, it's revealed that Jim Gordon is dead and that Dick Grayson had been tortured and murdered by the Joker. Then, Batman is reduced to a laughing stock after Selina Kyle cons and robs him. Finally, as he travels into the Batcave (traveling downward in the cave symbolizes Bruce going deeper into his own psyche), his mind lashes out and his torturers have to allow him to return to his memories.

The narrative then gets to the part in Batman's history where all of the darkest stories are told. Batman relives Jason Todd's death and Barbara Gordon's paralysis. He is broken by Bane, rehabilitated, and then battles the Azrael Batman. Gotham City is destroyed after an earthquake. Tim Drake is devastated after his father dies during the pages of *Identity Crisis*. At first, these memories elicit joy from Mokkari as he shouts, "raw emotional energy! More pain! Motivation!"

Mokkari may be a sick, demented lackey of an evil god, but his words symbolize the mentality that had driven Batman stories for years before Morrison rebuilt the character. Mokkari represents the ideology that Batman had to suffer and revel in darkness in order to be understood. He is the sick, sadistic side of readers who have allowed Batman stories to devolve into tales of Batman and his family being broken time and again. Yet, Mokkari is surprised when the clones of Batman begin to tear themselves apart. They rip at their eyes as he wonders, "How does Batman process this degree of stress?" We are meant to realize that the Batman stories we've read for years are far too dark and we should feel ashamed for wanting this.

Finally, as the immobile Batman turns the tables on his captors, Mokkari realizes that he has made a mistake as he wonders, "What kind of a man can turn even his life memories into a weapon?"

Even in the most helpless of circumstances, Batman manages to escape – a theme that Morrison began in "R.I.P." and that he has continued here, and will explore further in the ultimate test when Bruce Wayne travels through time.

The "Last Rites" issues are Morrison putting together as many references to the Batman history as he can one last time. From here, the theme of Batman will be looking forward to a new era using magic and mythology to reconstruct the character.

The Grayson Foils

In all great works of literature, the hero must have a foil: that special character designed to enhance the inherent heroic qualities of the protagonist. Oftentimes, the foil is cut from similar cloth to show the possible path the hero could have traveled down had he or she been so unfortunate. Superman and Lex Luthor, Hamlet and Laertes, Spy and Spy – the list goes on and on and on. While Batman and the Joker are the most classic pair of foils in the history of comics, there is nearly a mandated prerequisite of being a reflection of the Dark Knight in some way in order to be part of his rogue's gallery.

So, it should come as some surprise that despite Batman's long legacy of memorable villains it would take nearly 60 years to firmly establish powerful and meaningful foils for his first partner, Dick Grayson.

Foil Logic

There is a certain logic to creating a truly great foil and the basis of this logic is in the connection. The following are just a few simple ways for foils to connect with one another:

Personality / Methodology – The characters are similar in the way they act, but are different in ways beyond that. Sherlock Holmes and Moriarty are both brilliant minds, but they use their talents for very different goals.

Appearance – A similar appearance can often be strong enough to create a strong foil. The Green Lantern Corps and the Sinestro Corps have similar aesthetic designs, but they are enemies.

<u>Mission / Goal</u> – Both characters have similar goals, but different ways of going about them. The Punisher wants to stop crime, by killing the guilty while Spider-Man refuses to take a life. In a sense, Robin and Batman are foils for one another given that their mission is the same, but they have different methodology.

The exception to these would be that the characters in question have nothing in common, which in turn makes them perfect foils for one another. Batman and the Joker are nothing alike, yet they are perfectly alike. Batman is dark and brooding, yet heroic. The Joker is colorful and mirthful, yet he is a killer. They are foils for one another, but they have nothing in common outside of their commitments to very different ends and styles.

Previous to Dick Grayson's tenure as Batman, the only noteworthy foil for Dick Grayson was Deathstroke the Terminator. As the most common and dangerous enemy for the Teen Titans, Deathstroke's relationship is more complex than simply being a villain. At times, he saw himself as a kind of mentor to the team – teaching them even as he tested them with his insane plans. However, the Grayson / Deathstroke pairing only has significance when the added element of Batman is thrown in. Both Batman and Deathstroke are the pinnacle of human achievement and are prepared for any eventuality, so the two are very comparable. Batman trained Grayson as partners, while Deathstroke "trained" him in their various confrontations. Without Batman, Deathstroke would be just another villain to Dick Grayson – a great villain, but one without major significance nonetheless.

Other attempts at creating a foil for Dick Grayson were far less successful. The most laughable of these is Deathwing, who was supposedly a time traveling Dick Grayson from the future. While the ridiculous mirror name of Deathwing to Grayson's Nightwing is at least within the parameters of foil logic, the idea that he could be a time-traveling Dick Grayson (but later learns that he really isn't) is simply absurd.

During the *Nightwing* ongoing series, the villain Blockbuster was one of the recurring antagonists, but he was little more than a crime boss and could hardly be considered a mirror of Dick Grayson. He's a perfect example of how Dick Grayson has had good villains in the past, but none that are truly worthy of being Grayson's equal – until *Batman and Robin*.

The Circus of Strange

In his notes for first collection of *Batman and Robin* issues, *Batman and Robin: Batman Reborn*, Grant Morrison discusses pitting Dick against the Circus of Strange: "With Dick Grayson's origins as a circus aerialist, it felt right to pit him against a group of circus themed villains in his first adventure as Batman."

Individually, the Circus of Strange don't reveal new layers of depth to Dick Grayson's character, but when they are taken together, they present a challenge to him as the new Batman – one that shatters Grayson's self-confidence beneath the cowl.

"Nobody believes I'm Batman! I spent years building up respect as Nightwing and now they're looking at me like I'm one more psycho Batman impersonator," Dick explains to Alfred after Mr. Toad is murdered while under police custody following Batman and Robin's battle with the Circus of the Strange. Not only did Grayson have to put up with Damian's insubordination (something Bruce would not have had to endure), but Mr. Toad's lack of cooperation after being captured (interrogation scenes with Bruce always ended with the villain giving up some vital clue), combined with having to endure police criticism regarding his height and voice, all work in concert to bring Grayson to the point of giving up.

Ever the positive force in life, Alfred suggests, "Try to think of your Batman not as a memorial – you and I know he'd hate that – but as a performance. Think of Batman as a great role, like a Hamlet, or Willie Loman... or even James Bond. And play it to suit your strengths."

With this line, Alfred brings Dick back from the brink of self-destruction to help himself within the role of Batman, which is where the Circus of Strange as a whole becomes a foil for Dick Grayson.

While a toad man, conjoined triplets, a man on fire, and a fat man in a pink tutu don't reflect Grayson's personality individually, together they are a troupe of performers who play a role in crime. Grayson mirrors this by thinking of Batman as a performance. Taken together, the Circus of Strange is merely acting out the part of villains and he is acting out the part of the hero. If the actors could step aside and look at the absurdity of their situation, then they would see that none of it is necessary. They are actors in a play.

Furthering the motif of performance is the leader of the Circus of Strange, Professor Pyg. With his entourage of Dollotrons, Pyg plans on infecting all of Gotham City with an addictive identity-destroying drug. During the scene in which Pyg attempts to transform Damian into one of his Dollotron's, he won't begin until Damian is awake because Pyg must have an audience in order to work. And of course, before he can begin the operation, he has to turn on music and dance around like a mad man. To conclude his statement on performance, Pyg mutters, "I want to be sick in front of everyone" right before Damian breaks loose.

The connection between Grayson and Pyg doesn't end with the performances. While Bruce has been away, Dick has taken Damian under his wing in order to teach him how to be a hero. He uses his experience and kindness in hopes of being able to break through Damian's past. Meanwhile, Pyg uses his Dollotron method of transformation to create mindless drones to serve him. Both Pyg and Grayson are trying to transform others to agree with their particular ideologies.

While Professor Pyg may not be the physically impending menace like other Bat-villains, he presents a very important foil for Dick Grayson because the entire arc is based around identity. Dick Grayson is unsure of himself under the identity of Batman. Grayson has to shape and change Damian's identity. Professor Pyg is wrapped up in his own identity and transforming others into his perfect Dollotrons. Identity is so important that Pyg's virus explicitly destroys identity. The very threat itself is the destruction of identity, and that destruction is so powerful that it is addictive.

The idea of destroying one's own identity as being addictive is so immensely disturbing and cosmic that it could only have come from Grant Morrison and be properly told in a Batman comic where identity is everything. For years fans have debated whether or not Bruce Wayne's true self is a billionaire playboy or Batman. Dick Grayson has not only struggled with being Batman, but he has also struggled as Robin in Batman's shadow, and as Nightwing in forming his own identity.

Speaking of identity, the conclusion of the arc features Pyg's failure at completing the transformation of Sasha into his latest Dollotron. As she performs a mercy killing on her transformed father, Sasha has ended her old life and becomes transformed into the sidekick for Dick Grayson's next foil, the Red Hood.

The Red Hood

There is no one who could make a better foil for Dick Grayson than Jason Todd. The second Robin, Jason Todd entered the partnership of Batman and

Robin with a chip on his shoulder. He could never be as good as the original because nothing ever is. So, due to fan frustration with the character, DC infamously gave fans the choice of calling one of two 1-900 numbers to choose whether he lived or died. In the end, more fans opted for his death and comics went on.

Any comic fan worth his or her weight in Batarangs knows this story already, but it's interesting when one compares the choice to kill Jason Todd to the fan over the rumor of Dick Grayson's death at the end of *Infinite Crisis*. Dan Didio felt Grayson was redundant in the overall DC Universe and that his death would round out the event, but after much debate, he changed his mind. Phil Jimenez has perhaps the perfect statement regarding Grayson's impact in the DC Universe in an interview in the *Infinite Crisis* hardcover:

> Dick has so many connections to other characters. In many ways, even more than Superman or Batman, Nightwing is the soul, the linchpin, of the DCU. He's well respected by everyone, known to the JLA, the Titans, the Outsiders, Birds of Prey – everyone looks to him for advice, for friendship, for his skills. He's the natural leader of the DCU. His loss would devastate everyone and create ripples through the DCU. If it wasn't him, it had to be a hero that really impacted so many.

And as the natural leader of the DCU, he is perfect to oppose the natural bastard child. A character that was so hated, that fans not only voted, but had to pay to vote for him to die.

But Jason Todd's return as the Red Hood bears no aspirations toward a simple villainous get-rich-quick scheme. Jason Todd wants to become a next generation hero whose agenda is to kill criminals in order to prevent them from causing any more crime. Of course, other heroes throughout the history of comics have gone down this road before, but Jason plans on using viral marketing to get his message across. So, while the idea of Dick Grayson and Jason Todd being the surrogate sons of Batman is enough to unite them, Morrison takes it one step further by contrasting their respective marketing techniques.

With Batman, marketing isn't necessary. The symbol on his chest symbolizes that he will be an avenging angel – a hero that will never rest until villains are brought to justice. The only real "marketing" that the hero has comes in the form of the Batsignal which shines out into the night to let the people of Gotham City know that their hero will soon be on his way.

Meanwhile, the Red Hood employs a variety of tactics to replace the marketing of Batman. He updates a twitter feed that chronicles the exploits of the Red Hood and Scarlet. He speaks in catchphrases like "Let the punishment fit the crime," "The fight against crime grows up," and "cleansed by the red right hand of vengeance." He evens leaves a calling card of a red hand with the words "Vengeance arms against his red right hand."

After Scarlet criticizes Jason for getting all of his ideas from the book "Getting the Best Out of Your Brand," he explains, "That's all Batman is now – a brand, a logo, an idea gone past its sell-by date. We're the competition. We're making him obsolete like the iPod killed the Walkman."

Morrison is using Jason Todd to express his own ideas of corporations and branding as he stated in his article "Pop Magic!":

> Corporate sigils are super-breeders. They attack unbranded imaginative space. They invade Red Square, they infest the cranky streets of Tibet, they etch themselves into hairstyles. They breed across clothing, turning people into advertising hoardings. They are a very powerful development in the history of sigil magic, which dates back to the first bison drawn on the first cave wall.

> The logo or brand, like any sigil, is a condensation, a compressed, symbolic summoning up of the world of desire which the corporation intends to represent. The logo is the only visible sign of the corporate intelligence seething behind it. Walt Disney died long ago but his sigil, that familiar, cartoonish signature, persists, carrying its own vast weight of meanings, associations, nostalgia and significance. People are born and grow up to become Disney executives, mouthing jargon and the credo of a living corporate entity. Walt Disney the man is long dead and frozen (or so folkmyth would have it) but Disney, the immense invisible corporate egregore persists.[1]

In that very same conversation on branding between Jason and Sasha, Jason takes off his mask to reveal his hair had returned to its natural red color and that "Batman made me dye my hair to look more like Grayson." The corporate Batman model had effectively "etched" itself into his hairstyle just like in Morrison's "Pop Magic!" article. When Jason Todd was Robin, he was transformed by the brand, but now that he is the Red Hood, he is being transformed once more into what the Red Hood brand wants and needs.

So how is the Red Hood a "condensation, a compressed, symbolic summoning up of the world of desire which the corporation intends to represent?"

---

[1] Morrison, Grant. "Pop Magic!" *Book of Lies: The Disinformation Guide to Magick and the Occult*. Ed. Richard Metzger. New York: Disinformation Company Ltd., 2007. http://www.scribd.com/doc/24506/Pop-Magic-by-Grant-Morrison

Of course, on the surface level, the red hand symbol on Jason Todd's calling cards could be a reference to the old saying "caught red-handed," which refers criminals being caught in the act. The Red Hood catches the villain Lightning Bug in the act of stealing money and he is promptly executed. But the card is also made to resemble that of the Red Hand of Ulster – a symbol of the O'Neil clan. Legend has it that two chieftains raced one another across a stretch of water and the first to reach the land on the other side would claim it for himself. Realizing the other chieftain would land first, O'Neil cut off his own hand and flung it on to the land thereby inheriting it for himself. Today, the red hand is used as an emblem of Northern Ireland.

The phrase "vengeance arms against his red right hand" is from John Milton's Paradise Lost. It's spoken by the demon Belial in reference to God's vengeance against Hell if they went to war (Belial and other demons appear later in *Batman and Robin*, when Dr. Hurt returns). Furthermore, Christ sits at the right hand of God and therefore, the red right hand could very well be a representation of Christ the Redeemer, or more than likely in the case of Jason Todd, the Antichrist. If we consider Batman to be God the father and Dick Grayson is Jesus Christ the Savior, then Jason could very well be the Anti-Christ (of course, Damian is Bruce's real son, but he is hardly Christ-like especially when he is revealed to have sold his soul to the Devil in Batman #666 where he battles the Anti-Christ).

In addition, Nick Cave and the Bad Seeds have a song called "Red Right Hand" (released in 1994), in which the lyrics tell of "a tall handsome man in a dusty black coat with a red right hand." The character in the song has the ability to get you whatever you want, but the last verse seems to echo the idea of Jason Todd and his corporate sigils:

> You'll see him in your nightmares,
> you'll see him in your dreams
> He'll appear out of nowhere but
> he ain't what he seems
> You'll see him in your head,
> on the TV screen
> And hey buddy, I'm warning
> you to turn it off
> He's a ghost, he's a god,
> he's a man, he's a guru
> You're one microscopic cog

in his catastrophic plan
Designed and directed by
his red right hand

The song captures the mystery of the Red Hood while building a certain mystique around his plans. The repetition of where one would see him is a perfect example of corporate branding and how it infects people. Nick Cave and the Bad Seeds is a perfect band for Batman given that Batman operates out of a cave and Jason Todd is a "bad seed" in the Batman Family. Also, it's actually a perfect song to act as a soundtrack to the Red Hood story arc.

Children play the game "Red Hands" (also known as "slap hands" or "hot hands") where one player puts his hands above the other's and the bottom player is supposed to quickly slap the other's hands. The Red Hood is perhaps considering his competition with Batman as nothing more than a game.

Finally, the red hand is given an ironic meaning when considering that since 2002, every February 12 has been "Red Hand Day" which (according to the official "Red Hand Day" website) is a "worldwide initiative to stop child soldiers." Like Professor Pyg and his transformation of Dollotrons, Red Hood's interactions with Scarlet are meant to mirror Dick and Damian's partnership. While Dick and Damian bond over a rainy stakeout (where Dick informs Damian that a hood can easily become a blindfold, which echoes how blind Jason Todd is to anything but his mission), the Red Hood explains that Scarlet was chosen because of her twisted mask of a face. "You give the brand that genuine Nu-freak chic these try-hard Gotham wannabes just can't muster." Proof that all he ever cared about was the brand itself. Scarlet only matters because she improves the brand, especially with the double meaning of the first part of her name, "Scar" representing her appearance and her red costume.

Near the end of issue #5, the Red Hood captures Batman and Robin after shooting Dick Grayson in the chest. In the next issue, he advertises on television and the internet for people to call a hotline. After a certain number of calls, he threatens to reveal their secret identities. This is a not-so-subtle reference to *Batman* #427 where readers were to call one of two 1-900 numbers in order to vote on whether Todd would live or die. More readers voted for Todd's death, so the character was killed off in the next issue and stayed dead for 17 years until he was brought back as the new Red Hood.

Of course, Dick and Damian are set free, but once they suit up again, the Batman symbol is revealed to have been shot off of the suit. They find that the Red Hood and Scarlet are being beaten by an assassin known as the Flamingo.

Red Hood talks about corporate branding to Scarlet. From *Batman and Robin* Vol. 1 #4 (Nov 2009). Art by Philip Tan and Jonathan Glapion. Copyright © DC Comics.

After all of the corporate branding and symbolism, Dick and Jason are battling for their lives against someone far more fierce than they are. As Scarlet leaps on Flamingo's back, her cry, "Let the punishment fit the crime!" seems hollow as Flamingo easily defeats her. Still, the Red Hood is able to take down the assassin while saying his catchphrase, proving that even at its worst, good marketing will always win.

Finally, Jason admits what everyone knew all along. "I tried really hard to be what Batman wanted me to be… which was you." But he doesn't leave until he shakes Dick's faith by saying, "He's still dead because of something you can never admit! You just couldn't stand the fact that you were always gonna be in his shadow!"

Despite the confidence Dick gained after battling Professor Pyg, Jason's words shake him to the core. Only a true foil could do the damage to Dick's psyche that Jason is able to enact because only a true foil knows what the hero is thinking.

It's worth noting that Jason Todd's redesigned costume looks remarkably similar to a villain named "the Red Mask" that Morrison created for his *Animal Man* run. A user named "RedHoodsDen" on Comic Vine's forums noticed this and criticized the connection between the villains saying:

> Morrison ripped off one of his earlier characters from Animal Man, the Red Mask of Death. He had a lame ass red skull on his chest and red dome helmet and all his weaponry was red. He was old, out of shape, bald, and suicidal. He had a death touch which I would guess Morrison meant to, but never got around to using the phrase "Vengeances Arms Again His Red Right Hand." Basically, every idea Morrison had for Jason was just recycled. Substitute Mask being tired of being a loser supervillain with Jason's inferiority complex and you've got the same shtick.[2]

But it's a mistake to think that just because the characters share a visual link that Morrison has somehow ripped himself off. As Tim Callahan writes in *Grant Morrison: The Early Years*, this story is about "one character that didn't amount to much in the grand scheme of things, and while that may not be a mind-blowing idea, insignificance is a recurring theme in much of Morrison's work" (page 77). The Red Mask is a victim of circumstance with an origin not unlike Animal Man's, but having the power of a death touch made him into a villain because fate brought him to that point.

---

[2] http://www.comicvine.com/jason-todd/4005-6849/forums/batman-robin-24-solicits-cover-please-dc-lose-the--602539/

Though he was ruthlessly and mercilessly beaten by the Joker, Jason was resurrected and chose to be a villain. He had the option to return to being a hero but he didn't do it. This will be further echoed when Bruce Wayne returns from the dead and continues to be Batman. So, while he may look like Red Mask and they may be somewhat similar it is simply ignorant and foolish to state that Morrison is rehashing the same ideas. He is simply exploring the freedom and power of choice.

Dick Grayson's confrontations with Jason Todd work well because they are so multi-faceted. At the surface level, they are competitive brothers who hate one another. But just underneath lies a rich metaphor for corporate branding and heroism that sows the seeds for Grant Morrison's later *Batman, Inc.*

The first six issues of Grant Morrison's *Batman and Robin* expertly put Dick Grayson in a position that readers weren't used to seeing him in − one of vulnerability. The normally confident Grayson approaches heroism the way he approached the trapeze; with a grin and ready to put on a show. It's an interesting change of pace to see him uncomfortable as Batman and unsure of how to teach Damian morality. Even though Dick Grayson has been a super-hero since he was a kid, he is still developing. Morrison's ability to unveil a new psychological depth in a character that has been around since the '40s is a great accomplishment.

Bat-Lazarus

In the first arc of *Batman and Robin*, Dick Grayson learned to regard "Batman" as a great role. In the second arc, he reaffirmed his morality when it was tested by Jason Todd. In the third arc, Grayson literally faces his fear that Bruce might really be gone in order to complete his transformation into the role of Batman. While the third arc isn't the best of Morrison's run, it's important for a number of reasons.

First, while Grayson was uncomfortable as Batman in the beginning, it's clear he has adjusted by the sheer fact that he has left Gotham for London. Dick isn't being reactive in his heroism; instead, he is being proactive in his quest to revive Bruce Wayne. But this new mission creates an interesting paradox: If Dick Grayson is comfortable as Batman, then why does he look for an out by reviving Bruce Wayne? If he were truly comfortable, then he would accept Bruce's death as a natural part of life and move on.

Second, this is the first issue that Damian doesn't appear as Robin. In fact, he's only shown briefly during a scene where he is undergoing spinal surgery after being shot repeatedly by Flamingo at the end of the last arc. With Damian out of the story, Dick must learn to work with Knight and Squire (the Batman and Robin of London) and also Batwoman. The dynamic between the heroes doesn't quite work. This is either indicative of how the arc is awkwardly put together or proof that Dick and Damian play off of each other really well.

Third, the turf war between Charlie English and King Coal is never explored to a satisfactory degree. Their conflict is always in the background of the real plot of Dick Grayson trying to revive Bruce Wayne and so, their threat is never a real threat at all.

Ultimately, the arc has too many elements in play at one time and none of them really gel together into a strong, coherent story. Dick has to go to London to team up with too many people to revive Bruce Wayne in a Lazarus pit controlled by two London crime bosses. Yet, despite the oversaturation of story elements, Dick does manage to show some growth in this arc.

Once Bruce's body emerges from the Lazarus Pit, eliminate it's not the real Bruce Wayne. In a flashback within the fake Bruce's mind, the reader realizes that during Final Crisis, Darkseid had a clone made of Batman just in case he ever needed one. Whether Dick Grayson realizes this or not is unclear and the question of how this copy was replaced with Bruce's body at the end of Final Crisis #6 as the Omega Sanction blasts him is even less clear. What one needs to realize, however, is that these questions don't matter in the scheme of things. What matters is that a Bruce-like monster has appeared and Grayson has to stop him from killing Damian.

Of course, Dick saves the day, but rather than let this be a comfort to his doubts regarding whether or not he can be Batman, he considers it proof that Bruce is alive and worth searching for. As heroic as Dick Grayson is, he can never be comfortable as Batman. He can never embrace that darkness that haunted and fueled Bruce Wayne, and he will do what he can to pass the legacy back to his mentor.

Some might consider this to be Grayson giving up, but I would argue that it is proof that he is aware of himself. Grayson is selfless because he knows that Batman is essential to the world and if he must fill that void, then he will do so.

Deathstroke

The fourth arc continues Grayson's quest to resurrect Bruce Wayne and while Oberon Sexton and the 99 Fiends are major players in the story, Deathstroke's possession of Damian's body is the most noteworthy element to the story. As stated previously, Dick Grayson never really had a foil except for Deathstroke.

In the past, Deathstroke poisoned the mind of earth-manipulating heroine, Terra and other teens in order to strike against the Titans and Dick Grayson, but this time he quite literally takes control of Damian. It's a fascinating twist and one that perfectly shows the effect that Grayson has had on the son of Bruce Wayne. Despite not being in control of his own body, Damian is able to take what his partner has taught him and apply it to breaking the control of Deathstroke.

By this time, Grayson's identity as Batman had been established enough that to truly pit him against another foil would be unnecessary, but the Deathstroke interaction is a perfect conclusion to Dick Grayson's tenure as Batman.

Of course, there are four more issues of Dick Grayson as Batman under Morrison's guidance, and other writers contributed to him as a character afterward, but in terms of establishing foils for Dick Grayson, Morrison was the best.

By the end of *Batman and Robin,* Dick Grayson had grown as a character, but it would be foolish to only focus on his development because he is only half of the team.

Damian Wayne: More than Just the Son of the Bat

The very idea of Batman having a son was criticized before Damian ever made his first appearance. Technically, his first appearance was at the very end of Mike W. Barr's *Son of the Demon* back in 1987. The idea that Bruce Wayne would have a child out of wedlock was so controversial that it was immediately retconned. In Mark Waid and Alex Ross's *Kingdom Come*, the character made an appearance under the name Ibn al Xu-ffasch. But it wasn't until Grant Morrison started writing *Batman* that Damian was named in official continuity.

Morrison hardly names characters haphazardly, and Damian is no exception. The name "Damian" has taken on negative connotations after the film *The Omen* presented the Anti-Christ with that name. So before readers even know anything about the character, they assume Damian to be some sort of evil character; that name is now so associated with the idea of the Anti-Christ that readers immediately assume the worst about him. But the name actually means "to tame," which makes sense given that "Batman and Son" is about Bruce Wayne trying to tame his son and prevent him from succumbing to his assassin tendencies. One could easily argue that this first story arc is the true reason why so many fans were apprehensive with accepting Damian as part of the Bat-mythos.

When he's first revealed, Damian is holding a sword to Bruce's throat. Once Bruce brings Damian back to the Batcave, his son promptly challenges his father to a fight. He then threatens Tim Drake when Tim tries to be nice. When told that Alfred will help him unpack, Damian responds, "@#$% you." In short, Damian isn't very pleasant in his first full appearance. But Bruce still defends the boy by saying, "He was raised by international terrorists in his grandfather's League of Assassins. Brutalized, indoctrinated, then used as a weapon in his mother's insane war with me."

Morrison is almost directly telling the reader to give Damian a chance because he has both nature and nurture working against him so he will naturally be kind of a pain.

Combine the psychological trauma done to him with the fact that he has to learn to live with a father who has never been part of his life and you've got a recipe for disaster. Especially when that father happens to be Bruce Wayne – a ruthless taskmaster to children who *aren't* biologically his. "I've been sent here against my will! You can't make me do anything I don't want to do!" Damian screams as he throws a tantrum in Wayne Manor.

Even if you don't have children, you've probably seen Defiant children who have been raised without any boundaries – children who have been given everything and have never been told "no." The most common example is the child who throws fits in the grocery store and begs his or her parents for candy. These children can't be blamed for this lack of structure because it's up to parents to provide it. Therefore, Damian is never really to blame for his actions because he was raised wrong.

If Damian was a normal brat who disobeyed his father, he could be easily forgiven. As the son of the Dark Knight and a woman who is the leader of the League of Assassins, he is no normal child and therefore takes defiance to a new level as he decapitates a one-off villain by the name of the Spook. Then, Damian fights Tim Drake for the mantle of Robin. Even with an understanding of Damian's psychology, it's admittedly a little difficult to defend him after these two incidents, so many fans quickly made up their minds about what kind of a person Damian Wayne was with little to no room for improvement.

To make matters worse, his next appearance would be as Batman in a possible future depicted in *Batman* #666. Not only was Damian Wayne a character that was annoying to readers, but this single issue informed readers that he would be here to stay. Ironically, Damian battles the Anti-Christ (a reference to his namesake being associated with the horror film *The Omen*). Despite battling the Anti-Christ, having Damian as Batman in #666 still begets the interpretation that he might indeed be evil. So while Morrison establishes that Damian will one day be a hero, he still maintains the mystery that he might not be.

Beyond establishing Damian as a future Batman, issue #666 also plants the seeds for future arcs. This issue introduced Professor Pyg and the Flamingo for the first time, and also mentions that Dick Grayson was Batman for a time. The Anti-Christ Batman hints at the coming of the Devil which will later be revealed to be Dr. Hurt or the Black Glove. Most importantly, however, is the revelation that Damian sold his soul to the Devil when he was 14 on the night that Batman died – a point that will come up in Morrison's last issue of *Batman and Robin*.

While Damian Wayne is something of an annoyance in the early issues of Batman, his role is exceptionally important for a number of reasons. First, he is Morrison's initial assertion that all Batman stories from the past matter. While other writers might wish to ignore Damian's birth in *Son of the Demon*, Morrison embraced the story's potential and this is simply his first step towards explaining other more wild and bizarre stories from Batman's past like Zur-en-Arrh, Bat-Mite, and his relationship with the original Batwoman.

Next, Damian puts Bruce Wayne into an interesting position we had never seen before: that of the responsible father. Of course, Bruce has been a father to Dick, Jason, and Tim before, but those were always connected to the idea of a military drill sergeant training soldiers for the war on crime. With Damian, Bruce feels a certain degree of guilt for not knowing about his own son's existence, and for neglecting the boy who had turned into a monster because of his insane mother.

Damian also acts as a pawn in the game between Batman and Talia. After Talia had indoctrinated Damian, and she sent him to live with his father so that Bruce would feel attached to the boy, she then gave Batman an ultimatum: "Join me and I promise I'll never threaten civilization again. We'll found a dynasty that will rule the planet for a thousand years." When Bruce refuses, she responds rather cryptically, "Then it's war. And you're responsible... for people like us, the world is a gameboard and nations are pawns."

Because Bruce refused to join Talia, he is directly responsible for the foundation of the Leviathan organization and the war that would take place in *Batman, Inc.* Fortunately, even though Damian was poorly received by fans, he eventually lives up to his name and becomes "tamed" as he joins Dick Grayson in *Batman and Robin*.

While Dick Grayson's growth as Batman is certainly one way of interpreting *Batman and Robin,* one shouldn't forget the "Robin" part of the title. With this series, Morrison took on the seemingly impossible task of trying to make Damian Wayne into a likable character by giving him true development. His growth as a hero is an incredibly important factor in the narrative of the series because it is proof that even though fans may think they know what they want in terms of story, given the right character and circumstances, even the most hated character can be turned around.

Damian's first line in *Batman and Robin* is proof that the character had grown much since his first appearance. In a flying Batmobile while on the trail of Mr. Toad and his gang's getaway car, Damian coolly says, "I told you it would work. All I had to do was adapt my father's blueprints." He has accepted his father's mission and is working towards improving Batman's methodology.

Alfred furthers this notion when he compliments Damian by saying, "Remarkable work, young sir, if I may say so. The gyroscopic array was a source of endless frustration for your father, as I recall." To which Damian responds, "I promised I'd finish what he started" showing that he has not only accepted his Batman lineage as being more important than his role as assassin, but that he feels a sense of necessity to continue his father's work.

Additionally, note that Damian has improved a new Batmobile which harkens back to Morrison's first issue of *Batman* titled "Building a Better Batmobile." This Batmobile can fly, giving this series a whimsical feel.

But at the beginning of *Batman and Robin,* Damian shows that he isn't fully responsible just yet. He tells the frustrated Dick Grayson, "If you're not up to it, stand aside, Dick Grayson. I was bred for the job, and trained in the arts of war by the masters of my mother's League of Assassins. I could just as easily continue my father's work on my own," and later, "You can have respect if you earn it, that's all I'm saying." These instances show that even though Damian has grown into a more intelligent and calm person, he is still a defiant and impetuous child with room to grow.

In a sense, Damian and Dick are mirrors for one another. When Dick was Robin, he was cheerful and reminded Batman that there was good in the world. Now that Damian is Robin, he is too much of his father and Dick as Batman must remind Robin that the world isn't a horrible place. The dynamic of the Dark Knight and the Boy Wonder became inversed.

While battling the Circus of Strange, Damian's anger gets the best of him as he goes off on his own to battle and torture Big Top (a fat man in a pink tutu) and doing so allows Mr. Toad to be murdered by the Domino Killer causing a rift between Dick and Damian. "I already promised my father I wouldn't kill. Now I'm supposed to be nice to the police as well?" Damian asks, showing that he had taken his father's lessons of not killing to heart, but he is still ignorant about what it really takes to be a hero.

Damian represents Dick Grayson's first true challenge as Batman. If Dick can't get his partner to believe he is Batman, then no one will. He leaves the partnership to find Professor Pyg on his own which causes Dick Grayson to question his effectiveness as Batman. It isn't the Circus of Strange that shatters Grayson's confidence, but the actions of his own partner.

After being captured by Professor Pyg, Damian never breaks a sweat or shows one sign of fear as he makes his escape and nearly defeats Pyg and his Dollotrons all on his own. It's an interesting scene because in a typical story, after the arrogant partner is captured, it takes the calm, collected partner to come save him. In this case, Damian is ambushed, and captured, but he is still able to break out on his own and fight Pyg. All in all, he would have been successful in his mission, but despite his capabilities, he isn't able to save Sasha from the Dollotron horde which causes her to murder her own father and become the Red Hood's sidekick, Scarlet.

So the first arc of *Batman and Robin* has established that while Damian has grown, he still has a lot of learning to do, and the end of the Professor Pyg encounter finally teaches him that there are consequences for not being perfect, but the message won't be fully received until the next arc with the Red Hood.

Of all the arcs in *Batman and Robin*, the Red Hood is the most profound — not just because of the parallels created between Dick Grayson and Jason Todd, but for what it represents to Damian's growth as a hero. In their first interaction together in issue #4 on a rooftop stakeout, Dick and Damian seem to bond in the rain. It's a brief moment in which Dick criticizes Damian for wearing a hood and Damian proves that he can fight blind. The two grin and while it isn't a syrupy Hallmark moment, the reader gets a sense that the two have developed a sense of respect for one another since their conflict with Pyg.

Batman and Robin then face off against the Red Hood and Scarlet for the first time. After their battle, a visibly shaken Damian mutters, "That was her.

That was the girl from the circus I tried to save." The consequences of Damian's actions at the end of the Professor Pyg encounter were dire, but important to his growth as a character. For the first time, Damian is shown with genuine remorse for something he had done wrong.

Sasha is Damian's first real failure as a hero, and she acts as a foil of sorts for him. She murders her father (as opposed to Damian honoring his), she partners with a villainous former Robin, and she adopts an extreme stance on murdering criminals. And while she is an excellent lens to help readers better understand Damian, she is by no means alone in this.

After their first encounter with the Red Hood and Scarlet, Damian mentions that Bruce "made some very strange choices when it came to partners" and Dick explains, "Bruce thought he could save Jason..." This one sentence perfectly echoes Damian's introduction into the Batman universe. Bruce knew Damian had been raised wrong and he took it upon himself to rewire his son and make him into a hero. Jason is a representation of what Damian could have become if he would have continued down the path of killing crime. Furthermore, both Jason and Damian were hated by the fans and so there is a sort of meta-connection between the two that exists because of that hatred.

But despite the comparisons between Damian and Jason, Damian says, "It's not about him. It's that girl. I feel responsible." Damian faced the frighteningly creepy Professor Pyg and survived without the slightest psychological effect, but in failing to save Sasha, he finally feels guilt.

It's also worth noting that despite his faith in his abilities being shaken, Damian never once suggests that he isn't fit to do the job. Where other super-heroes have questioned their ability to perform their duties, Damian never does. He's so confident in his role that he resolves to redeem himself where others might have toyed with the idea of hanging up the costume.

At the end of the Red Hood story, Damian is damaged once more, but this time, rather than being damaged psychologically due to his failure, he is paralyzed after being shot in the spine by the Flamingo. Surely even the most stone-hearted reader could empathize with this once hated character as he is hurt while trying to do the right thing. After six issues of *Batman and Robin*, Damian has gone from the arrogant, hated, bastard child of Bruce Wayne to a slightly more mature character with mental and physical battle scars.

While Damian's name can be interpreted as "to tame," it can also be interpreted as "to conquer," which seems to be Talia's reasoning for his name when she says in issue #7, "Damian will stride across the 21st century like a new Alexander." As he is undergoes spine surgery after being paralyzed by Flamingo at the end of the previous arc, we learn that Talia's plans for Damian don't include his role as Robin. She sees it as a "phase," but with Bruce Wayne gone, she whispers not to her son, but to her idea of what her son should be. "Soon then, my dear. Soon."

Talia is more than Damian's mother in this instance; she represents everyone who ever had preconceived notions about who Damian is as a character. Like all of the fans who doubted that Damian would be a worthy successor to the Batman name, Talia doesn't want Damian to be Robin. She wants him to take his place as the heir of the al Ghul empire.

Damian is barely in the three-part "Blackest Knight" until the final issue, where he must defend himself against a mutilated, insane, resurrected clone of his father. Even though he is recovering from spine surgery and must single-handedly fight a monstrosity that appears to be his father, Damian shows that he is worthy to be the son of Batman through his bravery in battle. In this way, he has established that he is capable of Batman's abilities even when he isn't in the Robin costume. Meanwhile, at the beginning of the "Batman vs. Robin" story, Damian is shown taking on the role of chairman of Wayne Enterprises as he points out an error in finances that others should have caught. So, not only have his abilities as a fighter been proven, he has also proven to be a capable businessman as well (something that Dick Grayson has been avoiding throughout the entire series thus far).

The main focus of "Batman vs. Robin" revolves around Dick and Damian uncovering a mystery to bring Bruce Wayne back from the dead. While searching for clues in Wayne manor, Damian asks, "If my father returns we can't be Batman and Robin anymore, can we?" to which Dick replies, "No, I guess not. It's a small price to pay for getting him back alive."

From there, Damian continues to worry that he won't be Robin any longer and Dick cracks jokes so that he can avoid the tough questions while still trying to teach Damian to be a detective. Finally, a frustrated Damian says, "Do you know what I gave up for this? It's not just nothing to me." Afterward, there is a flashback to a conversation between Damian and Talia after his spine surgery.

Talia perfectly explains Damian's inner conflict when she says, "Their plan is to tame and brainwash you until nothing is left but a spineless puppet. The world could be yours."

The tame or the conqueror – the two possibilities of Damian's namesake – are the options that Talia presents to her son. While in his most vulnerable state after having spine surgery, she invokes the idea of destiny and that Damian has no choice but to follow her plans for his life. But ever defiant, Damian foreshadows the remainder of this arc when he says, "I won't be your weapon against them, mother."

Of course, Damian's new spine is just another weapon in Talia's war against Batman (or "game" to quote her from the end of "Batman and Son") and she is able to take control of Damian's body in an attempt to kill Dick Grayson. After he regains control, Batman and Robin confront Talia. She claims that Grayson's indoctrination of Damian is no different than her own.

The idea that Damian has somehow been indoctrinated into heroism is interesting because it presumes he has no free will. As a child of 10, one could further argue that this is true, because he is dependent upon others. Still, the guilt he felt for failing Sasha wasn't an indoctrinated emotion; it was his own. He felt genuinely sorry for his mistake without being told to by Dick Grayson, so perhaps Damian does indeed have the will and ability necessary to make his own decisions.

It's during the private conversation between Damian and Talia that he truly completes his transformation, however. He shows how serious he takes his role when he tells her, "Being Robin is the best thing I've ever done, mother." Talia responds by showing that she is growing a new child that will be Damian's genetic duplicate. In a way, she has cloned her own son just in case of the occasion that he would ultimately betray her.

When she offers him one last chance to inherit her empire, he replies, "Can't you just love me for who I am? Not what you want me to be?" Even though Damian has proven himself to be an exceptional fighter without emotion, this scene shows he is still vulnerable. Underneath his tough exterior, all he wants is to be loved and accepted by his parents. With Bruce Wayne gone, Damian chooses to be Robin to honor his father, but this decision goes against his mother's wishes.

Their conversation concludes with Talia declaring that Damian would be "an enemy of the house of al Ghul" and he completes his transformation by saying, "Very well. I hope I can be a worthy one, mother."

Finally, after so long, Morrison hit upon the raw, emotional core of the character and it was well worth the wait. Damian's struggle between "the

Damian tells Talia that he hopes he can be a worthy enemy of the al Ghul empire. From *Batman and Robin* Vol. 1 #12 (July 2010). Art by Andy Clarke and Scott Hanna. Copyright © DC Comics.

tame" and "the conqueror" was never overdramatized, but rather bubbled just below the surface of the character throughout Morrison's Batman run. That struggle concludes in the final issue of *Batman and Robin* as Damian defies reader expectations by becoming a hero worth rooting for. Though at times a frustrating brat, Damian grew emotionally. Despite fans virtually begging for him to be retconned or killed off, he became an unexpected and surprising hero.

Batman and Robin was a title that constructed Dick Grayson's rogue's gallery and accomplished much in establishing a stronger identity for the hero while he was under the Batman cowl, and accomplished the seemingly impossible task of transitioning Damian Wayne from brat to hero, but don't be fooled into thinking that this was the real goal; it was merely a façade. Underneath the shiny veneer of character development, a war was being waged. Creeping between the panels and bleeding out onto the page in glorious, four-color symbolism, two players manipulated the events of the comic in a game of dominoes, and chess.

So, while *Batman and Robin* was a fun read about how Dick Grayson and Damian Wayne grew as characters and became heroes, when read again and more closely, it's not really about that at all. It's simply a ruse.

A trick.

A joke.

A Game of Villainy: The War Between the Joker and Dr. Hurt

While Dick Grayson and Damian Wayne were busy learning how to adjust to their new identities, a secret war was being waged between Dr. Thomas Hurt and the Joker. Reading Morrison's run on *Batman and Robin* for the story of their titular characters is a satisfying and complete experience, but upon subsequent readings, the clues to the game between villains become more apparent.

But before discussing the game itself, one must delve into the history of the conflict between the Clown Prince of Crime and the Devil himself, which stretches all the way back to Morrison's first issue of *Batman* (#655).

Though Dr. Hurt wouldn't be introduced until much later into Morrison's run on *Batman*, the game between Hurt and the Joker technically begins with Morrison's first issue. The Joker stands with bloody crowbar in hand before a broken Batman and proclaims, "I did it! I finally killed Batman! In front of a bunch of vulnerable, disabled kids!"

Everything about this image is classic, iconic Joker: the purple suit complete with absurd green bow tie. The wild green hair. The crowbar to remind readers of "Death in the Family" and the Joker's triumph in killing Jason Todd (Batman's greatest failure). In the background, a group of children impossibly tied together and dangling from a helicopter sporting the Joker's smile. Even the subject of the image itself (the Joker's hubris allowing him to believe that he

A double page spread of the Joker holding a crowbar over a beaten Batman. From *Batman* Vol. 1 #655 (Sept 2006). Art by Andy Kubert. Copyright © DC Comics.

had finally conquered his nemesis under such absurd, bizarre circumstances) just screams of classic Joker.

All of these work in concert to form one final image of Batman's greatest villain before his transformation. Suddenly, the fallen Batman pulls a gun out of his utility belt and says one word, "die," and then he shoots the villain in the head which is a significant symbol because it specifically calls attention to the Joker's psyche.

Wait... in order to understand *this* development, it's perhaps more important to go back even further.

Before *Before*

During a conversation between Batman and Dr. Ruth Adams in Grant Morrison's *Batman: Arkham Asylum*, the doctor explains the Joker's condition as possibly being:

> a neurological disorder, similar to Tourette's syndrome. It's quite possible we may actually be looking at some kind of super-sanity here. A brilliant new modification of human perception. More suited to urban life at the end of the twentieth century... unlike you and I, the Joker seems to have

no control over the sensory information he's receiving from the outside world. He can only cope with that chaotic barrage of input by going with the flow. That's why some days he's a mischievous clown, others a psychopathic killer. He has no real personality. He creates himself each day. He sees himself as the lord of misrule, and the world as the theatre of the absurd.

While *Arkham Asylum* is more of a Batman story than a Joker story, this explanation for the Joker's behavior serves as the foundation for every story that Morrison has written about the character. It establishes a psychological reasoning for why the Joker can have so many different incarnations. The Joker shifts personalities because he has none. Our world moves at such a fast pace that the Joker has developed a hyper-personality that allows him to cope with the information overload. He can be anything he needs to be given the situation.

Transformation

The next time the Joker appears during Morrison's tenure is in a *very* different kind of story altogether – the first prose issue in a comic book "The Clown at Midnight" in *Batman* #663. The Joker's transformation is so complete that it requires a total change from the standard comic book in order to fully capture this change.

Chapter 1 of the issue's story begins with a funeral for Bozzo the Bandit (a former henchman for the Joker) and ends with the deaths of everyone at the funeral. While the funeral may be for Bozzo on the surface level, Morrison really means for this funeral to be for the Joker's old personality. This is also the first time the "red and black" motif appears and it will be not only a driving plot point in this story, but it will continually reappear all the way through Morrison's *Batman and Robin* run. Here, there are black and red flowers as well as a reference to "black and red voltage" as a clown dies. Each of the locations in the story follows the motif and each murder site features one of these two colors.

In chapter 3, Batman visits a broken and bandaged up Joker in Arkham Asylum much to the dismay of Jeremiah Arkham. Under his bandages, the Joker isn't ready to be revealed just yet. He is like a pupa in his chrysalis, patiently awaiting his development to complete. Even as an invalid, the Joker insults his doctor by blinking inappropriate things in Morse code. Arkham reveals that the Joker has been working with a speech therapist by the name of "Miss Wisakedjak" and she apparently graduated from "the Rose Bruford School."

Batman notes that "Wisakedjak is the name of the Cree Indian trickster god," but he neglects to inform Arkham that the Rose Bruford School is an acting school in Southeast London or that the Anglicized version of Wisakedjak is "Whiskey Jack" which is another name for a type of bird known as the "Gray Jay." The Joker, of course, is pale-skinned and called "Mister Jay" by his sidekick, Harley Quinn.

This reference to the Cree Indian trickster god isn't simply a wink and a nod to show how clever Morrison is with his names, nor is it meant to show how clever Batman's mind is. Morrison is deliberately including this god in order to help establish a mythological connection between a trickster of the ancient world to the trickster god of comics. Morrison further tries to establish the Joker as a kind of god through the invocation of the Joker's various nicknames. Throughout the issue, he is referred to as: the Clown Prince of Cruelty, the Picasso of Crime, the Master of Mirth, the Deathly Dandy, the Laughing Leper, the Clown Prince of Pain, and finally, the Clown at Midnight. All of these nicknames act as epithets in the same way that Greek Gods were called upon by different names depending on what people were requesting.

In chapter 4, two little people named Solomon and Sheba are introduced. They are described as dwarves from "the Joker's short-lived ringmaster-from-Hell phase," which shows that this latest transformation for the Joker is just one in a very long line. After the dwarves are murdered by toxins combined from red and black flowers, Commissioner Gordon seems to feel no pity towards them.

"You remember what this little creep did to me?" He shudders. "The Joker and his whole circus can go to Hell as far as I'm concerned."

From this little bit of dialogue, one can reasonably assume that the reason for Gordon's hostility stems from *The Killing Joke* and that Solomon and Sheba were the dwarves that abused Gordon as he rode naked in a car through a fun house of pictures of his shot and tortured daughter, Barbara. The Joker's motivations in *The Killing Joke* and in this story are similar: he wants to break the heroes and bring them to madness. For all of his intelligence and emphasis on his own personality, the Joker is strange in his motivations. Considering that he is comfortable in his madness, it's odd that he would be so insistent in others sharing in this madness. To bring others to his way of thinking would destroy the idea of his autonomy and self-reliance because he would be making them just like him.

Chapter 6 is a brief and frightening look into the mind of the Joker and the cocoon imagery is explicitly spelled out, "like a grub growing all wrong in a tiled cocoon, like a caterpillar liquefying to filth in its own nightmares, or a fetus dissolving in sewage and sour milk, the Joker dreams, awake."

This is also the first mention of an epithet for the Joker; the first moment where Morrison begins to assert the Joker's role as trickster god.

During chapter 7, there is a bit of a retcon of Morrison's own *Arkham Asylum* (depending on one's perspective). Batman says, "He's changed again. You know how he changes every few years. You wrote the book, Doctor Quinzel. He has no real personality, remember, only a series of 'superpersonas.' That's what you called them, right?" If the reference is to *Arkham Asylum*, then Harley has replaced Dr. Ruth Adams, but perhaps the Adams conversation still occurred and Quinn wrote her book outside of that interaction. Then again, since Dr. Ruth Adams is actually the same name of the female lead in the classic B-movie *This Island Earth* and Harley Quinn is known for disguises, it would be fun if she had taken the name as a joke (this is impossible, of course, given that *Arkham Asylum* was written four years *before* Harley Quinn's appearance in *Batman: The Animated Series*, but it's still fun to think about).

In addition to solidifying the psychological background to the Joker's transformation, this chapter establishes Harley as a blind follower to the Joker's insane ideology. She is a woman who has been transformed into an almost religious fanatic who worships a trickster god and is unable to see past the flaws in her own dogma.

Finally, the Joker is revealed in Chapter 8 as he removes his cocoon, and the Clown at Midnight is revealed at last. He first cries out, "I'm a cockroach!" and begins to dance the can-can in celebration. The scene is a dark reflection of Franz Kafka's *The Metamorphosis* where Gregor Samsa's learns that he has been transformed into a bug. Whereas Samsa was horrified by being changed into a monster, the Joker is thrilled. Samsa was alienated by his transformation, but the Joker never feels alienation because he is without a conscience. Or, as Morrison writes in the issue:

> He tries to remember how the doctors in Arkham say he has no Self, and maybe they're right, or maybe they're just guessing. Maybe he is a new human mutation, bred of slimy industrial waters, spawned in a world of bright carcinogens and acid rains. Maybe is the model for the 21st-century big-time multiplex man, shuffling selves like a croupier deals cards, to buffer the shocks and work some alchemy that might just turn the lead of

tragedy and horror into the fierce, chaotic gold of the laughter of the damned.

The red and black motif is explained as the Joker telegraphs his plans to kill Harley Quinn. One can't help but feel sorry for her as she realizes that she had been worshipping a false god all along. The Joker and Batman finally face off as the Joker "drags his foot like Asmodeus, the lame demon, the tempter and destroyer." Again, Morrison is being deliberate by invoking a demon and connecting it to the Joker. He is far more explicit, however, when the Joker thinks, "Why be a disfigured outcast when I can be a notorious Crime God?"

It's at this point that the terrifying transformation of the Joker is complete and he has solidified his status as a trickster god of a new era of crime.

One gets the sense that Morrison isn't presenting the Joker as a villain so much as he is the next step of evolution. He respects the Joker perhaps because he sees some of himself in the character. Of course, Morrison isn't a homicidal clown, but he is a man who has undergone many transformations in his own life (*Talking With Gods* is evidence of this). Whatever the case, Morrison seems to hold the Joker in high-esteem; in a kind of reverence. As Morrison explains in his (previously mentioned) interview with *Playboy*:

> I identify with the Joker to a certain extent—at least the way I write him, which is as this cosmic fool. He's Batman's perfect opposite, and because of that he's as sexy as Batman, if not more so. When the Joker was introduced in 1940, he was a scowling homicidal maniac. Then they took out the violence and death, and he became the chuckling clown, driving around in his Joker-mobile. Then he was the giggling mental-patient version from the TV show: Cesar Romero with his mustache covered in greasepaint. Suddenly in the 1970s he was killing his henchmen again. And in the 1980s he was a gender-bending transvestite. I said, Okay, we've had all these varied versions of the Joker. Let's say it's the same person who just changes his head every day. I rationalized that by saying he's supersane, the first man of the 21st century who's dealing with this overload of information by changing his entire personality. I quite like him, because he's a pop star—he's like Bowie.

One almost gets the sense that the Joker could very well have been part of the Invisibles if he would just drop the whole "homicidal psychopath" act. Unlike the characters of Morrison's *The Invisibles*, the Joker doesn't need a "fictionsuit" to change who he is, because the Joker's personality can shift so dramatically and powerfully that he is already enlightened. And if he's not, then he surely could be very easily.

Whereas Bruce Wayne will later go through a transformative experience in *Return of Bruce Wayne*, the Joker has already attained enlightenment. He is able to attain his god-like status through his own actions while Bruce Wayne had to endure the Omega Sanction caused by Darkseid in order to attain his own status as "Bat-God."

The Devil and the Ghosts of Batman

While the Black Glove doesn't actually make an appearance until later in the series, the presence of Dr. Hurt can be felt in the Morrison's first issue as Batman throws the Joker into a dumpster and the hypnotic trigger words "Zur-en-Arrh" are written in graffiti on a nearby brick wall. This is a subtle clue for readers that can be revisited once the trigger is revealed in "R.I.P.," but more importantly, they are the signature of Dr. Hurt; they indicate that he had a hand in whatever had occurred.

In"Three Ghosts of Batman," Batman investigates a group of crooked cops who are hiring prostitutes to "pacify" a venom-enhanced cop who dresses as Batman, and the "Zur-en-Arrh" graffiti appears again. Both the Gun Batman from the first issue and the Monstrous Batman are part of a deliberate attack on Batman's psyche by Dr. Hurt. They are used to corrupt Batman's colors and to twist what he represents. Not only are they physical threats, but they are damaging to his reputation and his state of mind. If Batman somehow caused all of this evil, then what does that say about him as a hero? As Bruce Wayne recovers from the beating he received at the hands of the monstrous Batman, he has a hallucination where the three Batmen are with Damian and his son says, "The Third is the worst of all." However, we won't see the third Batman interact with Bruce Wayne until later.

At the end of the conflict with the Monstrous Batman, Commissioner Gordon's dialogue foreshadows the revelation of the ultimate evil when he says, "Why did you have to choose an enemy that's as old as time and bigger than all of us, Batman?"

The Black Glove

The Black Glove is finally mentioned when Batman and Robin meet with the International Club of Heroes on Mayhew's Island. The story, a classic mystery story (in the vein of Agatha Christie's *And Then There Were None*), is perfect for intriguing readers with the identity of the Black Glove.

On page one of the story, the black and red motif established by "the Clown at Midnight" issue returns in the form of a roulette wheel. A man hangs upside down and someone says,

> The Black Glove is a seal of absolute quality and ruthlessness. The Black Glove aims to deliver a deluxe-service, high-stakes experience at the very highest levels of the international game. Our esteemed clientele see no virtue in thinking small, nor do we. This weekend the Black Glove settles the age-old questions once and for all. Which is strongest? Good? Or evil?

This may seem like generic villain banter, but it's incredibly important because it establishes the game motif that continues in *Batman and Robin*. The Black Glove is a gambler and is willing to bet that evil can triumph over good. He is playing a game of chance while the Joker plays chess. Therefore, the real conflict seems to stem from two different games being played; chance and strategy.

Nothing is left to chance in the Joker's manipulations because he has all of his moves and Batman's moves planned out. But the Black Glove sets things into motion to see how they will interact with one another. He puts a gun in the hand of a drugged-out cop in a Batman suit and instructs him to shoot the Joker just so he can see what the outcome will be.

But who exactly is the Black Glove? He seems to be Jonathan Mayhew, a "mega-rich daredevil from the old school" who financed a film known as the "Black Glove" starring Mangrove Pierce and Marsha Lamarr. He is a wealthy man who seems to have done everything that money can buy (including putting together his own private super-team of International heroes) and has become a recluse on his private island. That notion is quickly destroyed when the heroes watch a video of a man wearing Mayhew's skin as he tells them, "Can the world's greatest crimebusters solve John Mayhew's savage murder? Or will they all die here, one by one, begging for mercy? Place your bets. The Black Glove points at you. By this time tomorrow, you will all be dead."

After he destroys all of their transportation, the Black Glove murders the Centurion by stabbing him in the back 23 times. He leaves a scrap of paper reading "et tu, Morte?" and announces to the heroes, "Advantage: evil. Place your bets with the Black Glove."

As the former club of heroes fight to survive, we begin to learn more about them and (more importantly) their adversaries. Names like Pierrot Lunaire, Scorpiana, Spring-heeled Jack, Charlie Caligula, and El Sombrero are dropped casually into conversation, but these villains will all return to plague Batman during "R.I.P." Once again, Morrison is shown to be establishing small story elements early on so that they will pay off much later. For now, the name-dropping of villains not only expands the mythology of the International Club of Heroes, but it also shows the Black Glove's influence goes beyond Gotham City. Whoever the Black Glove is, he has a far-extending reach.

The real threat, however, isn't a Club of Villains so much as it is the heroes themselves. One of them must be the killer, but their paranoia leads them to accuse each other. The Black Glove simply needed to murder one of them and plant the seed of doubt in the minds of the heroes so that they will suspect one another.

In the third installment of the Black Glove mystery, Robin, Cyril, and Red Raven have been captured by El Sombrero and put into an old-fashioned death trap and Dark Ranger is revealed to be Wingman. Apparently, Wingman had been working for the Black Glove so he killed Dark Ranger, and switched outfits with him because he was upset that Batman had ruined his chance of becoming a hero. Wingman might also have been the actor Mangrove Pierce who starred in "The Black Glove" movie. It is further revealed that El Sombrero is not who he appears to be. He is really John Mayhew dressed up as the hero. However, John Mayhew wasn't the Black Glove; he was simply working for the Black Glove. In the end, Mayhew is apparently killed in an explosion and the International Club of Heroes escapes to fight another day.

Admittedly, it's a rather confusing mystery with no real clear motivation for any of the villains involved, but it perfectly establishes the Black Glove as a threat to Batman. The mystery of John Mayhew and the Black Glove has many twists and turns, not because it is poorly written, but because it is establishing the mystery of Dr. Hurt. While the confusion may be frustrating now, it is essential in establishing the mystery for the identity of Dr. Hurt, the Black Glove, and Batman's ultimate enemy.

But the corruption of the International Club of Heroes also echoes the corruption of Batman's colors by the Three Ghosts of Batman. The Black Glove causes the heroes to question one another and twists the idea of an International Club of Heroes into a Club of Villains because the heroes can't work together. In that instant, the idea of Batman becomes corrupted and evil, something we will see more of in later issues.

The Third Ghost

The first appearance of the Third Ghost of Batman appears in the future as he battles Damian Wayne in *Batman* #666. It's there that he is revealed as the Anti-Christ who has been sent by the Devil to destroy Gotham City. In that story, Damian murders the Anti-Christ and explains that he sold his own soul to protect Gotham.

In the present, the Third Ghost makes his first appearance in *Batman* #672 and is referred to as "The Third Man" by a policeman (perhaps an allusion in name only to the classic noir film). He attacks GCPD Headquarters and is confused that Commissioner Gordon is in charge instead of Commissioner Vane. Once he finally faces off against Batman, he says, "This police department... this city betrayed me... sent me to hell to learn from the Devil" – which hints at who he works for. He shoots Batman in the chest and as the Dark Knight goes into shock, he visualizes the words "Zur-en-Arrh" and Bat-Mite as he passes out.

The next issue has Bruce hallucinating and reliving moments in his life, and Dr. Hurt is revealed for the first time. He explains that the hallucinations Bruce underwent during the isolation chamber:

> One of man's most primitive fears is loneliness. When a man is isolated too long, the mind plays strange tricks. In your case, you imagined that you were indirectly guilty of Robin's death. Your constant concern about the boy's safety came to the surface in your hallucinations."

Perhaps this is true, or perhaps this is Dr. Hurt planting the idea in Bruce's mind. Given the manipulations of Dr. Hurt, it could easily be asserted that everything he says is simply designed to toy with Bruce Wayne's mind.

Batman has his own reasons for experiencing the isolation chamber. He explains to Robin that he "wanted a glimpse of how the Joker's mind worked." In a way, the statement is a bit of a joke because the Joker's purpose for living is for that *exact* thing. The Joker tortures Batman in the hopes that the Dark Knight will see things from his perspective. Batman wants to torture himself to see from the Joker's perspective and Hurt is more than willing to give him the opportunity. If Batman's psyche falls apart, then evil wins. If Dr. Hurt is really the Devil himself, then the corruption of Batman's soul due to the Joker's machinations can do nothing but benefit evil. In this way, Dr. Hurt is using the Joker for his own ends which is something that the Joker won't like later on.

In *Batman* #674, the Third Ghost explains that Dr. Hurt had created the three ghosts of Batman just in case something ever happened to the Dark

Knight. He chillingly says, "It will be my privilege to turn you all into fearsome creatures of the night." Little do they know that they will become the pawns of the Devil himself, designed to be activated when it is necessary to destroy Batman.

Hurt's psychological warfare began by placing commands in Batman's head which caused him to doubt himself and resulted in Bruce quitting as Batman. Hurt tested the replacement Batmen against Bruce Wayne and the first two couldn't compare, but the third Batman, Michael Washington Lane, was put through the ultimate test. His family was slaughtered by Satanists in order to put him through the same emotional trauma that Batman endured. Eventually, the experiments of Dr. Hurt were put to a halt, but the damage had already been done to Michael Lane.

The Third Ghost outright states, "Dr. Hurt was the Devil. Sometimes he visits this world to destroy the good and make slaves of men like me," and he doesn't mean this in a figurative sense. Quite literally, Dr. Hurt is the Devil himself, and while he may have been playing a game of chance during the Black Glove storyline, in the case of the Three Ghosts of Batman, he is most definitely playing a game of chess.

Dr. Hurt's first pawn is the First Ghost of Batman who shot the Joker in the head which triggered the Clown Prince of Crime's transformation into the Clown at Midnight. This was his first move in the game between himself and Batman, but it also inadvertently causes the Joker to set his sights on the Devil. The First Ghost causes public distrust of Batman as the rumor spreads that Batman is a murderer.

Hurt's next pawn, the Second Ghost, was meant to trigger fear in Bruce through his resemblance to Bane. This causes doubt in Batman as he remembers what it was like to be crippled.

The assault on the International Club of Heroes and the distrust it causes between the heroes further shakes Batman's nerves as he begins to realize that there is a mastermind behind all of this.

As he escapes the Third Ghost, Batman begins to wonder, "What if there were an ultimate villain out there, unseen? An absolute mastermind, closing in for the kill? And as the Third Ghosts disappears, Batman ponders, "If the king of crime is real, is he telling me his name?"

Of course, Dr. Hurt has revealed his real name through the Third Ghost's dialogue, but Gordon surmised it long ago; the Devil has come to Gotham and he is there to corrupt Batman's soul.

Unfortunately for Dr. Hurt, he didn't take into account that the Joker might not be so willing to allow his nemesis to be corrupted.

"R.I.P."

While the gambling motif was first established in the "Black Glove" storyline, "R.I.P." (*Batman* #676-681) begins more overt references to games. The key players in "R.I.P." are Batman and Dr. Hurt who are both masters of order and preparation. Dr. Hurt's plans stretch back to Morrison's first issue and even further back to years before Morrison was writing the title when Batman was trapped in Hurt's isolation chamber. While the Joker is known for elaborate plans as well, none have been as far-reaching as Dr. Hurt's. Their goals are similar in that they both want to break Batman, but their intentions differ; Dr. Hurt wants to break Batman in order to recruit him while the Joker wants to break Batman because the two characters are intrinsically linked.

Identity remains the central theme in these issues beyond the Batman and Bruce Wayne dynamic. Time and again, the Joker is established as a villain with a super-identity that can adapt to his surroundings. Dr. Hurt, on the other hand, is a villain who has no true identity. He goes by many names and pretends to be many people so that no one really knows who he is. The Joker and Dr. Hurt don't have many scenes together until the end of the story, but these are essential in understanding the conflict that occurs between the panels in *Batman and Robin*.

Technically, the story begins with *DC Universe* #0 with a short, three-page scene between the Batman and the Joker. On the first page, the two are juxtaposed to heighten their opposition to one another. Batman is bathed in red light and looking rather grim. The Joker sits in darkness with playing cards in hand and that eerie smile on his face.

Batman says, "Red and black. Life and death. The joke and the punch line." More importantly, what Batman means to say here is "death and rebirth" because the events with Dr. Hurt will set him on the path toward his death in *Final Crisis* and lead to his eventual rebirth as the Bat-God.

As the Joker deals a dead man's hand of aces and eights, Batman says, "Someone's hunting me. I can feel it. Someone who thinks they can do your job better than you." And ultimately, this is where the central conflict between the

Joker and Dr. Hurt lies. The Joker fancies himself an expert on ruining Batman, but Dr. Hurt believes that the Joker is a fool. Hurt believes he can be better than the Joker and this doesn't sit right with the Clown Prince of Pain.

The Joker responds, "Some very, very bad people have decided to hurt you. Hurt you so bad you'll never recover." The deliberate use of the word "hurt" is the Joker's way of working in a pun about Dr. Hurt in his conversation with Batman. Not a great joke, but don't tell him that.

Coincidentally (or perhaps not so coincidentally, given the attention to detail that Morrison has given to connecting his *Batman* run to past stories), the scene is reminiscent of the opening scene to *Batman: The Killing Joke*, where Batman tries to compromise with the Joker and reason with him. This time, however, instead of rationalizing with the Joker and getting him to enter a truce, Batman seems to be coming to him for advice. Both scenes seem uncharacteristic of Batman, but they enhance their symbiotic relationship. They are connected intrinsically to one another and by the end of "R.I.P.," we'll see exactly how far their symbiosis goes.

Issue #676 is the official beginning to "R.I.P.," and the first page features Batman and Robin bathed in black and red with lightning striking behind them as Batman declares, "Batman and Robin will never die!" We won't know that this is Dick Grayson and Damian Wayne until the end of the third issue of *Batman and Robin*, but their victim is foreshadowed on the next page with the appearance of Le Bossu.

The hunchbacked criminal explains to Dr. Hurt that he had to kill a man and Hurt's first line exemplifies the Black Glove's power and influence:

> The dead man's medical files are already being edited to include a documented history of paranoid schizophrenia, M'sieur Le Bossu. A suicide note he left for his disabled wife is being composed and will be secreted upon his person... eyewitnesses will be bribed or killed, the widow ruined. We are the operators at the highest level.

The scene gives credibility to Batman's fears at the end of his encounter with the Third Ghost. It shows that there could be an organization far-reaching enough to buy their way out of anything.

Notice that the Club of Villains is made up of eight members – much like the eight key pieces of a chess set. Throughout this story, Batman will be facing plenty of pawns in the form of Le Bossu's gargoyles. The checkerboard floor in Gotham in the story's climax enhances the chess motif later on.

Where the Joker wishes to be infamous, Dr. Hurt and the Black Glove wish to remain anonymous. To use Dungeons and Dragons terminology, Dr. Hurt is lawful evil in that he operates under very strict rules and always seems to have the situation under control. The Joke is chaotic evil because he kills indiscriminately and sometimes without provocation. What makes the Joker so dangerous is that he sometimes acts within an orderly manner. The "Clown at Midnight" story is a perfect example of the Joker using order to enact his chaos. One could argue that this frame of mind, this enlightened balance of order and chaos, is exactly why the Joker can gain the advantage over Dr. Hurt.

After the introduction of the Black Glove, the scene shifts to a black car racing through the Gotham streets. The driver (a deranged, red-haired man) struggles with a green bird mask and screams, "Leave 'em crazy clues they'll never work out! Get me some hot psycho groupies with bells in their hair! Bodycount! Bodycount!"

As strange as this dialogue is, it eerily echoes the Joker in some ways. The Joker leaves obscure clues for Batman to figure out; Harley Quinn could be considered a "hot psycho groupie" with bells in her hair; and the Joker is awfully proud of how many people he has killed.

After taking care of the Green Vulture, Bruce and Tim return home and Alfred remarks that "every Tom, Dick, or Harry with a make-up box and rampant Tourette's fancies himself the next Joker." The Joker invocation is blatant, but it is also meant to subtly contrast the Joker and Dr. Hurt. Some of Batman's villains are *exactly* as Alfred described, but Dr. Hurt is the furthest thing from it.

In the Joker's fantasy, he envisions himself killing Robin, Nightwing, and Commissioner Gordon and his vision is colored in black, white, and red. Notice that Batman is nowhere to be found in the hallucination because the Joker doesn't want his death because then the game would be over. To the Joker, Batman is his opponent, not his enemy. Without Batman, the Joker wouldn't have any fun.

In *Batman* #677, the Club of Villains only makes a brief appearance. A roulette wheel is the transition image that shifts the narrative from Batman and Commissioner Gordon to the Black Glove to remind readers that Dr. Hurt views the destruction of Batman's soul as nothing more than a game. Dr. Hurt's identity as the Devil comes through when he says, "What we are about to do will be a work of art. Nothing less than the complete and utter ruination of a noble human spirit."

Trivializing Batman's soul into nothing more than a game is a small, but important insight into Dr. Hurt's evil. The audience doesn't have to even see Hurt do anything, but the concept of him gambling with Batman's honor is enough to establish him as a frightening villain.

Dr. Hurt only makes brief appearances in #678, once in Bruce's fractured memory, and again near the end of the issue as Club of Villains takes over the Batcave. At the end of the issue, Hurt puts on Thomas Wayne's old Batman costume to create a visual link between himself and Batman (the two most prepared players in this game) and to also enhance his satanic appearance. The satanic imagery of Dr. Hurt comes to a head in issue #680. He had previously put on Thomas Wayne's bat costume, poured champagne on Alfred and called him "betrayer" (a not-so-subtle allusion to Hurt being Lucifer), and had taken the Batcave as his own personal headquarters (the new lord of the underworld).

Not content with simply destroying Batman, Dr. Hurt knows he has to take the rest of Batman's chess pieces off the board as well. He captures Nightwing and sends him to Arkham Asylum, keeps Tim Drake on the run, traps Commissioner Gordon in a booby-trapped Wayne Manor, and abuses Alfred in the cave. Anyone who could even possibly help Batman has been taken care of in some way and Hurt's lies have destroyed the Wayne family reputation as well.

The Club of Villains admires the Joker, but none so much as Le Bossu. In a conversation with the Joker, Le Bossu says as he undresses, "You are so perfect, so complete... a product of random circumstance." Le Bossu explains to the Joker how in his normal life, he is a respected neuro-surgeon and that no one knows who he is on the inside. He envies the Joker because the Thin White Duke of Death never hides his identity. The Joker embraces who he is while Le Bossu cannot. All the while, Le Bossu changes from his doctor identity into his super-villain identity and says, "I trust you will do me the honor of witnessing my transformation," showing that Le Bossu craves justification from the Joker. Le Bossu's identity is predicated on being validated by the greatest villain of them all. Of course, the Joker only yawns.

Once the Joker and Batman finally face off against one another, it is almost as if the Joker is on Batman's side. While the Joker isn't powerless, he isn't in charge at all; a point that is emphatic as Dr. Hurt places his hand on the Joker's shoulder and commands, "Stop there. My good and faithful servant." The look on the Joker's face is one of anger that Hurt would dare place a hand on him. Maybe the Joker was having fun to this point as Batman was being broken, but it's clear that he refuses to be known as anyone's servant as in the final issue of the story, the Joker executes one of the Black Glove's members so that he can join. If the Joker was only a pawn in the story thus far, he has made his way across the chessboard and has assumed a new role.

Then, almost immediately after he suggests joining, the Joker changes his mind and begins discussing the symbolism of red and black:

> It's simple, it preys on the mind... the ultimate gag... now you here, now you ain't... Get it?! But it doesn't matter, see, because every single time I try to think outside his toybox, he builds a new box around me. Apophenia. I've been driven literally insane trying to get him to loosen up.

Apophenia is the experience of seeing meaningful patterns in random information. Batman's mind is trained to find patterns and associate the symbolism with everything while the Joker is able to create meaning from seemingly meaningless information. In the realm of semiotics, the Joker creates signifiers, and Batman interprets the signified. Together, the two are one. Not only does the Joker change personalities and identities, but Batman has done the same to keep up. The shifting identities is what keeps the two characters connected, and also what has kept fans interested in the characters for years. Each generation gets a new Batman and a new Joker.

At the end of his confrontation with Dr. Hurt, the Joker says, "I'm saying adieu. Pleased to meet you, admire your work but don't. Don't call me servant. I'll collect my winnings from all of you in due course." And with that, the Joker disappears and hauntingly foreshadows his role in *Batman and Robin*.

During the final conflict between Bruce and Dr. Hurt, the identity of the Black Glove is further muddied. Dr. Hurt still claims to be Thomas Wayne, but he also refers to himself as Mangrove Pierce and "the hole in things." As Batman attacks Hurt's helicopter, he begins to wonder if he isn't battling the Devil himself – an answer that won't come until the end of *Batman and Robin*.

The most significant motif to come from "R.I.P." is the idea of gaming as a narrative. The conflict between Batman and Dr. Hurt is a game of chess and the scene where the two finally face off against one another exemplifies this through the use of the checkerboard red and black motif. Even the characters involved can be considered particular chess pieces. Jezebel Jet is the black

Dr. Hurt waits for his helicopter and offers Batman the chance to join him. From *Batman* Vol. 1 #681 (Dec 2008). Art by Tony Daniel and Sandu Florea. Copyright © DC Comics.

queen, while Talia al Ghul is the (albeit somewhat unconventional) white queen. Dick Grayson and Tim Drake are rooks.

One of the most interesting comparisons is the first ghost of Batman that shoots the Joker could easily be a knight given that they move unconventionally and the character might dress as Batman, but he is far from conventional. The second ghost of Batman could also be a knight, and the third ghost could be considered a bishop, considering that in *Batman* #666 he acts as a prophet for the Devil. The Club of Heroes and the Club of Villains are all pawns in the game and are taken out as such in the Black Glove storyline and "R.I.P."

Comparisons between the characters and chess pieces are numerous and could be pondered on for quite some time, but the game really is afoot during *Batman and Robin*.

Batman and Robin

In his footnotes for the first volume of *Batman and Robin*, Grant Morrison discusses the strange coincidence of the third issue's cover resembling an image of the Joker that Brian Bolland had done years previous. Morrison writes that the cover was not an intentional image, but he does note that the series

> *was* intended to feel 'haunted' by the Joker from the very beginning. Although he does not appear in person in this volume, you will find numerous deliberate and carefully inserted traces of the Clown Prince of Crime's sinister presence throughout the series, some in the form of scenes that hint at or recall famous Joker moments of the past.

Up until "R.I.P.," Dr. Hurt fulfilled a similar role to the Joker's in *Batman and Robin*; both characters seem to exist in the background, between the panels, secretly plotting something that our heroes can't quite comprehend.

The first issue is titled "Domino Effect" and just as Dr. Hurt set off a chain reaction that lead to "R.I.P." by having a Batman imposter shoot the Joker in the head, the Joker will set off a chain reaction by setting up Mr. Toad and his men with a bad drug deal. As Batman and Robin chase Mr. Toad, one of Toad's henchmen shouts, "You said this would be easy! A simple exchange, you said!"

After Toad is captured and Batman and Robin punch him out, Toad's suitcase explodes open and dominoes fly everywhere. Dick Grayson wonders, "What kind of a drug dealer gets paid in dominoes?" As it turns out, Mr. Toad was part of the Circus of Strange that works for Professor Pyg who works for Dr. Hurt. The dominoes are actually a clue from the Joker telegraphing that he had set Mr. Toad up as part of his game against Dr. Hurt and the Black Glove.

Professor Pyg, upset that Toad fails him, comes to the home of Niko (one of Toad's men) and tortures Niko by transforming him into one of his dollotrons. This scene is meant to show Pyg as a frightening villain, but it also establishes Sasha's own transformation into Scarlet in the next arc with the Red Hood. So the dominoes keep falling down as Toad's capture has greater consequences.

In the next issue, the Circus of Strange attacks GCPD Headquarters and our heroes have to stop them from freeing Mr. Toad. During the battle, Mr. Toad is somehow murdered and left with a domino in his hand. While it's unclear how Mr. Toad is murdered, the police officer who declares, "The Toad. He croaked," almost HAS to be the Joker in disguise. The pun is a perfect joke and even though this is the first actual victim of the Domino Killer, it should be obvious that it's the Joker.

While Professor Pyg is a bizarre and wonderful villain on his own, he seems to be somewhat inspired by the Joker. Pyg's lair is a similar circus to the one the Joker operated from during *Batman: The Killing Joke* (during what "The Clown at Midnight" issue seemed to dub the "ringmaster-from-Hell phase"). The point seems further enhanced by Commissioner Gordon when he says, "I hate it here. They should have let the whole damn place burn to the ground."

Pyg's plan is to infect the city with an addictive, identity-destroying drug in the form of a virus that will be spread by his dollotrons. Many of the Joker's own plans revolve around Joker gas or other forms of drugs to infect people. Also, since the drug is "identity-destroying," the character is part of the theme of identity exemplified by Batman and the Joker and their ability to alter their own identities to survive. Pyg's plan (which is also Dr. Hurt's plan) is a direct result of the conclusion of "R.I.P." as Dr. Hurt tries to combat the superpersonas of his enemies.

In the end, Batman finds the antidote to the virus next to the next domino in the sequence. So, even though the Joker is the "domino killer," he is slightly mislabeled because he is also aiding Batman in protecting Gotham City. After all, the Joker was the one who set up Mr. Toad, which led to his capture and lured out the Circus of Crime, which led Batman and Robin to Professor Pyg, which allowed for Gotham City to be saved from losing its identity. Domino effect.

Red Hood

The Joker connection is far more apparent and blatant in the next arc with Jason Todd as the Red Hood. Making a reference (once again) to *The Killing*

Joke, the Red Hood was the Joker's identity prior to his transformation. Furthermore, during "A Death in the Family," the Joker was responsible for killing Jason Todd. So Todd can be considered to be a pawn of the Joker because his identity is completely defined by the Clown Prince of Crime. And considering that Jason Todd is also the perfect foil for Dick Grayson, this three-issue arc is a new generation of Batman versus the Joker.

Issue #4 introduces a British author by the name of Oberon Sexton who informs Dick Grayson, "It seems we have a mutual interest in crime." The black clothing, white gloves, and red glasses are dead giveaways to the Joker's identity, but the nick-name of "the Gravedigger" connects Sexton to the dominoes which are also called "bones."

As Batman and Robin are staking out a meeting between Gotham crime bosses, a mobster by the name of Gabriel Santo mentions his boss, "El Penitente." The name is in reference to a member of a Roman Catholic brotherhood in parts of the Southwest, of Native American and Hispanic origin, who celebrates the Passion with rites involving fasting and self-flagellation. But Gabriel Santo is also a name worth noting. His name literally means "St. Gabriel." Biblically, Gabriel is an angel and God's messenger, but in this case, he is acting as the Devil's messenger.

Santo goes on to say that El Penitente believes, "The new model of crime is grass roots, viral." If we consider the words "Zur-en-Arrh" to be magic sigils that act as a virus implanted in Bruce Wayne's mind, then this latest plan of viral narcotics follows right along with Hurt's previous plans. He has seen the power of the virus on Bruce Wayne and how it is able to break the greatest man in the world, and now he will use the same tactics on the general population.

Oberon Sexton reappears in issue #5 as part of a Gotham City talk show where he discusses Batman and Robin "shielding criminals from two killers, let's not forget. The Red Hood is a name used by more than one notorious Gotham criminal in the past. Is this any different?"

Sexton is reminding us that the Joker was the Red Hood originally, but he is also setting up that there is a real Oberon Sexton and the Joker has stolen that identity now.

The Red Hood and Scarlet are about to murder Santo in an act of irony by pouring bleach in his IV drip (a move that is more appropriate to the Joker) when Batman and Robin save the day and are promptly captured. El Penitente's assassin, the Flamingo comes to Gotham to kill the Red Hood. Flamingo is a silent, insane killer who can be compared to the Joker for his ruthless methods (he eats a man's face) and his flamboyant sense of style.

Jason apparently kills Flamingo in the end and even though he regrets the path his life had gone down, he still remarks, "Tonight, I did something even Batman couldn't do. I beat my arch-enemy."

His words are a bitter attack on Batman, who was unwilling to kill the Joker even after he beat and murdered Jason.

At the end of the arc, Oberon Sexton receives a phone call from El Penitente. Penitente is shown with a "W" scar on his back and the end of a whip over his shoulder to symbolize the self-flagellation of his name. He says, "Your little secret is no secret to me... no... say nothing and listen very carefully. I have unfinished business in Gotham City, and scores to settle. Here's what you're going to do."

Again, Dr. Hurt feels as if he can order the Joker around. He believes that the Joker is somehow under his employ.

And the domino effect goes on. Pyg created Scarlet who joined the Red Hood's crusade against crime and the two struck out against the El Penitente Crime Syndicate. All of this because of the Joker's deal with Mr. Toad, but there would be much more to come.

"Blackest Knight"

While it could be argued that *R.I.P.* is a game of chess between Batman and Dr. Hurt, the game of dominoes is at the forefront of *Batman and Robin*. Oberon Sexton and El Penitente aren't mentioned in this arc, but their conflict is mirrored by the war between the Pearly King and King Coal. The white and black imagery of the dominoes is built into the names of the Pearly (white) King and King (black as) Coal, and their conflict of two criminal empires at war with each other with Batman caught in the middle is a hint as to the underlying conflict of the Joker and Dr. Hurt.

After rescuing Eddie English, the Pearly Prince from King Coal's runaway train of death, Batman visits the Pearly King in prison. The Pearly King won't give a straight answer as to the location of a mystical pit, nor will he reveal what it actually contains, but he does continue to play a game of dominoes called the "Mexican Train" (a clue as to the whereabouts of El Penitente, Dr. Hurt). Batman summarizes the conflict between the Pearls and the Coals by saying, "Eddie says there was a game of cards played using real people. Coal gambled and lost." Somehow, the two families were gambling with lives and now the

Pearls are in control of the pit. Though there isn't any direct comparison between the Joker and Dr. Hurt here, it does mirror the chess game played during "R.I.P."

The scene mirrors the many times Batman has visited the Joker in Arkham for answers. Both the Pearly King and the Clown Prince of Crime have given themselves names of royalty. So, given that the Pearly King speaks in riddles and helps Batman take down King Coal, we can further understand that while the Joker is still certainly interested in his own gains, he is willing to help Batman out in the war against their common enemy. Of course, last time he wasn't so keen on the idea, telling Batman, "You might be thinking this is the part where you join forces with your old enemy to turn the tables on these upstart newcomers but you shot me." However, given that Dick Grayson is now Batman instead of the Joker's true foil, perhaps the Joker feels as if Batman is at a disadvantage.

If the Pearly King represents the Joker, then it stands to reason that King Coal is Dr. Hurt, and not surprisingly, his dialogue reflects the satanic imagery of Dr. Hurt. In issue #8 as he straps a bomb to the Pearly Prince and claims that "NewCastle'll be capital city of wor New Jerusalem of crime soon enough, like," (an idea that Mannheim had for Gotham during 52) but then King Coal explains to the Prince, "Divvent yr knaa there's a hole in everything, smooth Eddie." Both Hurt and Darkseid refer to themselves as the "hole in things." Later in the issue, Coal boasts, "The beast is loose, the new age of crime has come and the broon's on me!" This claim echoes the ideas of Dr. Hurt.

As Dick Grayson explores the Pit, he realizes that during his conversation with the Pearly King, the King had made a map of the underground using the dominoes in front of him. The map looks like a reverse swastika which is a symbol of life (as Wonder Woman explains in Morrison's *JLA* #8 some 13 *years* before this story... an impressive callback to say the least) and it turns out this map leads our heroes to a Lazarus Pit for them to revive Bruce Wayne.

Of course, it's not really Bruce Wayne at all, but one of Darkseid's clones, but even this clone acts as a narrative foil of sorts. In "R.I.P.," Bruce Wayne had created the Batman of Zur-en-Arrh to protect his mind from being destroyed. In this story, a clone of Bruce Wayne already has his mind destroyed and he is on a rampage. Even his first dialogue of "Heer U. RRR" looks remarkably similar to "Zur-en-Arrh."

One final minor mirror comes at the end of the story when Knight and Squire locate King Coal to bring him to justice. Throughout the series, Dick and Damian finish their opponents with a simultaneous punch or kick away from the panel, but Knight and Squire simultaneously punch Coal toward the reader and claim that he will be thrown into prison across from the Pearly King – like two dominoes.

As I've said before, the "Blackest Knight" story isn't the best in Morrison's run, but structurally, it is an interesting piece. The story doesn't have much impact as a whole, but the narrative mirrors enhance the themes Morrison has established in the series so far. In fact, these narrative mirrors are so complete that the conflict between the white and black kings leads to the return of a grotesque and twisted Batman. But it's the real conflict between the Joker and Dr. Hurt that will lead to the return of the real Batman.

"Batman Vs. Robin"

Oberon Sexton and Dick Grayson examine the evidence of the Domino Killer, and it seems that Grayson probably knows that Sexton is the Joker. He makes the comment that "the so-called 'evidence' against the Waynes was a joke." While the victims of the Domino Killer may seem to be unconnected, a quick return to the pages of "R.I.P." shows that they are all members of the Black Glove. The Russian General, oil sheikh, media guy, and cardinal are all shown at Batman's funeral near the end of the arc. Also, since they wear domino masks, so it's pretty clear as to why the Joker chose this latest nom-de-crime.

In terms of the game itself, the Joker's domino effect is about to run its course. He pushed the first domino down by setting up Mr. Toad which lead to Batman discovering Professor Pyg, which led to the creation of the Red Hood and Scarlet, which led to Grayson questioning his mission and attempting to bring back Bruce Wayne, which failed and led him to the mystery of Wayne Manor in this story. The Joker has stopped El Penitente's drug trade in Gotham City and killed the members of the Black Glove – all of which has happened behind the scenes of the main narrative – and now, Dr. Hurt will strike back.

Prior to the scene with Grayson and Sexton, Damian takes control of a Wayne Enterprises board meeting and reveals, "I discovered a fund for victims of railroad accidents established in the name of Thomas Wayne." The scene is a little odd and seems out of place, but it's important for a number of reasons.

First, in terms of plot, it establishes that some of Wayne's money is being filtered out for Dr. Hurt's use.

In terms of symbols, the specific use of a fund for railroad victims calls the reader to be mindful of the Mexican Train that has been brought up throughout *Batman and Robin*.

More importantly, Morrison uses trains as transformative experiences in his fiction. Trains are important in *The Invisibles*, during the Manhattan Guardian storyline of *Seven Soldiers*, and most recently in his *Action Comics* run, Superman's first real challenge from Lex Luthor is to save a runaway train which completes his transformation as a hero to Metropolis. By bringing this imagery into the story, Morrison is setting readers up for Bruce Wayne's return and transformation into Bat-God.

Back at Wayne Manor, Dick becomes obsessed with clues that seem to be hidden within the home. Damian notices a picture is missing and Alfred spoils the true identity of Dr. Hurt (a.k.a. El Penitente, the Black Glove, Mangrove Pierce, the Devil, Lucifer, the Hole in Things, or Bruce's father) when he says,

> That gap is the only acknowledgment of the existence of Thomas Wayne, the black sheep of the family. Back in the 1760s, Thomas led a rather distinguished sect of Devil worshippers apparently. They summoned an ancient Bat-demon of the Miagani tribe and all kinds of terrible and bloody bargains were struck, or so the story goes.

All of this foreshadows the revelations that will come in the final story arc and in *Batman: The Return of Bruce Wayne*.

Oberon Sexton receives a phone call from El Penitente at the Gotham Grand Hotel. "I reached out to you 'Mr. Sexton' and you rejected my offer. Do you know what you've done? The Mexican train is on its way." At this point, Morrison is trying to throw in some mystery about who Oberon Sexton is, but it's too little too late for those who have been paying attention. Hurt offered to recruit both the Joker and Bruce Wayne, but all of the signs clearly point to the Joker. The final image in the issue is of Oberon Sexton side by side with Robin in a graveyard (or as the term goes in "Mexican Train" dominoes, the "Boneyard").

Issue #11 begins with Dr. Hurt being blessed by a priest as his drug mansion is being raided by D.E.A. agents. He has carved a "W" into his back to "remind me who I am." He calls it the "mark of the shadow" and the "dark twin" and demands that a priest bless him so that he may commit further sins. It's a curious development because if Dr. Hurt really were the Devil, then he wouldn't want absolution. Then again, it could be that he was manipulating the priest into committing blasphemy just before the mortal's death.

Damian and Oberon Sexton fight some of the fiends in the graveyard while Dick Grayson finds a tunnel built by the Wayne family and used by The Underground Railroad. Again, the use of trains is used to foreshadow the transformative experience that Bruce Wayne is going through. Damian demonstrates a lack of detective skills as he inquires if Oberon Sexton is actually Bruce Wayne. Sexton responds by showing the signature of the domino killer and claims the killer is after Bruce Wayne.

Near the end of issue #12, one of the four fiends who battled Damian and Sexton asks, "And the Batman?", to which another replies, "It's already too late for him. This train started rolling a long, long time ago."

Dr. Hurt is shown on an elevated train which connects the idea of the transformative experience. He feels redeemed and ready to take Gotham for his own. Curiously, he doesn't mention Batman at all in his discussion with Senator Vine, and only hints at the Joker when he says, "Coming at us out of the East. But he has a knack for engaging foes he cannot defeat."

In all of his talk of taking back Gotham, Dr. Hurt never mentions Batman because he is no longer a threat. In a way, it's a little insulting. As much as Morrison built up Dick Grayson's mythology by pitting him against foils along the way, he undoes all of this by having Dr. Hurt never worry about him. Hurt is completely focused on the Joker as his nemesis to the point Batman isn't even on his mind.

The arc concludes with the "revelation" that the Joker is indeed Oberon Sexton, but the clues were there the whole time. Oberon is the name of the Fairy King in Shakespeare's *A Midsummer Night's Dream*, but as Tim Callahan once pointed out, Oberon is also known as the "Fey-king" which sounds like "faking" – which is a pretty clever pun. A sexton is one who digs graves hence the nickname of "Gravedigger," but also ties nicely into the dominoes which are also known as "bones." Still, despite the fact that all of the clues were right there in front of us the entire time, many readers (myself included) were guessing right up until that last page. It's only upon rereading that one can see the clearly telegraphed message of the Joker, but that's why this series is so brilliant.

As the series goes on, however, the subtle game between the Joker and Dr. Hurt deteriorates and becomes a much more straightforward contest. While the Joker started by playing dominoes with his nemesis, the game evolves into another game of chess with the Devil.

"Batman and Robin Must Die!"

During the final arc on *Batman and Robin*, gossip columnist Rich Johnston wrote an article on 29 July 2010 titled "Grant Morrison and Game Theory" on his website, Bleeding Cool, about Morrison's use of Game Theory during his *Batman* run. Johnston challenges his readers, "Little Bleeders, you have your mission. Looking for games and game references in DC comics, especially Morrison written titles or by close compatriots. Then working out who has won. Then stepping back and seeing the big pictures."[1]

During *Batman*, the chess motif was prevalent as the characters were pawns being moved by the Black Glove. In *Batman and Robin*, dominoes have been used to symbolize the chain of events that the Joker has set off and the use of the "Mexican Train" has been used to literally call for Dr. Hurt's return under the name El Penitente and to foreshadow Bruce Wayne's transformation into Bat-God.

In Morrison's final *Batman and Robin* storyline, Dick Grayson explains all of the domino puns the Joker had been using throughout the run:

> Dominoes. Fact 1: Informally known as bones. The box they come in is the Boneyard. Fact 2: Masked detective Oberon Sexton turns up in Gotham allegedly investigating, or maybe I should call it drawing attention to, crimes you committed. Sexton 'The Gravedigger.' Coincidence? Sexton, who conveniently arrived in time to poison Mr. Toad and set up Gabriel Santo. A branching trail. It's that cranky, creepy attention to detail that always gives you away. Throw in the double meaning of 'domino' as in Robin's mask... I know you like to leave clues, but I'm kind of insulted you made it so obvious.

As we all should, really. Even though Grayson has effectively dissected all of the main meanings behind the Domino Killer identity, he neglected to mention the domino masks that the members of the Black Glove wore to conceal their identities, and also the chain of events that followed. But the Joker is kind enough to explain, "If only you could trust me, just this once. I'm too late to stop the chain reaction I started with the first little domino of death. And now it's all fall down time."

The games don't stop there, however. At the beginning of issue #14, the very first panel has Alfred looking to a mantle at Wayne Manor where a large,

---

[1] http://www.bleedingcool.com/2010/07/29/grant-morrison-and-game-theory/

white knight chess piece stands. This symbolizes the shift in games to a chess match between the Joker and Dr. Hurt. The Joker has manipulated Batman and Robin into taking Dr. Hurt's chess pieces off the board, Grayson is captured by Dr. Hurt near the end of the issue, and Hurt calls out, "You're next, you hear me? Your knights have fallen and the board is mine! You have nothing left to fight with!"

The Joker cackles as he replies, "Give yourself a big hand, Black Glove! It's all getting way too serious for me! So who do I know that's good with serious?" The Joker is referring to Damian Wayne who has spent the entire run of *Batman and Robin* transforming into the kind of hero his father would be proud of. Talia envisions that he will one day be like Alexander the Great, and he has almost finished his transformation into a full-fledged hero, but not yet.

"Stop poking me with that gun," he tells the Joker in issue #15, "I'm not a pawn in your stupid game."

The wit Morrison puts into the Joker's dialogue is delightful as he replies, "In the hands of a grandmaster, the prawn can be the most dangerous piece on the plate. No fancy moves, hear?" implying that Damian is a "shrimp" and also solidifying his pawn status by saying "no fancy moves."

"Being a pawn is your best option, trust me," Joker continues, "I offered Dr. Hurt dominoes, but he wants to play chess. Chess with the Joker," the Clown Prince of Crime then orders Damian around by saying, "Pawn to tree! Your move!" This sets Damian off on a quest to save Commissioner Gordon, which leads him to getting trapped by Dr. Hurt, which allows him to save Dick Grayson. Even in chess the Joker seems to play dominoes.

Finally, near the end of issue #16, the Joker confronts Dr. Hurt in the graveyard of Wayne Manor and once again, Morrison packs meaning into every word the Joker says. Hurt tries reasoning with the Joker by suggesting that they could build a new Black Glove together. The Joker replies, "No games. Mano a mano. Betcha can't reach the gun before me, gambler." Of course, "mano a mano" means "hand to hand" which is a pun on the Black Glove.

Dr. Hurt races toward the gun and slips on a banana peel which Morrison explains in the afterword that the most common banana pratfall was used with a banana known as the "Big Mike" which could mean "St. Michael" the angel who cast Lucifer out of Heaven after the Fall. If Dr. Hurt is really Lucifer (or Barbatos / Darkseid / any demon), then the Joker has caused his second fall which he also refers to as the "primal joke." The Joker wraps up their conflict by saying "Batman's gone, in case you hadn't figured out what all this is about... I thought you'd make a 'worthy adversary' but who am I kidding? I go to all this trouble and you haven't made me laugh once!"

Ultimately, the Joker's games with Dr. Hurt stem from an absence of Batman. Without Batman, the Joker has no one to play games with, so he turned to Dr. Hurt. Notice that Hurt isn't defeated until after his origin story has been revealed. In the games between the super-identity and the man with no identity, the Joker wins once Dr. Hurt is able to be defined. Before, Dr. Hurt was dangerous because he was a man of many names. His greatest weapon was that he was unable to be defined, but in the same issue we learn that he is merely the human host for Darkseid, the Joker is able to defeat him. The unknown is frightening, but once the unknown is revealed and becomes known, it holds no more power.

After defeating Hurt by burying him alive in a coffin with the oh-so-significant number six in the shape of a domino on Hurt's coffin, the Joker declares that he will become a crime-fighting hero. With no one left to play games with, the Joker has taken the transformative Mexican Train to his new identity as a hero... until he is punched out by Batman.

Back to Rich's initial challenge about who is playing these games and who has won. Obviously, the Joker and Dr. Hurt were opposed to one another and the Joker was the winner, but during this game, Damian Wayne completed his transformation from pawn to something else as he single-handedly disarmed a nuclear bomb on a train (once again symbolizing transformation) speeding through an underground railroad. Bruce Wayne had gone through his own transformation into Bat-God as well, but he wasn't truly part of this game. The only loser outside of Dr. Hurt is probably Dick Grayson.

During his tenure on *Batman and Robin*, Morrison transformed Damian from a hated character to a hero and also added new dimensions to Dick Grayson by pitting him against numerous foils. But in the end, Grayson is shot in the back of the head by Dr. Hurt. He somehow survives, but the failure suggests that Bruce Wayne is a better Batman than he is. But what do all of these games *mean*?

A game known as the "Angel Problem" is directly applicable to Batman and the Joker. Essentially, the angel wins by being able to move indefinitely and the Devil wins by trapping the angel so that he can't move anymore. In a role reversal, the Joker is the angel who is constantly on the move and trying to be

The Joker buries Dr. Hurt. From *Batman and Robin* Vol. 1 #16 (Early Jan 2011).
Art by Frazer Irving. Copyright © DC Comics.

pinned down by the devil who is Batman. In fact, the Joker's constant maneuvering has resulted in its own trope in fiction known as "Joker Immunity" which states that sometimes a character is so popular that no matter what the situation appears to look like, the character will always survive to return another day.

Furthermore, Game Theory supposes that the players in the game are rational – meaning that they will choose the options that yield the greatest outcomes. So, in a sense, it's ironic (or, given the circumstances, one could say "humorous") that the Joker is one of the rational characters in question. The Joker isn't supposed to be *rational*. He is supposedly an agent of chaos; a character who thrives upon inflicting misery upon others without any rhyme or reason. Damian confronts the Joker in a holding cell about this very idea. "You say you're a force of chaos and you don't plan anything, it just happens. But I've read your files and everything's a plan. So what is it this time? Because I don't think you know what chaos is."

This is hardly an all-encompassing symbolic statement over Game Theory in *Batman,* however. My mind kept spinning round and round as I pondered what these symbols could mean. It got to the point where I felt like Batman in "R.I.P." as the Joker called out, "The real joke is your stubborn, bone deep conviction that somehow, somewhere all of this makes sense! That's what cracks me up every time!" Maybe there was no real method to this madness.

Then I went back and reread Rich Johnston's initial post one last time and something stood out to me. Rich writes,

> One of Alan Moore's recent arguments is that no one is writing or creating comic books, let alone superhero comics, as complex as *Watchmen* twenty-five years ago... But one of Alan Moore's nemeses, Grant Morrison, is certainly doing something very interesting on a wider canvas. He's playing games. Seriously.

Suddenly, new layers of meaning were revealed to me.

Dr. Hurt is Alan Moore. Sure, visually they look nothing alike, but consider their actions. During his tenure in the DCU, Moore made a habit of breaking characters and dragging them through the mud. The central plot points around his work revolved around breaking super-heroes and finding their humanity. Hurt's goal is to break Batman and drag other human souls to Hell.

Meanwhile, the Joker is Grant Morrison – chaotic, mad, and always changing his identity. The Joker isn't necessarily played as a villain when Morrison handles him. Of course, he had changed into an even more ruthless killer during "The Clown at Midnight" but it was all part of his mental disorder that helped him cope with an ever-changing world.

For years now, Morrison has been playing games with Moore. In his run on *Doom Patrol*, Morrison poked fun at Moore's beard through the use of the Beardhunter. In the *Manhattan Guardian* issues of *Seven Soldiers*, the titular hero battles two subway pirates named "All-Beard" and "No-Beard" – perhaps an allegory for Moore and Morrison that certainly follows Morrison's love of the transformative train motif that he uses in *Batman and Robin*. Perhaps more significantly, Morrison is using a methodology similar to Moore in order to prove a point.

In a 1988 interview with Vincent Eno and El Csawza in *Strange Things are Happening* Vol. 1 # 2 (May-June 1988), Moore cites writer / magician William S. Burroughs as an influence on *Watchmen* in "the way that the word and the image are used to control, and their possible more subversive effect."[2] Essentially, Moore and Gibbons established a few symbols that would keep recurring throughout the series for readers to return to and interpret as they will.

Obviously no stranger to magic and William S. Burroughs (who Morrison cited as his influence on *Doom Patrol* by using cut-up technique), Morrison is using a similar technique of symbolism for readers to interpret the meanings behind. In a 30 July 2011 interview with the Mindless Ones titled "Grant Morrison Supergods interview transcript," Morrison took the comparison to Moore to the next level by saying in reference to his stories, "they're all my *Watchmen*. He just did one and I do one a week!"

With Moore, the symbolism was used to tell the ultimate revisionism tale, and with Morrison, it was used to tell the ultimate reconstructionist tale. Moore tears super-heroes apart to see how they work and Morrison celebrates them to show that they do work. Two sides of he same coin, or more significantly, two sides to the domino.

Maybe Morrison didn't *exactly* intend to cast Moore as Dr. Hurt, but given that Moore and Morrison have been rivals for years, and Moore and Hurt have deconstructed identities of heroes, perhaps Morrison was subconsciously attacking not just Moore, but the entire notion of revisionism. It would certainly go along with his assertions that every Batman story that has ever been written

---

[2] http://www.johncoulthart.com/feuilleton/2006/02/20/alan-moore-interview-1988/

is still in continuity. So perhaps Dr. Hurt isn't *exactly* Alan Moore but is instead, a representation of all writers who have taken a joy in tearing apart and deconstructing super-heroes and perhaps the Joker isn't *exactly* Grant Morrison either, but rather reconstructionism having fun with revisionism.

Building a Better Batman

Grant Morrison's tenure with Batman is a series of stages. The first stage during his run on *Batman* was meant to explore forgotten stories in a new light. It can be viewed as a transition period between the darker themes of years before and the light-hearted, wild adventures that Morrison would create after. With *Batman and Robin,* the writer explored a new dynamic by casting the light-hearted Dick Grayson as Batman and the grim Damian Wayne as Robin. But as Morrison explored their relationship, he was also recreating Bruce Wayne. *Batman* #700-702 and the mini-series *Batman: The Return of Bruce Wayne* take the hero away from the dark streets of Gotham City and launch him into the realm of mythology. This is the final journey from costumed crimefighter to full Bat-God. Yet as strange as it may seem for the world's greatest detective to travel through time and ascend to godhood, Morrison makes it work by keeping the hero close to the elements that have always been part of the Batman mythology.

Batman #700

Of all of Grant Morrison's issues of *Batman*, none have so expertly expressed the idea that "Batman and Robin will never die" as this one. A sort of thematic sequel to issue #666, this is the story of three generations of Batmen, but it features many more.

The first part of the story has Bruce Wayne as Batman and Dick Grayson as Robin. The dynamic duo has been captured by the Joker, Scarecrow, Riddler, Catwoman, and Mad Hatter and strapped to a "Maybe Machine" which "generates visions of how things might have been." Developed by Dr. Carter Nichols (a scientist who first appeared in *Batman* #24, Aug-Sept 1944, and has appeared over the years in time-travel stories) according to Batman, the machine "generates visions of how things might have been."

While Bruce Wayne is Batman in this section, and he is important, the Joker is the real star. There are a number of significant ideas that come to light when he is studied closely. First, the Joker fluctuates between personalities, suggesting that he is undergoing his next transformation. Second, Morrison deepens the Joker's connection to Batman through the Joker's Joke Book and Batman's Black Casebook; Joker's joke book is a collection of his methods while the Black Casebook is a collection of Batman's wildest adventures. Finally, the Joker's plot of sending Batman back in time to undo himself mirrors Darkseid's own plot of sending Batman back in time during *Batman: The Return of Bruce Wayne*.

In the second part of the story, Dick Grayson has become Batman and Damian Wayne is now Robin. Their section begins with an investigation into the death of Carter Nichols. Grayson asks Officer Bailey about his son Max, and the Officer replies that he's "hoping to get him outta the wheelchair soon." When Batman and Robin patrol Crime Alley, they run into a gang meant to resemble the mutant gang from Frank Miller's *Dark Knight Returns*. It's a subtle reference, but one that continues Morrison's assertion that every Batman story occurs and is important. Furthermore, considering how Morrison tampers with the future of the Batman Universe with Damian Wayne, the mutant gang is a very important reference to show that Miller's Batman has the potential to still exist.

Finally, the third part returns to the world of issue #666 where Damian is a different kind of Batman. The future is still presented as dangerous. A villain named January (also called "2-Face-2") has tampered with the city's climate control machines and forced them to rain Joker toxin. After interrogating Max Roboto (perhaps Officer Bailey's once-crippled son who Dick Grayson enquired about in the previous part), Damian leaves the villain to be eaten by cannibal rats. Damian's methods are somewhat disheartening in there extremity, but there is a sign of redemption in him as he contacts "Brother-I" from the *OMAC*

Project (a prequel to *Infinite Crisis*). In that story, Bruce Wayne built a satellite to monitor super-heroes all over the world but his creation was hijacked by the organization Checkmate, led by the evil Max Lord. It's a story that spotlights one of Batman's biggest sins, and it appears that Damian has redeemed the satellite by having it work for him. However, that redemption is somewhat undermined as he uses the satellite to exterminate some henchmen hopped up on Joker and Monster venom.

After issue #666 was released, there were some readers who criticized the story due to the paradox it created with Terry McGinnis and the *Batman Beyond* continuity. If Damian Wayne becomes Batman in the future after Bruce Wayne dies, then how would an elderly Bruce train a young Terry McGinnis? Morrison attempts to reconcile this by featuring Terry McGinnis as the child that January had mistakenly kidnapped and also as Batman in one of David Finch's future Batman pages. While it should still leave a few purists scratching their heads, it is also the first example that Batman will always live on.

Batman #701-702

Months after "R.I.P." and *Final Crisis* had concluded, *Batman* #701 attempted to fill the gap between the two stories. Even though a connection between them seems somewhat unnecessary, Morrison makes these issues essential reading by asserting that Bruce Wayne is more than a man in a mask – he is the archetypal hero whose roots are firmly planted in classical mythology. After deconstructing Batman by placing him next to the villainous Three Ghosts of Batman, and the International Club of Heroes, and by experimenting with what Batman would be without Bruce Wayne, Morrison is ready to finally and definitively state who Batman truly is at his core.

The issue begins with Batman diving into Gotham harbor as he did at the end of "R.I.P." and he thinks, "Surviving is easy. Surviving is what I do. Ever since that first night when Joe Chill turned his gun on Dad and Mom. I've been surviving."

The words "Dad and Mom" are the most interesting because they convey a sense of vulnerability that is rarely seen in Bruce Wayne. At times, he refers to the murder as the death of "Thomas and Martha Wayne" which gives the incident a sense of distance. Here, they are "Dad and Mom" – people Bruce Wayne loved who had been ripped from his life. Even though the origin story of Batman is exceptionally well-known, it's easy to forget that meaning behind the death of Bruce Wayne's parents, but Morrison reminds us of that pain in three simple words.

Once Batman makes it to the docks, he's greeted by the painted face of former prostitute, Ellie, who asks if he remembered her. Batman reassures her and she says, "We thought it was you, and I just came over to say 'hi' and... well, just to see if you were okay..." It's a touching scene and one that's not common in *Batman* comics. Normally, Batman is feared by the general populace, yet Ellie not only doesn't fear him, she wants to thank him for his kindness.

When Batman returns to Wayne Manor, he notices Alfred's bruises and asks, "How's the whole 'extreme butlering' thing working out for you, Alfred? Tell me you didn't use up *all* the Band-Aids" to which Alfred corrects, "I believe the correct term is 'butling,' sir."

Their good-natured back and forth adds an element of levity to what should otherwise be a bleak return from near death. Bruce reflects upon the events of "R.I.P." and while he is haunted by them, the scene with Alfred shows that perhaps this is just another night in a long string of nights that were similar.

After an unsuccessful search for Dr. Hurt's body, and a reminder that the next time he wears the costume will be his last, Bruce is alerted to the red skies shown in *Final Crisis*. Superman summons Bruce and demands his help in investigating the death of Orion and Bruce thinks, "I've worked so hard to gain their respect, they sometimes forget I'm flesh and blood. In Superman's world, everything is mythology."

All of this (the invocation of Bruce Wayne's parents, the thank you from Ellie, the joking between Alfred and Bruce, the interaction with Superman) is meant to emphasize Batman's humanity. No longer the confident man who is perfectly capable of holding his own with the gods, Bruce has created a distance from them and himself, exemplified by his referring to them as "Super-people." After the events of "R.I.P.," Bruce Wayne faced his own mortality. After *Batman* #700 and its central message that "Batman and Robin will never die," the reader is made to fear for Bruce Wayne and empathize with his own fear, despite the fact that *Final Crisis* concluded his story a few months earlier. Morrison emphasizes Bruce Wayne's humanity in order to greater emphasize his mythology in the next issue.

In #701, Bruce spends the majority of the issue out of the mask, but in #702 he has moved past his fear and embraced the role of Batman fully for one last time. The issue begins with Batman standing alongside the Justice League which symbolizes that he is ready to take his place in the pantheon of their mythology. He doesn't stand in the front (which would give the appearance of being outside of the pantheon), but rather amongst the other gods.

In a conversation with the Flash, Batman explains that the bullet that killed Orion was "an all-purpose god-killing projectile that can be loaded and fired over and over again from any gun ever invented. Essence of bullet" and that the bullet is a "blueprint, the template for every bullet there had ever been."

Batman goes on to list the people who had been killed by this idea of the bullet, including JFK, Martin Luther King, John Lennon, Gandhi, Archduke Ferdinand, and most importantly (for this narrative, at least), "Thomas and Martha Wayne."

Note that Batman doesn't say, "My Dad and Mom," but actually says their names. The distance of the Bruce Wayne and Batman identities is restored with this. No longer is the reader meant to think of him as a mere human; instead, Batman is meant to be thought of as a god. Therefore, Batman defines the New Gods as "incredibly powerful living ideas from a kind of platonic, archetypal world." Essentially, the New Gods are ideas made manifest. If Batman is meant to take his place as an extraordinary human, then he has to embrace the ideology present within the idea of Batman.

Batman is captured by Granny Goodness in the form of Alpha Lantern Kraken and placed into the machine used to control Darkseid's forces. When he is finally freed, he thinks, "That Hole in Things was everywhere. It was there in every best laid plan."

This motif of the "hole in things" is used to describe Dr. Hurt and Darkseid's fall through time. The hole connects Hurt and Darkseid thematically well before they are connected via plot later.

The events of *Batman* #682 and #683 occur in the middle of this issue, explaining Batman's escape from Mokkari's torture. Batman wanders through the corridors of Darkseid's lair and once he finally finds the dark god, he says, "I stepped through that door into a bigger, simpler world." After his confusion, and his search for meaning, Batman steps into the world of mythology, "A world where the stakes were ultimate stakes, where each moment was heavy with the massive weight of unfolding myth and everything had a thousand extra layers of meaning. Like Darkseid. He might have been a wolf once, a dragon, or a tyrant. How many times in human history had this moment played out?"

Batman faces off against Darkseid. From *Batman* Vol. 1 #702 (Oct 2010). Art by Tony Daniel. Copyright © DC Comics.

Not quite ready to accept himself as a New God and therefore a representation of an idea, Batman steps into the role that humanity has had to fill countless times. He plays the part of the only hero able to stand up to an evil that by all rights should be more powerful than himself. In the past, Batman had been written off as a great character, but one that could never live up to Justice League status. Yet there he is, far from the streets of Gotham City and facing an evil that is far more powerful than he could imagine. But as a representation of the indomitable human spirit, Batman refuses to give up. No longer beholden to his own identity, Batman is the idea that mankind will always triumph over the oppressive Other.

Or as Batman puts it, he has created a new myth, "A myth where the Ultimate Evil turns its gaze on humanity and humanity gazes right back and says 'gotcha.'"

After being blasted by the Omega Sanction, Batman is thrown back in time as Darkseid unleashes the "Hyper-Adapter" that follows Bruce Wayne through time during *Batman: The Return of Bruce Wayne* mini-series.

Batman mistakenly believes that through the Omega Sanction, Darkseid has manipulated the events of Batman's life in order to lead him to this point. What he doesn't realize is that Bruce Wayne will manipulate events as a sort of Batsignal through time.

Batman: The Return of Bruce Wayne #1: Shadow on Stone

Batman: The Return of Bruce Wayne finds Gotham's protector sent back in time where he battles to piece together his memory. If Morrison's run on *Batman* angered some fans due to its premise that even the strangest Batman stories were still in continuity, then this far-out concept of Batman as time traveler was downright blasphemy. To some, Batman only ever works as a detective. A story that features Batman as a caveman is just beyond the realm of believability (as if comics ever needed to be believable). But as bizarre as the premise may be, Morrison uses the concept to distill Batman into his basic elements, completely freed from his supporting cast. The plot may be about Batman traveling through time, but the story is really about all of the symbolism and magic that is the essence of Batman.

At the beginning of Grant Morrison's run on *Batman*, the writer established that Batman is much more than Gotham City. Now that he is rebuilding Bruce Wayne, he has to take him back to Gotham and establish him in the city throughout time. Batman and Gotham City are intrinsically linked to one another and are inseparable throughout time.

Reading *Final Crisis* isn't necessarily essential before getting into *Batman: The Return of Bruce Wayne*, but it provides context for the story. The main beats for the purpose of this story are that *Final Crisis* begins with a caveman named Anthro the First Boy being visited by the New God Metron who has taught humans how to use fire. Batman has been sent back through time via Darkseid's Omega Sanction and the final page has Bruce Wayne in a cave along with an old man version of Anthro. This is where *Batman: The Return of Bruce Wayne* begins.

The first issue begins with a group of cavemen investigating a crashed blue rocket. Through their dialogue, we learn a number of important elements of their world. One explains that the rocket is a "shining cart" and that it is "same as brought down the fire, in old man's story. 'made without stitch or seam'" which directs the reader back to the events in *Final Crisis*. The gods visited this tribe and gave them a gift, but one caveman recounts a prophecy where, "when shining ones come again, it's the all-over."

Even at the beginning of man, these people fear the end of the world. When there is literally a world of potential set before them, they still fear the future because they know it will end when the gods return. It's a rather sad and sobering thought that there was never a time when humanity wasn't afraid of the future, and because of this fear, the idea of the super-hero was born. We have to believe in the idea that there are selfless, altruistic beings who exist to protect us or the only future is one that will simply end.

The cavemen identify themselves as being Deer Country People and they are in conflict with the Blood Mob whose Blood Chief is a "devil." Later, this tribe will be transformed into the "Bat-Tribe," and the transformation strangely reflects a moment in *Arkham Asylum* when Batman rushes through the asylum and flashes back to when he was a boy watching *Bambi* with his family. Thomas Wayne scolds his son for crying at a cartoon – a sign that Bruce's innocence was coming to an end. The next film he remembers seeing is *Zorro* on the night his parents were killed and he became Batman. Before Bruce's contact with the tribe, they were innocent deer, but after his contact with them, they became the bat just as he did.

The symbolism of Bruce Wayne stepping out of a cave as a horde of bats flies out is overwhelming. It directly connects Bruce to the image of Christ emerging from the tomb after resurrection. Symbolically, the cave is like a womb giving birth to a new, fresh Bruce Wayne; one without memories and desperately fighting to reestablish his identity.

The Deer Country men are astonished by his strange looks and his indecipherable way of speaking. The men introduce themselves and we learn that their names are reflections of their personalities. It appears that the leader is the most Aryan of them all – he is the tallest, the only blonde and he calls himself "Giant." Another, known as "Surly," studies Bruce's strange boot tracks. Anthro was called "Old Man" and his son is known as "Man." Man's son is "Boy" who is learning to be "Young Man." Finally, there is one called "Joker" who causes Bruce to growl.

The members of the tribe are distinct character types that are prevalent throughout time. They are enhanced by the appearance of Superman, Green Lantern, and Booster Gold at the end of the issue. Of course, Superman is like "Giant" because he is so far beyond everyone else. The detective skills of "Surly" could be the early prototype for Batman. Or, if he is a parallel to the time travelers at the end, he could be connected to Green Lantern, given that GL is a space cop. And even though "Joker" is clearly meant to be the archetype for the Clown Prince of Crime, because he is part of the Deer Country People Tribe and therefore seen as heroic, he also represents Booster Gold's personality. Then again, given that Booster Gold is Rip Hunter's father, they could represent "Man" and "Boy." Obviously, there are a number of ways to interpret the archetypes and their application to the heroes at the end of the story, but the important thing to remember is that Morrison is playing with the idea of identity here. At the dawn of man, names reflect identity just as the names of super-heroes are identities. While the names are simple, they seem to suggest that we can all be heroes if we distill our names down to our essence. It's a perfect place to start when the focus of the series itself is the distillation of Batman.

Man and Boy investigate the cave that Bruce emerged from. Man says, "I smell death. Stay, Boy." To which Boy asks, "Am I learning to be a Man now?" The implication is that only through the confrontation of death can one truly learn what being a man is about. Not only is this a common theme throughout the history of Batman, but of super-heroes altogether. In order for Bruce Wayne to become Batman, he had to be confronted with the deaths of his parents – an idea that he had to pass on to Dick Grayson and Tim Drake. Just as

Man has taught Boy to be a man by confronting death, Batman has taught Robin to confront mortality.

Bruce investigates the rocket and finds a disintegrating Batsignal in a hidden compartment along with Superman's cape. Even though the world's greatest detective is silent, it is clear that he is taking this evidence into consideration and piecing it together in order to understand what has happened to him. In "R.I.P.," Bruce proved himself the world's greatest detective as his drug-addled mind was still able to deduce his true identity. Now, faced with an even greater challenge, Bruce must once again prove his detective skills are unmatched as he is completely out of his element.

After the tribe buries Old Man, they set up camp and are attacked by the Blood Mob. Bruce gets Boy to safety only to get captured himself. Back at the Blood Mob, we learn that the Blood Chief is the immortal DC villain, Vandal Savage. Using Savage as a foil for Batman is perfect. Vandal Savage is an immortal who has built an empire to destroy the world and Batman is on a journey to establish the Bat-symbol as immortal in order to build an empire to protect the world.

Savage refers to Bruce as the "sky man" and the "man-god" and clearly considers himself more powerful than a god. He has his people tie Bruce down and he plans to eat Bruce in the morning sun. During the night, Bruce is visited by the Hyper-Adapter in the form of the giant bat that had been slain by Savage. The bat speaks in single words, but each one is essential in the makeup of the Batman identity. The words are: night, terror, superstitious, omen, creature, black, terrible, bat, disguise, and man. Eventually, Boy appears with a domino mask on his face, utility belt over his shoulder, and bat-shield. The idea of Batman has taken hold of Boy to make him into something more.

The next day, Bruce (wearing the skin of the giant bat) and Boy lead an assault on the Blood Mob. Batman uses his gadgets to defeat Savage and Boy declares that the Deer People have been renamed "the Bat People." And as the two heroes end their assault and run from the Blood Mob, the eclipsing sun signals Bruce Wayne's jump through time to his next destination.

Just after Bruce disappears, Superman, Green Lantern, Booster Gold, and Rip Hunter appear after tracing Bruce's Omega Energy to that place in time. In order to add to the drama, Superman mysteriously states that "if Batman makes it back to the 21st century on his own... everyone dies." It is unclear what he means by this, but it gives the narrative a sense of urgency and consequences beyond just Batman traveling through time.

Strangely, everything that makes Batman a hero is present in this caveman tale. Bruce Wayne acts as a detective, leads a boy into battle against a mob, and uses gadgets to defeat an enemy far stronger than himself. Not only has Bruce Wayne survived the dawn of man, but he has established his sigil as the protection of the innocent and it has been adopted by a tribe, who considers him a god.

The Return of Bruce Wayne #2: Until the End of Time

Puritan times have a rich, symbolic literary history. From Nathaniel Hawthorne's *The Scarlet Letter* to Arthur Miller's *The Crucible*, the time period is characterized by the oppressive rule of Puritanical law created to suppress individuality. Amidst strict Christian values, there was a burning desire for individuality and a fetishistic desire to rebel against the church. And since Batman is a symbol of rugged individualism in rebellion against authority, the Puritan era is the perfect setting to explore Batman's symbolism.

While European Gothic was characterized by ancient cathedrals with long, dark passages and satanic monks, American Gothic had to be something different. The new world was without the cathedrals of the old and so, the woods became the setting for gothic horror in America. In Arthur Miller's *The Crucible*, the author describes the woods as a place where the Puritans believed to be "the Devil's last preserve, his home base and the citadel of his final stand." The woods were the location where people were able to hide from society and bear their souls to one another. The secretive nature of the woods led to using the location metaphorically for a place where evil dwelt because anything unknown and secret was presented as evil. Pathways in the woods were analogous to the passages of cathedrals. Rather than monks turning their souls to Satan, Christianity as an oppressive force became a common motif, in addition to the standard personification of evil in the form of monsters.

The issue begins where the last left off as Batman battles a large, squid-like monster in a lake. We will later learn that this is Darkseid's Hyper-Adapter that was sent through time with Bruce Wayne. As such, it is the embodiment of evil in the form of a monster. After their battle, Bruce passes out and awakes in the home of a young witch named Annie. A ferret acts as her magical animal familiar on her shoulder. Her prayers over Bruce evoke the feeling of a Lovecraftian language that compliments the Cthulhuesque Hyper-Adapter.

Bruce sees a necklace that has a Superman and Wonder Woman symbol, and his detective mind naturally begins to piece itself back together. The "W" causes him to begin remembering his name. The necklace acts as a protective sigil and is meant to resemble the cross. By connecting super-hero symbols to the image of Christ and the cross, Morrison is emphasizing the idea of super-heroes as gods that can be invoked for protection.

Annie tells Bruce, "A great dark god has set his hand upon you. But stay with me and I'll love you. Until the end of time." Darkseid is the "great dark god" Annie refers to, and there is something perfect about the idea that he is the one who has caused Bruce to travel through time in order to transform Batman into a god-like symbol. Batman uses fear and horror as weapons in his arsenal against crime – weapons that villains would use. Yet, even though his trip through time is part of a plot for Darkseid to weaponize Batman, Bruce will still turn events to his advantage and use the villain's methods in order to reshape Batman into a more powerful idea.

In the village, a bat has been nailed to the door of the church and Bruce (under the guise of Witch hunter Mordecai Wayne) is on the case. Though his memory might not have returned, his detective skills are still unmatched and Bruce deduces that a goodwife has murdered her husband. Another witch hunter named Malleus Wayne condemns her as a witch, but Bruce stops her execution and insists that she be tried for murder after being abused by her husband. Here, Bruce is affirming his stance on operating outside the conventional wisdom of the law. Even though the standard reaction in this time period would be to condemn her as a witch, Bruce's passion for the truth is ever-present and a reminder of the type of hero that he is.

Annie and Bruce talk in the woods where the scene falls perfectly into the American Gothic motif. Annie fears that she has been implicated in the crime of the bat on the church. She reveals that she has felt rejected by God since coming to America and has come to be a non-believer. Just as in *The Scarlet Letter*, the heroine only feels comfortable admitting her true feelings away from society in the woods. Society would shun her for being who she really is and so she must flee to the only place she can share her secret. No doubt, the Puritans considered the woods to be a place of evil because secrets could be kept there.

Later, Bruce commissions a painting from Brother Martin Van Derm. Somehow, subconsciously, Bruce is trying to send a message to the future through this painting. The message will be received by Dick and Damian in

Batman and Robin #10. Malleus interrupts the painting and tries to convince Bruce to be more vigilant in their hunt for witches. Fearing the worst for Annie, Bruce returns to her. It is revealed that she dressed him as Mordecai and he has been posing as a detective ever since.

Annie reveals that she had feared for her life and that she had summoned the Hyper-Adapter and Bruce to save her. She says, "I begged my bright gods to send a man to end my loneliness." Her words are similar to the description of the "shining ones" that the cavemen recounted in regards to the New Gods. She distances herself further by saying that she worships different gods and devils than the Puritans and that she asked them to "send an avenging angel." But both she and Bruce misinterpret the situation because they both believe the Hyper-Adapter to be the Avenging Angel in question rather than Batman.

In the previous issue, Morrison had established the primal roots of the Batman myth, and here, he is establishing how the idea of Batman will endure. When the defenseless need him, he can be summoned. The first and second issue, and their magical revelations, are connected with one another through the Miagani tribe's cave. It is the home of the cavemen from the first issue and the location of Annie's revelations to Bruce, and will one day be the location of the Batcave. All of these ideas are working in concert with one another to reinforce that Batman is an enduring idea.

The Hyper-Adapter returns to the cave and Bruce battles it again, as Annie runs out and is captured by Malleus. Years later, Gotham legends say that, "If not for our mysterious Brother Mordecai, Gotham might have died before she was born."

Here even at Gotham's beginning, Batman protects his city and ensures her survival. It's a beautiful moment, but Annie steals the show when, just before she is put to death, she reveals Malleus's real name as she cries out, "A curse on you, Nathaniel Wayne! My curse on you and all your kin! Until the end of time!"

Perhaps if Bruce had given up on the Hyper-Adapter, he could have saved Annie from Malleus, and therefore could have saved his family line from being cursed. But because he chooses to save Gotham, he curses his family line for all eternity. It's a classic Batman tale of sacrifice for the greater good and perfectly explains the bad luck that seems to follow Bruce.

Meanwhile, Superman, Green Lantern, Booster Gold, and Rip Hunter travel to Vanishing Point, "the final instant before universal heat death." A shadowy figure known as the Archivist informs the travelers that the timeline will terminate in less than 10 minutes. He then begins to explain the time anomaly that is occurring with Batman (which shouldn't take more than 10 minutes, surely). Without going into the specifics of the Archivist's timeline mumbo-jumbo, he is essentially describing a combination of string theory along with Morrison's own observations about how 2D and 3D space can be used to explain man's own relationship with higher beings in the fourth dimension. To which Superman replies, "It certainly fits with what I've experienced" (of course).

And so, at the end of time, the heroes search for the Omega sanction energy that will lead them to Batman.

As the Archivist searches for Bruce, he stops where Annie dies. He reveals that he is actually Bruce Wayne and that even here at the end of time, Annie's death haunts him. Batman is so obsessed with protecting the innocent that even the death of one woman countless of millennia before still haunts him. Superman tries to reason with Bruce by revealing that Darkseid has weaponized Batman (and counting Batman's role in *Final Crisis*, that makes it Darkseid's second attempt at turning Bruce into a weapon). But Superman's plea falls on deaf ears; Bruce steals the time sphere the heroes were using and leaves them behind with two minutes left until universal heat death.

The focus of first issue was to establish the basics of the Batman identity, and this issue is meant to establish the Wayne family identity along with establishing Batman's connection with Gotham City. And so, Bruce's magical journey continues.

The Return of Bruce Wayne #3: The Bones of Bristol Bay

Like the previous issue, Bruce has been summoned to another time period by a person in need of Batman's assistance. This time, however, his memory seems to be piecing itself together as Bruce remembers his "death" from *Final Crisis*. Captured by the pirate Blackbeard and mistaken for the Black Pirate, Jack Valor, Bruce is forced to lead the pirates into the caves of the Miagani tribe in search for treasure. Along for the ride is a 15-year-old cabin boy by the name of Jack Loggins who serves as the story's narrator and whom we later learn to be the real Black Pirate.

The majority of the action takes place within the Batcave itself which serves multiple purposes. First, while the Batcave was featured in the previous issue, the focus was on Batman and his relationship to Gotham City. This issue is meant to definitively establish the Batcave in Batman mythology and to give it a history of its own. Morrison is giving the Batcave its own stories and history outside of Batman, but he still uses it to connect back to the hero.

The Batcave issue works on a deeper level as well. Taking place in the third issue, the story of the Batcave is at the halfway point of the series and therefore represents Bruce's last major turning point in piecing his mind back together. The challenge of the cave is part of the hero's journey and serves a similar structure to Batman entering the underworld during *Arkham Asylum* or Superman traveling to Bizarroworld in *All-Star Superman*. The hero must enter the underworld and return triumphant. There is no better symbol for this than the symbol of the cave. Bruce was reborn in the cave in the first issue of this series and he must return to the cave in order to face his mortality.

Inside the cave, the sigils of Superman, Wonder Woman, Batman, and the sigil from *Final Crisis* remain on the walls. Bruce triggers traps set in the cave by whistling (a sort-of narrative connection to the song Superman sings in *Final Crisis*). As the pirates pass an alcove, Bruce notes the bat droppings have filled the cave with methane which directly connects to *Batman* #657 where Batman had a conversation with Damian regarding how he handles the methane levels of the cave (coincidentally, that was Morrison's *third* issue). The Batcave's traps indicate that it has been protected long before Batman and it will be protected later once the Dark Knight uses it as his base of operations.

Along the way, Bruce continues to demonstrate his detective skills. He surmises that Jack Loggins isn't wealthy based on the condition of his clothing. Jack reveals his real name is Jack Valor and he is the real Black Pirate. His grandfather was Jon Valor and he had been the Black Pirate 100 years before Jack and had operated out of the Miagani cave. The Black Pirate mirrors what will become of Batman in the future. Batman is an idea that will endure and be passed down from generation to generation just as the Black Pirate had been passed down from father to son. The Black Pirate, however, didn't endure as an idea for a number of reasons.

First, the Black Pirate seems to just be a mask and cape, and without a sigil to base his magic on, the Black Pirate lacks enduring power. Also, the Black Pirate is such a simple idea in comparison to Batman. Batman is a complex idea that is made from many different sources – pulp novels, gothic horror, detective fiction, etc. – but the Black Pirate seems to simply be a pirate. However, the swash-buckling, altruistic, masked hero is at the heart of the Batman identity just as the methodical detective from issue #2, and the raw, primal, warrior of issue #1. Each issue unveils another layer of meaning that is inherent in Batman.

Bruce escapes the pirates and takes the Black Pirate costume with him. Blackbeard and his men search for Bruce and their search leads them to a bridge made of bones which will take them to the treasure of the Miagani tribe. At the end of the bridge, Bruce stands in the Black Pirate costume under an archway of bones surrounded by bats. While Bruce had been a primal Batman in the first issue, this is the first we've seen him in something more traditionally resembling the Batman costume. The message is clear – this cave is hell itself and Batman is the king of hell. Here at the halfway point of the series, Bruce embraces his role as Batman. If he is going to be reborn as a god, then he is the god of the underworld.

After Bruce and Jack defeat Blackbeard and his men, Jack introduces Bruce to the Miagani tribe. Bruce's inadvertent influence is apparent in that all of them have masks painted on their faces and their weapons are adorned with bats as well. A carving of their god, "lord of night and the dark sun," marks the entrance to the deepest part of their caves and though Jack isn't allowed in, the Miagani somehow recognize Bruce as their god and permit him to enter. However, the mystery inside the cave must never leave because it will lead to the "All-over" first mentioned in the first issue of the series.

As Bruce discovers his cape, cowl, books and belt, the Miagani bow in a kind of prayer to him. Suddenly, Bruce's memory has returned and he is aware of his jumps through time. As he prepares for the eclipse that will cause his next jump through time, Jack explains that he has called upon his grandfather's spirit for help and that Bruce was sent to him, proving once again that Bruce comes to the aid of those in need. When Jack says that he is thinking of giving up the role of the Black Pirate, Bruce encourages him to never give up.

Blackbeard and his first mate Israel Hands row back to their ship and Hands notes that "Gotham's a bad place. Some places are born under a black sun." – this invocation recalls the god of the Miagani, the "lord of the night and the dark sun." Since Gotham was saved by Bruce in Puritan times, it was literally born under "the dark sun." Although it will be a place cursed with crime, it will remain protected.

Jack closes his narrative by revealing that he retired years later and that he married, had a child, and finally completed the task that Bruce left for him. His notes were placed "solemnly within a casket marked with a bat-design" and inside the casket was an old book. This casket was the object that Dr. Hurt's 99 Fiends had battled Batman and Robin for. At the end of his life, Jack notes that he can hear the bells of the "All-Over."

Like the other issues, this one ends setting Bruce up in his next time period. Two men approach a haunted house and one remarks that it had been haunted since "Judge Solomon's brother died in the caves" which is both an allusion to DC villain Solomon Grundy who had died and been reborn, and also a reminder that the caves themselves are a place of death and rebirth.

Inside the house, the western anti-hero Jonah Hex sits in the parlor and has dealt a dead man's hand to himself with the Joker as the last card. The image is a subtle reminder of Batman's confrontation with the Joker just before "R.I.P." where the Joker had dealt the same hand. Rather than the red and black motif of the Joker's deal, however, Hex has dealt all black. The men are there to hire Jonah to take down a stranger who has been disrupting their boss's operations. Of course, the last page reveal is of Bruce Wayne, but unlike the previous issues where Bruce is thrown into a situation he doesn't understand, we are shown a very confident Bruce Wayne dressed as Cowboy Batman, riding atop a horse with bats flying around him. It's the final, necessary symbol that Bruce has changed from his encounter in the cave and fully remembers who he is.

The Return of Bruce Wayne #4: Dark Night, Dark Rider

One of the remarkable things about each issue of *Batman: The Return of Bruce Wayne* is how expertly Grant Morrison is able to insert Batman into a different genre. While Bruce may be a man out of time, the concept of Batman is still one that seamlessly fits into each genre he is placed into. As bizarre as it may seem for Bruce to be depicted as a caveman, Puritan, and pirate, it somehow works. Batman is such a multi-faceted character that he can slide into any genre experiment Morrison comes up with. Issue #4 is no exception.

By this point, the rules of the game Morrison is playing are clearly laid out; the genre conventions are firmly established and the Batman identity is bent and manipulated to best suit those conditions. Like all great westerns, this one begins with a standard revenge story. A group of thieves has attacked a small farm, slaughtered the family (including the requisite hanging and execution of a young, innocent boy), and stolen something valuable. There's even a stage coach present to reemphasize the wild west motif.

It turns out that the members of this family are the ancestors of the Puritan painter who made the painting of Mordecai Wayne in the second issue. They have been tasked with taking care of the bat-casket. After the violent murder, the mother Van Derm prays for God to send his "darkest, truest angel of retribution", and once again, Bruce appears to help a defenseless Gothamite. This time, however, he is in costume because of the realization and transformation that happened in the previous issue. He may not look exactly like Zorro, but the resemblance is there and connects Batman to one of the influences on the character (both in story and in real life).

Gotham has become a far more populated city, but with that increase in population comes an increase in crime. The killers bring Jonah Hex to their hideout – a saloon and whorehouse run by the immortal Vandal Savage (who was last seen in the first issue of this series). Batman comes to Gotham to get revenge for the Van Derm family and to find the bat-coffin. The situation is similar to the one Joe Chill faced back in *Batman* #673: family killers hiding in fear of Batman as he plays mind games with them. One even says, "Bucky never should have shot that kid," which is the inverse of Chill's statement of "I shoulda shot the kid right there – I shoulda done him first."

Savage knows that the bat-coffin will bring about the end of the world, and he welcomes it. He has hired Dr. Thomas Wayne (who will later be Dr. Hurt, the Black Glove, and El Penitente) to torture Catherine Van Derm in order to unlock the secrets of the bat-coffin. In a dark room surrounded by skulls and candles, Thomas has begun a ritual that enhances the satanic symbolism that surrounds the character. Catherine claims to hear the bells that Jack heard in the previous issue and Thomas claims that they are the "bells of Barbatos." But Catherine believes that the bells are a sign of "a dark god... opening his box and there's bells but the bells at the end summon another from the shadows one who won't stop until the wicked are brought to account." The dark god is Darkseid, but it's unclear what she means by the rest and it won't be clear until the final issue of the series.

A Native American known as Midnight Horse tries to stop Thomas Wayne and calls him, "Old Gambler" suggesting that Thomas is Lucifer and also continuing the theme of games and gambling established in *Batman*. After Midnight Horse is killed, Savage suggests that Hex join his army in Mexico where he is building a new empire. This seems to foreshadow the role of El Penitente in *Batman and Robin*, though it's strange that Savage is the one who mentions the empire rather than Thomas.

Batman attacks Savage's men and is described in ghost-like terms. Aside from a few grunts, he is silent for the entire issue. Most of Batman's appearances in this issue are accompanied by smoke. All of this works in concert to explore the mysterious spirit of vengeance aspect of Batman. This layer is perhaps the most superficial, but is also the one that is most associated with Batman. Yes, Batman is the world's greatest detective, but he is also the embodiment of fear.

The climax of the issue centers on Thomas Wayne kidnapping Catherine Van Derm and Batman saving her along with his ancestor, Alan Wayne, who seems to be contemplating suicide. Not only has Batman created a tribe of bat-cavemen, saved Gotham before its birth, protected the secrets of the Batcave, but now he has saved his own family tree. Batman gives Catherine her mother's necklace (which seems similar to Bruce's own mother's pearl necklace worn on the night she was murdered) and Catherine opens the bat-casket by singing the song of the Miagani. She says, "All the days of the world is one day and he must be strong for us all!" – a sentiment that echoes Morrison's philosophy in *The Invisibles*, *Batman* #673, and the scene at Vanishing Point in the second issue of this series.

In the end, Batman is shot by Jonah Hex and he falls into Gotham bay. Thomas Wayne travels to Liverpool by way of the S.S. Orion, a subtle reference to Thomas's connection to Darkseid. Catherine and Alan build what will become Wayne Manor. Finally, Bruce appears in a more modern Gotham City complete with seedy adult film theatres.

The Return of Bruce Wayne #5: Masquerade

The issue begins with the requisite scene of what is going on with other heroes. Red Robin (Tim Drake) recaps that Darkseid is using Bruce as a weapon and that as he travels through time, he is "accumulating enough energy to blow a hole in time."

These threats have been seeded along throughout this series with little evidence to support them and little conviction to make the reader worry. If they are meant to give Bruce's return some dramatic tension, they fail. More than likely, they exist only to give the series a necessary through-line so that an overarching story exists beyond Batman being placed in a different context. They are slight distractions from the main focus of rediscovering the various facets of Batman.

The real story begins with Bruce in a hospital after being shot in the previous issue. His narration begins with typical noir nonsense, "When you think about it, life is like a detective story… it's all shadows and clues, mysteries and secrets. And it always starts with a dame."

It's this sort of hokey, hardened, and mysterious writing that defines noir, and of course, it's punctuated with the word "dame." Light seeps through the window blinds of Bruce's hospital room and the floor is cracked and dirty. This image alone is enough to firmly establish the detective genre that has informed Bruce's thinking throughout this series. While Bruce has been presented as an object of sexual desire, and is dark and mysterious at times, it's his naturally inquisitive and analytical mind that has been absolutely present in each issue. By constantly reminding the reader of Bruce's intelligence, Morrison is presenting an argument that the key to his survival has always been his mind. While he may be a wealthy, philanthropic master of all martial arts, at his heart Batman is a detective.

When actress Marsha Lamarr (the woman who starred in the film *The Black Glove* along with Mangrove Pierce) enters Bruce's hospital room and claims, "My best friend was murdered. Her name was Martha Wayne. I want you to help me expose her killer," it may be surprising that he doesn't question her motivations. A detective needs clues, however, to form a case and this woman is his best lead. Her only requirement is that Bruce has to wear the same bat costume his father had worn in *Untold Tales of Batman* and that Dr. Hurt had worn during "R.I.P."

Bruce wonders how he got to the hospital when a nurse explains that he had been shot. A book he had been carrying stopped the bullet from killing him. Bruce growls when he sees a hole in the center of the book. This is a subtle clue to the issue's villain Dr. Hurt who describes himself as the "hole in things." The nurse then gives Bruce a gangster suit and he goes on his way. Bruce thumbs through the book and realizes that even though it was written by a Pilgrim named "Mordecai," the book seems new and was clearly written by himself.

There has been some criticism of this issue due to its historical inaccuracies. The look of the issue comes out of 1930s and 1940s noir stories. If Bruce is in his 30s, that would mean his family was murdered sometime in the 1970s, which completely negates the look of Gotham in this issue. For the sake of the noir genre, this story *had* to have a 1940s aesthetic. The alternative would have been for Bruce to investigate the death of his family in a *Starsky and Hutch* or

Hawaii Five-O sort of manner (which would have been entertaining, I suppose), but it wouldn't have fit with the style of writing when Batman first appeared in *Detective Comics* #27 (May 1939).

In short, continuity be damned, Batman *is* noir, and putting him in any other detective setting would just be wrong.

Marsha takes Bruce to meet Martha Wayne's mother, Betsy Kane, in order to glean more information about her killer. The signs of Marsha's eventual betrayal are numerous. Her car is sexy, sleek, and red and she insists upon chain smoking inside because "cigarettes are packed full of vitamins and give children pep" – both of which seem to suggest a demonic, evil side to her. She tells Bruce that he needs to play along in "a game of bluff" which recalls the gambling motif that Black Glove uses. Marsha even references John Mayhew and *The Black Glove* film that she will eventually star in. All are signs that Marsha is more than she seems.

At the Kane estate, Bruce's grandmother discusses her belief that Thomas Wayne murdered his wife. Of course, this was a similar theory that was presented to Commissioner Gordon during "R.I.P." She further reveals that the pearls Martha was wearing the night of her death were a "worthless Van Derm heirloom" which suggests that they were the same pearls worn by Catherine at the end of the previous issue. Betsy lists all of Thomas's faults including his cover up of "the secret room where they treated him for months while my grandson was sent away to a boarding school" – a direct reference to Morrison's own "Gothic" story, in which a young Bruce attended a boarding school that was run by a Satanic, mad monk. Yet despite her hate-filled words, the tea leaves in her cup reveal the bat-symbol and a "W" that could either stand for "Wayne" or it may suggest the "Wonder Woman" magic sigil that has followed Bruce each issue.

Meanwhile, Bruce's grandpa Roddy sits in an iron lung and gasps for life. He is plagued by wasps surrounding him. The scene with Bruce's grandparents ends with Betsy lamenting the fact that her husband doesn't realize their daughter is dead and she curiously says, "These awful wasps. They don't care, do they?"

The swarm of wasps could be interpreted as agents of Dr. Hurt. They plague the Kanes like Betsy's false notion of Thomas Wayne's guilty nature. And later, at Willowood Psychiatric Hospital, Dr. Hurt offers fame and wealth to Dr. Carter Nichols (the time traveling doctor from *Batman* #700) in exchange for his soul and then threatens him by saying, "Think about what happened when Roderick Kane chose not to play." Though it is never revealed what Roddy Kane did to incur the wrath of the Black Glove, Betsy did reveal that he had gotten sick after selling Kane Chemical to Ace, so the reader can act as detective and presume this to be the reason.

Finally, Bruce dresses in his father's bat costume and confronts the Satanists who had killed his parents. On his way, he seems to recall "R.I.P." as he thinks, "I couldn't help thinking I'd done this before." Like Jezebel Jet, Marsha betrays Bruce for the Black Glove and he is tied down to be the sacrifice in what Dr. Hurt describes as the "ceremony of the bat." Unlike the modern Black Glove, the members of this Black Glove incarnation seem to be exclusive to Gotham. Dr. Hurt and Dr. Carter Nichols both work at Willowood and Marsha implicates Commissioner Loeb and Mayor Jessop as well.

If this issue is meant to spotlight Batman's abilities as a detective, then it is unfortunately disappointing in that regard. Bruce is dragged along from location to location by Marsha and despite every clue presented to him, he is still surprised by her betrayal. After all, he is told where the Satanists will be meeting, he investigates and he is still taken captive; definitely not the best way to establish that he is the world's greatest detective.

After being drugged, Bruce awakens to the murmurs of the Black Glove: "200 years ago Barbatos was beyond our abilities to explain or comprehend – a demon, a myth. Now we have a dark science on our side. A new understanding of time and unearthly lifeforms."

Once we learn that Barbatos is just another name for Darkseid, these statements take on a new meaning. If the New Gods are just ideas made incarnate as *Batman* #701-702 suggests, then Darkseid is the idea of evil and he has existed since the dawn of time. As the Black Glove pours gasoline on Bruce, they use the language of the followers of the Crime Bible from *52* as they call upon "the name of the first red rock and the rage, and the angels and dukes of the dark side inferno pits." The red rock is the first murder weapon that Cain used to slay his brother Able, and this invocation of Cain connects Darkseid to the first murderer.

John Mayhew films Marsha dressed as Martha Wayne as she attempts to murder Bruce and someone says, "Destroy a reputation, destroy a soul" – a philosophy that will be the basis for the creation of the Three Ghosts of Batman later in Dr. Hurt's career, but applies here to the reputation of the Waynes.

They set fire to Bruce. As Betsy points out the eclipse to Roddy and comments on the sound of bells, and Dr. Hurt demands that Carter Nichols "open the hole in time" to "call down Barbatos, the hunter, the finder of great treasure." Carter refuses and Bruce takes the box and disappears through time. So, even though Carter was a party to the Black Glove initially, his refusal to summon Darkseid means that he has beaten Dr. Hurt and proven that good can overcome evil, but the price will come much later as we have seen in *Batman* #700.

The final two pages return the narrative to modern day with Batman's arrival which will set up his battle with the Justice League in the next issue.

The detective genre is a perfect fit for Batman and solving the murder of his own family is the perfect case, so it's unfortunate that there are so many missteps in the story. While this issue suffers from logical inconsistencies, it is, however, a fun look at an early version of the Black Glove and returns to some of the plot threads that had been left open at the end of "R.I.P."

The Return of Bruce Wayne #6: The All-Over

The threat of the All-Over that the cavemen predicted in the first issue has finally arrived. At Vanishing Point near the end of time, the archivists record Bruce's story. They describe it as the last story which is fitting given that Morrison portrays Batman as the prototypical human. When he battled Darkseid, Batman says that he had stepped into a "simpler world" where characters are pure representations of whatever they represent. Darkseid is evil. Batman is mankind and he has triumphed over evil in *Final Crisis* and here again, he will triumph.

Now that Bruce Wayne has traveled through time and the identity of Batman has been examined in layers, all that is left are the symbols of the character himself. The archivists catalogue Batman's story with items that are "representations of its defining elements." Each archived item is part of the mythology that has created Batman. The first item to be archived is Martha Wayne's pearl necklace, which is shaped like DNA. It is the image most associated with Batman's origin. Next, curiously, is a bell. Finally, a gun that signals the birth of Batman at the hands of Joe Chill and also his end as he had shot Darkseid just before the Omega Sanction sent him through time.

Bruce appears at Vanishing Point via the Nichols time box and on the verge of death. His magical transformation is almost complete and in order to prevent his death, the archivists place him in an archivists suit to "proceed with Lazarus

The Archivist drops pearls, a bell, and a gun. The first page of *Batman: The Return of Bruce Wayne* #6 (Dec 2010). Art by Lee Garbett, Alejandro Sicat, and Walden Wong. Copyright © DC Comics.

transfusion." Once again, Bruce must take on another identity in order to save himself just as the identity of Batman saved Bruce and the colorful Batman of Zur-en-Arrh saved him from madness. This time, the suit seems to resemble a sarcophagus of sorts. The archivists "assume cardinal configuration" which is meant to act as a magic circle during his transformation.

The Hyper-Adapter from issue #2 has followed Bruce to Vanishing Point where it will become more significant and much more powerful. Batman divulges his plan to the archivists who erase his memory. One of the archivists bonds with him saying, "May I say how honored I am to be a significant part of Batman's final adventure... and his new beginning."

Not only has Morrison transformed the character when he first joined the title in 2006, but four years later, he is transforming the character again into what he will become during *Batman, Inc.* Greg Rucka described Batman's transformation during *52* as "from the dour-faced humorless vigilante and bringing some light back into his life." This transformation will bring Batman still farther away from the "humorless vigilante" he had been.

Before Batman returns to modern time to battle the Justice League, there is a brief flashback to Frank Miller's *Batman: Year One.* Bruce's first night out as a vigilante has failed. He sits in his study, severely injured and on the verge of death when the significance of the bell finally becomes clear as Bruce says, "If I ring this bell, Alfred will come." This line is directly from Miller's script. However, the line that follows is different than Miller's version. Instead of copying the original line, "He can stop the bleeding in time," Morrison divides the line in two, making it "He can stop the bleeding. The bleeding in time." We'll learn the full significance of this statement later in the issue, but for now, an on-looking bat says in Darkseid's voice "There you are."

The narrative returns to resolving the cliffhanger at the end of the previous issue. The Justice League interrupts a reunion between archivist Batman and Red Robin, but are easily defeated thanks to Batman's new defenses which adapt to each new threat. After the fight, Red Robin removes his mask to reveal to Batman that he is Tim Drake, Bruce's adopted son. Tim shares his faith in Bruce and says, "I prayed every night you'd come back to us," which connects Tim to all of the people throughout time who had summoned Bruce through prayer.

Wonder Woman arrives and questions Bruce. He explains that he had been followed throughout time by a hunter-killer called the "Hyper-Adapter" and that he had tricked it to come to this time period so that the Justice League could stop it. Diana seems to understand and further explains the ideas that Morrison first presented in *Batman* #701-702: "Gods and New Gods like Darkseid are self-aware ideas. They use concept-weapons, anti-life equations, hunter-killer metaphors."

So if the Hyper-Adapter is a weapon derived from the literal meaning of its name, then its power comes from being able to adapt to any situation. That's why at Vanishing Point it would become unstoppable – all ideas are at their purest and most powerful there. That's why the Hyper-Adapter defeated the Justice League so easily – because it could adapt to each individual that attacked it. It has haunted Batman throughout time because Batman can adapt to his own surroundings. Batman is so good at this, in fact, that eventually he defeats the Hyper-Adapter at its own game.

As the Hyper-Adapter launches its assault, all of the symbols of Batman are unleashed in a flood of meaning. Martha's pearls, a bullet, and a rose all represent the traditional ideas of the origin story. Panels of laughter, a panel of a black glove, a black spade from a deck of cards, and the word "Apophenia" are all symbolic of Batman's turmoil during "R.I.P." The crescent moon (or perhaps a solar eclipse image), and the Wonder Woman and Superman sigils are reminders of Bruce's journey. The Batman symbol is the smallest panel showing that it is just a small part of what Batman really is.

The Hanged Man tarot card is a prominent image on the page that epitomizes Bruce's journey. Traditionally the 12th card of the Tarot, it is the inverse of the World card (which is the 21st card) which represents an outward journey. It is a card of transformation as a person goes through great suffering in order to change. The card is often interpreted as a representation of the Norse God Odin's suffering on the world tree for nine days – a connection that is enhanced by Batman having one eye in his archivist armor. It shouldn't come as a surprise that this singular image connects Batman once again to *the Invisibles.* In issue #19 of that series (Apr 1996), King Mob (as Gideon Stargrave) hangs upside down as London burns. Finally, the hanged man image mirrors the final image on the page of the bat hanging upside down from the branch.

Superman and the other time travelers from Vanishing Point are saved from oblivion because Batman has the archivists create a time sphere for them to escape in. Rip Hunter realizes that "the archivists were rebooting the universe... using the black hole to loop the timeline's end through its beginning..." and as the universe experiences heat death, the page turns completely white. It's a similar motif that Morrison used in *Final Crisis*; if characters experienced the end of the world, they would experience a blank page because the antithesis of story is the white page. Now that the heroes are back to their own time, they begin to beat the Hyper-Adapter out of Bruce and then they trap it in the time sphere to shoot it back in time.

Wonder Woman insists that Batman must die because he had the hubris to strike down the god, Darkseid. Meanwhile, the panels are fractured and broken to signal that the Omega inside of Bruce is tearing reality apart as it did in *Final Crisis*. Bruce hallucinates and sees Darkseid, and his own rebirth at the hands of the Ten Eyed Tribe. He speaks with Metron who asks, "Can man confront evil's challenge? Turn it upside down and end it? Tell me the first truth of Batman. Take control of Darkseid's design. Summon the All-Over."

Suddenly, we are taken back to Frank Miller's *Batman: Year One* with Bruce holding the bell, staring at a bat in his study.

After the Hyper-Adapter sent back through time, we see a single panel where it attacks Dick Grayson as Batman from the pages of *Batman and Robin* #12 and Bruce says, "Whatever they touch turns to myth." The Hyper-Adapter travels farther back to the first issue of *Batman: The Return of Bruce Wayne* where it is killed by Vandal Savage and will later serve as Bruce's caveman Batman costume. But it is also the bat in Bruce Wayne's study when he discovers that he will become Batman. The ring of the bell reverberates throughout the globe (and throughout time as evidenced by the various characters who had heard bells throughout the series) and will summon Alfred, who will patch up Bruce so he can begin his crusade as Batman.

While it was always apparent that Batman channeled fear to drive his mission against crime, Morrison has now established that Batman not only channeled fear, but he is deliberately invoking the spirit of Darkseid himself in order to fight evil. Darkseid, in the form of the Hyper-Adapter bat, touched Batman and turned him into myth. Bruce took an inherently evil idea and transformed it to do good things. So, when Metron challenges Bruce to turn evil "upside down and end it," it's something that Bruce has done all along. Darkseid tried turning Batman into a weapon in *Final Crisis* and again in *Batman: The Return of Bruce Wayne*, but in the end, Batman was created when Bruce turned Darkseid into a weapon.

Superman and Wonder Woman try reviving Batman, but it's Tim's suggestion to "tell him Gotham's in trouble" that does the trick. Before reviving, Bruce realizes that the Hyper-Adapter infected Dr. Hurt, but also that even though gunshots had made him an orphan, he had help along the way, "The first truth of Batman... the saving grace. I was never alone."

With those words, Bruce revives and vomits blackness from deep within his soul. The very last remnants of Batman's darkness are finally purged from him as Bruce realizes he has never been alone. The death of his parents doesn't define Batman even if that is the beginning of his origin. Alfred, Tim, Dick, Damian, Commissioner Gordon, and his friends within the Justice League have always been there for Bruce. It's an epiphany that was a long time coming and beautifully done. It also sets up what's to come in *Batman, Inc.*

The issue ends with Bruce in the Batman costume without the mask, showing that this was never just a story about Batman, but a story about the man under the mask. Bruce's transformation is essentially complete, but he still must defeat Darkseid's avatar, Dr. Hurt, before he can be whole.

Batman and Robin #16

Though *Batman and Robin* #15 featured Bruce Wayne's full return as Batman (complete with Dick Grayson introducing him as a "Bat-God" and Bruce's perfect line of "It's all over" to remind readers of "the All-Over" phrase repeated in *Batman: The Return of Bruce Wayne*), it's issue #16 that firmly reestablishes Bruce into the DC Universe. But first, since *Batman and Robin* is a series of foils, Morrison has some plot threads to tie up in order to fully round out Dr. Hurt's status as Batman's opposite.

Dr. Hurt's origin is finally revealed at the beginning of the issue. The year is 1765 and in the basement of a barn, a group of men has summoned the dark god, Barbatos. The leader of these men is Thomas Wayne who will later become Dr. Hurt. He is described as "the black sheep of the family" by Alfred in issue #10. As he summons Barbatos, Thomas says, "By my blackened hand I summon ye in seek of knowledge of the inner world, my daemon." The blackened hand refers to his later identity as the Black Glove and the knowledge of the inner world parallels Bruce Wayne's own journey into the inner world during his transformation. Darkseid commands Thomas to "drink deep dark twin" which acknowledges that he is Bruce's "twin" and could be a slight reference to the insane brother of Bruce Wayne in 1975's *World's Finest* #223 (if so, that would be the second reference to this forgotten story as

Thomas Wayne Jr. was a resident of Willowood Asylum and Dr. Hurt worked at Willowood in *Batman: The Return of Bruce Wayne* #5).

After Dr. Hurt completes the ritual to Barbatos, he becomes the avatar for Darkseid on Earth. The connections between Bruce and Dr. Hurt are rich and powerful. Dr. Hurt's real name is Thomas Wayne making him part of Bruce's family. Bruce had transformed Darkseid's symbolism into a weapon for his war on crime and to make the bat-symbol immortal, and Thomas had embraced Darkseid's evil in the form of the dark god Barbatos in order to give himself immortality and to build an empire of evil. And technically, Bruce created Dr. Hurt when he sent the Hyper-Adapter through time. When the two finally meet again, their meeting is framed in a way to enhance their connection as foils. Dr. Hurt stands to the left in Bruce's father's bat costume (the same costume Bruce had worn during issue #5 of *Batman: The Return of Bruce Wayne*) and he holds a gun. Batman stands to the right with his fists raised and ready to fight.

From here, the action is light and breezy to reflect the new era of Batman. Artist Cameron Stewart returns for a few pages in this issue for the battle between the 99 Fiends and the two Batmen and Damian. His pages are quickly followed by Chris Burnham whose art is defined by a kinetic energy and exaggerated expressions that are devoid of all traces of gothic gloom and fully embrace four-color frenzy.

Batman chases Dr. Hurt through Wayne Manor and into the Batcave. Hurt has captured Alfred and it's up to Batman to find his mentor before he drowns. Meanwhile, Hurt taunts Batman saying, "One of man's most primitive fears is loneliness, Bruce," but he doesn't realize that Bruce had an epiphany and he is no longer alone. The same old tricks that Hurt pulled on Batman during "R.I.P." don't work anymore, but that won't stop him from trying. He cries out that he is Bruce's father and that he is the "hole in things" but they are cries of a desperate man. Bruce knows Dr. Hurt's real name and because of that, Hurt no longer has any power. He may be Darkseid incarnate, but Batman uses Darkseid as a weapon. So, it is fitting that he slips on a banana peel and falls in defeat to the Joker – now that Batman has returned as a Bat-God who has transformed the power of an evil god, Dr. Hurt's boogeyman tactics are nothing more than a joke.

Meanwhile, the Joker had been helping Dick and Damian during this arc and after burying Dr. Hurt alive, he swears to fight crime. Before the Joker can be a hero, Batman punches him out and arrests him. It's a signal that everything is back to normal once more; evil has been defeated and Batman has returned. But the last two pages also signal a significant game change.

Bruce Wayne takes the stage and explains to the press that he has been funding Batman all this time. This act shows us that his transformation into a new, more whole person is complete. It has the effect of making the Bruce Wayne identity in control over the Batman identity. The Batman of Zur-en-Arrh was Batman without Bruce Wayne and the Batman going into *Batman, Inc.* is one that is more balanced and stable than the hero has ever been.

Beside the more human identity that Batman has adopted, Bruce has also (almost paradoxically) ascended to god-like status. If the New Gods were as "incredibly powerful living ideas from a kind of platonic, archetypal world," then Batman has become a New God. The idea of Batman will spread like a religion throughout the world in *Batman, Inc.* with the bat-symbol acting like a cross for people to worship. Both man and Bat-God; perfect human and benevolent corporation – Batman has synthesized into something new and global.

Batman, Inc.: Where Everything is Hyper-Mega!

Grant Morrison's Batman saga can be divided up into three distinct phases: *Batman* explored the identity of the hero; *Batman and Robin* established a new dynamic duo into a fun, pop-fueled adventure series while also exploring the mythology of the hero in *Batman: The Return of Bruce Wayne;* and *Batman, Inc.* fully embraces the madness and absurdity of the previous two phases to create a wholly new Batman experience. Amongst fans, *Batman, Inc.* is a polarizing storyline. Morrison doesn't meditate on the Batman identity as he did in his first phase and during *Batman: The Return of Bruce Wayne* in the second phase. The pop adventure of *Batman and Robin* is kicked into overdrive as Batman stars as an international super-hero rather than gritty Gotham detective. *Batman, Inc.* is a departure from the norm and this could be where the criticism of the series comes from; because it is unfamiliar, it is held to unfair criticism.

While *Batman, Inc.* is a different take on Batman, it is a change that Morrison had logically been building towards after Bruce Wayne returned from his time-traveling adventure to become a Bat-God. Bruce Wayne has gone through meditation rituals like Thogal, had his identity stripped away by Dr. Hurt, and has returned from the time stream – to take the character back to solving mysteries in Gotham or to have him face off against the same old rogue's gallery again would be anticlimactic. This new era of Batman is a light romp through the more bizarre corners of the DC Universe as the hero recruits agents into his organization and battles the mysterious terrorist organization, Leviathan.

On the surface, the conflict between Batman Incorporated and Leviathan is no different than G.I. Joe versus Cobra, James Bond versus SPECTRE, or Spy versus Spy. But beneath the colorful heroes, dastardly villains, and devious double-agents is Morrison's commentary on corporations, branding, and magic sigils. In "Pop Magic!" — Morrison's manifesto on how to be a modern magician — the author writes about the power of viral sigils. He writes, "The viral sigil also known as the *brand* or *logo* is not of recent development (see 'Christianity,' 'the Nazis' and any flag of any nation) but has become an inescapable global phenomenon in recent years." He further goes on to write, "The McDonald's Golden Arches, the Nike swoosh, and the Virgin autograph are all corporate viral sigils."

Essentially, the symbols that are associated with these corporations have certain connotations, feelings, and ideas connected to them. The feelings that one has towards that corporation are summoned forth once they see the symbol. For instance, seeing the McDonald's golden arches can bring forth feelings of nostalgia for childhood, feelings of hunger, or perhaps feelings of queasiness. By simply observing this symbol (or viral corporate sigil), one can feel a mix of emotions. He goes on to write:

> The logo or brand, like any sigil, is a condensation, a compressed, symbolic summoning up of the world of desire which the corporation intends to represent. The logo is the only visible sign of the corporate intelligence seething behind it. Walt Disney died long ago but his sigil, that familiar, cartoonish signature, persists, carrying its own vast weight of meanings, associations, nostalgia and significance. People are born and grow up to become Disney executives, mouthing jargon and the credo of a living corporate entity. Walt Disney the man is long dead and frozen (or so folkmyth would have it) but Disney, the immense invisible corporate egregore persists.

With *Batman, Inc.*, Morrison has taken this concept of using corporations as a magic sigil to further an idea to a new level. The comic begs the question, "What if there were a corporation completely dedicated to saving lives?" *Batman, Inc.* is a sigil itself. By creating a corporate Batman, Morrison is trying to send out his idea of corporations being used for the good of the people rather than profit. Clearly, it's not meant to be a literal idea of super-heroes in our world, but rather, a figurative idea where corporations don't have to be strictly for profit.

Batman: The Return #1

The new era of Batman begins with a look back at the hero's origin story. Three bats are fighting in the night sky and the narrative focuses on one particular bat that is described as a "common creature at the end of his forty-year lifespan." The bat is seriously wounded by the two other bats and the narration explains that he was beaten because "something bigger ... faster. Smarter. Younger. Hungrier. Better came along." As the bat flies off to die, it finds the home of Bruce Wayne and it is revealed that this is the bat that inspired Bruce to become Batman.

This five-page sequence is a significant and highly symbolic new beginning. Batman's origin story is frequently revisited in comics, but by focusing the origin from the perspective of the bat, Morrison is challenging our expectations. The bat was never a character before, despite how vital and important it is to the creation of Batman. Before seeing the bat, Bruce Wayne is described as "a warrior without a totem" and now this bat will bring meaning into his life; it will become the sigil that Bruce adopts to strike fear into the hearts of criminals. But it will also expand into a corporate sigil that will span the globe for Batman Incorporated.

Numbers play a significant role in this sequence as well. The bat is described as "at the end of his forty-year lifespan" and the typical Batman narrative is nearing the end of its own lifespan as *Batman, Inc.* begins a new era. There are three bats fighting and the number three will be a number of significance throughout *Batman, Inc.* It takes two bats to kill the older one and these two bats are described as superior in every way, foreshadowing Leviathan's own superiority and showing that the odds will be against Batman. Furthermore, the two bats are younger and represent the generation conflict motif that will be present throughout the run.

After the opening sequence, Batman's new costume is revealed in a double-page spread. The most important change to the costume is the symbol on his chest; while it was a black bat before, it is now a black bat with a spotlight behind it. The spotlight works as a symbol for a new era of Batman that loses the dark, brooding hero in favor of a brighter, more fun mood. It draws attention to the hero and signals that innocents shouldn't be afraid. Symbolically, the spotlight lets the world know that Batman is shining his light in the darkest corners and will protect everyone.

Instead of battling a costumed super-villain, Batman faces off against a terrorist named Hussain Mohammed who holds a boy at gunpoint. Batman's first line seems to be addressing the audience as he asks, "You didn't expect to see me here, did you?"

Again, Morrison is challenging our expectations with this sequence of Batman rescuing the son of Sheikh Farouk from a terrorist. Most would assume that Bruce Wayne's first adventure back as Batman would pit him against a colorful super-villain, but the battle with a Middle Eastern terrorist is a visual cue for the new international, anti-terrorist Batman. Also, Hussain Mohammad is the first to name the terrorist organization Leviathan and claims that he'd "rather die" than face them.

Back at the Batcave, the entire Batman family meets as Bruce explains his plan. "Starting today, we fight ideas with better ideas. The idea of crime with the idea of Batman." This scene marks the change in Bruce's mentality. Just as Darkseid and the New Gods were living ideas in *Final Crisis*, Batman has become an idea now that he has gone through his transformation in *Batman: The Return of Bruce Wayne*. The Batman idea will become a corporate sigil that will span the globe. This echoes Morrison's introduction from *Supergods*, "Before it was a Bomb, the Bomb was an Idea. Superman, however, was a Faster, Stronger, Better Idea" (xv). The idea of Superman is stronger than the bomb, and the idea of Batman is stronger than crime.

Bruce then visits Waynetech R&D with Damian to view the new weapons in his crime-fighting arsenal. Lucius Fox shows off their G.I. Robot program (a subtle reference to the robot soldier G.I. Robot from the pages of *Star-Spangled War Stories* #101) and new jet-suits. After a paint-job to the jet-suits, Bruce and Damian fly off to Yemen to investigate illegal experiments financed by Sheikh Farouk. Batman explains to Robin that the dead bodies they have found are "surgically engineered superhuman bodyguards – all the rage amongst the mega-wealthy. Ask your mother." This seems to be a throwaway line, but it also implicates Talia in the experiments.

During their investigation, Batman and Robin meet two genetically altered super-humans named Traktir and Spidra. Traktir's appearance makes him seem evil, but he is afraid of someone called "The Fatherless," or "The Heretic," who was born from a whale carcass. Robin meets the Heretic who looks like a robot Batman in Middle Eastern robes, but before he can get any answers, the Heretic escapes saying, "You will know me. But not yet!"

The investigation in Yemen is another example of Morrison playing with our expectations. Spidra and Traktir seem evil based upon their freakish appearances, but they aren't. The Heretic is a mysterious figure but he won't appear again until the last page of *Batman, Inc.: Leviathan Strikes* #1. All of this feels like set-up for the first issue of *Batman, Inc.* but it isn't. Just as villains have been playing games with Batman in Morrison's run, the writer is now playing games with his audience. We expect *Batman: The Return* to establish characters and themes to look for in *Batman, Inc.*, but we are left with a number of elements that won't pay off until much later during the New 52's relaunch of *Batman, Inc.*

The final scene of the issue shows Sheikh Ibn Ali Farouk speaking to a mysterious, shadowed figure. The Heretic brings in the boy Batman saved earlier in the issue, Farouk's son Omar. The boy has a vacant look in his eyes as he points a gun at his father and says, "I was saved to purify the world in Leviathan's name. In the name of all that is pure and true, strong and young, you can only die." Omar then kills his father and pledges himself to Leviathan.

Cyclical narratives are a motif in *Batman, Inc.* Here, this last scene has returned to the generational conflict that was first established in the opening scene between the bats; a new generation is rising up and killing their parents. It is also a scene that is the inverse of Batman's origin story. Bruce Wayne was devastated when his parents were killed and now this new generation is killing their parents. However, Omar didn't kill his father willingly; Leviathan brainwashed him into becoming a violent child willing to commit patricide.

In this final scene, we see the first glimpse of the overarching brand conflict. Batman Incorporated is a brand designed to protect and save lives. Leviathan is a brand that promotes terrorism and violence. If we view both brands as real world symbols for pop culture, then Batman Incorporated can influence average people to be heroes while Leviathan is a synthesis of the most violent, horrible parts of popular culture infecting youth. Leviathan is every M-rated video game and R-rated movie that minors are exposed to. Leviathan is the culture of gun violence that America embraces. Leviathan is violent pop culture personified while Batman is the personification of heroic pop culture. So, in a way, Morrison is arguing that kids should read more Batman comics to become better people.

Batman, Inc. Vol. 1 #1

Morrison sets an explosive action tone for *Batman, Inc.* as the first issue features four different action scenes. The series begins on a dark note as skeleton-based super-villain Lord Death Man murders the Japanese hero, Mr. Unknown. Lord Death Man, with the power to enter a death-like trance, was originally known as just "Death Man" in Robert Kanigher and Sheldon Moldoff's story "Death Knocks Three Times" from *Batman* #180 (cover date May 1966). Later, Jiro Kuwata named the character "Lord Death Man" in Batman's Japanese adventures for *Shonen Ace* magazine in 1966 and later reprinted in Chip Kidd's *Bat-Manga!: The Secret History of Batman in Japan*. By using Lord Death Man, Morrison is returning to his belief that all Batman stories deserve to be in continuity, no matter how ridiculous.

The death of Mr. Unknown is symbolic to both Batman and Leviathan. For Batman, the death of Mr. Unknown represents the unity of Batman's identity. He knows who he is and doesn't question his mission. Meanwhile, the leader of Leviathan is unknown and after Mr. Unknown is murdered, we learn that a man named Jiro Osamu is *also* Mr. Unknown, showing that the identity of Leviathan will also feature many twists and turns. Later, we learn that Lord Death Man works for Leviathan, so killing Mr. Unknown before Batman can recruit the hero shows that Leviathan is always one step ahead of Batman.

Batman first appears in the issue alongside Catwoman, showing readers that this series will center on Batman teaming up with unexpected allies. At the end of *Batman: The Return*, Bruce enlists Catwoman to help him steal a mad scientist's invention and now they have infiltrated Dr. Sivana's laboratory to steal a magic diamond. The pairing of Batman and Catwoman is meant to ease readers into the idea that this won't be a solo Batman title. By having them steal from Dr. Sivana (a villain from Shazam's rogue's gallery), we see that Batman is venturing outside of Gotham and into the wider DC Universe. Also, in terms of the cyclical narrative, the series begins and ends with a femme fatale. Here, Batman is partnering with his first femme fatale and the series will end with the revelation that Talia al Ghul is the leader of Leviathan.

When they arrive at Sivana's lab, they notice that the security had already been disabled and Catwoman remarks that it "looks like someone got the same big idea ahead of you." This shows that Leviathan is one step ahead of Batman just as they were with killing Mr. Unknown. However, Batman and Catwoman are still able to retrieve the blue diamond which will become important much later.

Then, Batman and Catwoman are off to Japan to recruit Mr. Unknown, only pausing for two pages for a brief conversation as they work out in their underwear. The two then find Mr. Unknown's hideout underneath a comic book store where they battle Lord Death Man's skeleton warriors. After the goons are defeated and interrogated, the narrative shifts to the apartment of Jiro Osamu, who seemingly kills Lord Death Man by shooting him numerous times. Lord Death Man crashes through a window and lands on the sidewalk outside as Batman and Catwoman arrive on the scene. As Jiro's girlfriend falls through a trapdoor, Catwoman wastes no time as she leaps into the trap to save the girl and finds the trap to be a flooded apartment with a giant killer octopus.

Structurally, the issue moves very quickly as our heroes bounce from fight to fight, but it works to establish the fun, pop attitude that Morrison is going for in the series. One can almost hear the voice of William Dozier (producer and narrator for the 1966 *Batman* TV series) as the first issue of *Batman, Inc.* ends with the narration, "Lord Death Man lives to take life, and he's only just begun! Can Batman solve the reaper's riddles? Or will curiosity kill the cat? Find out next month in *Batman Inc.*" Ending the issue with questions to entice the reader in the middle of an impossible deathtrap perfectly recalls the feeling of the 1966 *Batman* TV series and given how polarizing that television series is, it should come as no surprise that *Batman, Inc.* is also polarizing, but it's in the interest of telling a new kind of Batman story; albeit one that captures the feeling of a bygone era.

This Batman doesn't have time to brood over his own mortality; he's too busy battling skull-faced ninjas and fighting giant robot mice in a scientist's lair with his jewel-thief gal-pal. If any of this seems ridiculous, the reader just needs to remember that it's no more ridiculous than a man dressing as a bat and solving mysteries. If there is a line between what readers are will and will not accept as absurd in comics, then *Batman, Inc.* crosses that line for some. But, to his credit, Morrison never abandons the core concepts of Batman as an idea.

Batman, Inc. Vol. 1 #2

Batman and Jiro battle Lord Death Man's goons as Catwoman faces off against the giant octopus. In the previous issue, as Batman and Catwoman were entering Mr. Unknown's hideout under the comic book store, Catwoman picked up an issue of hentai which is a catch-all term that describes the bizarre and graphic sex acts illustrated in Japanese anime and manga. Catwoman's battle with the giant octopus is both a reference to the "tentacle-porn" hentai she saw in the previous issue, and more importantly, a reminder of the cyclical nature of the narrative of *Batman, Inc.* which is a spiral like the Leviathan eating its own tail.

After the villains are defeated, Catwoman is saved and Lord Death Man's body is taken away, Batman examines the crime scene for clues that will lead him to Lord Death Man's next target. Using a similar methodology that Adam West's Batman would use, Batman deduces that Lord Death Man's use of hydrochloric acid (also known as aqua regia or "royal waters") means that the next assassination will take place at the Poseidonis Jewels exhibit. Jiro then realizes that the target is Aquazon from Super Young Team (the Japanese team of super-heroes Morrison introduced in *Final Crisis*). Batman calls Lord Death Man's game an "elemental chain of death" which is an idea that will return in *Batman, Inc.: Leviathan Strikes*.

Jiro reveals that the other Mr. Unknown was the detective and that Jiro would do "all the physical stuff – patrols, stakeouts, street fighting." This relationship between the two Mr. Unknowns is similar to the relationship that Bruce Wayne will have with Terry McGinnis in the cartoon *Batman Beyond*. Whether this allusion was intentional or not, it is still an interesting connection.

Despite Jiro's pleas to help avenge Mr. Unknown, Batman denies him: "You used a gun. Rule number one: no guns. My people have to be better than that." If Leviathan is a terrorist organization that brainwashes children to kill their parents, then the Batman brand is nonlethal and has to stay as such if it is to mean anything.

Lord Death Man rises from the dead, slaughters the doctors examining him in the hospital and says, "No grave's deep enough to hold mighty Lord Death Man" and then adds, "Put that on a t-shirt. It's all souvenirs in the end." It's a curious statement and one that cuts to the core of the branding that comes with super-hero comic books. Batman is a brand that makes billions of dollars in merchandise each year. Toys, t-shirts, bath products, and all sorts of odds and ends are created in the image of Batman which furthers the brand. With every product sold, there should be an underlying endorsement of heroism and justice, but perhaps all of that is forsaken in exchange for capitalism. Along with the Batman brand, the Joker is used to sell products. In terms of story, Lord

Death Man has the potential to be as interesting as the Joker, but he has been largely forgotten. However, through good enough merchandizing, Lord Death Man could be a recognizable pop culture figure.

With a Tommy Gun in hand, Lord Death Man exits the hospital as he detonates an explosive and races off in his super car. The villain continues the motif of reeducating youth as he says, "I read somewhere that violent, antisocial crime's almost unheard of in Japan. How's about we take them to school! Lord Death Man! I am the Headmaster!"

As the issue begins to reach a climax, the narrative cuts to the Poseidonis exhibit where Aquazon introduces the jewels. In one panel, Aquazon looks directly at the reader and says, "Don't forget! Everything is hyper-mega! Everybody have fun!" Her words serve as a reminder for readers to relax and not take *Batman, Inc.* too seriously. The best way to enjoy the comic is to embrace the "hyper-mega" of a Tommy Gun-wielding skull man crashing through apartments in his race car.

Lord Death Man tries to kill Aquazon, but Batman and Jiro-dressed-as-Mr. Unknown arrive to save the day. Mr. Unknown fakes his death in order to get a fresh start and become the Batman of Japan (seen again much later in Chris Burnam's issue of *Batman, Inc.* Vol. 2 #11) and Catwoman traps Lord Death Man in a safe and shoots him off into space. Catwoman asks, "What will you do when Batman's enemies come after Bruce Wayne?" Bruce replies, "You'll see," and we eventually will in issue #6.

Finally, Bruce reveals that he knew Catwoman had tried to steal the Poseidonis jewels, but that they had been liquefied. This final, playful exchange between Batman and Catwoman plays upon their relationship as crime-fighter and criminal and because there are no real consequences for Catwoman, it reestablishes the playful nature of the series itself. Sure, Catwoman is a thief, but Batman doesn't hold it against her because she isn't evil, necessarily.

The first arc of *Batman, Inc.* is short, but it establishes the mood of the series. It moves quickly and dares the audience to keep up. But, even though it is a fast-paced adventure, it still holds substance when read alongside the rest of the run. The motifs of the education of violence, the number three, and the cyclical narrative are all present in these first two issues and will continue to permeate the series. And as the Batman brand grows, we see the effect it has on identity.

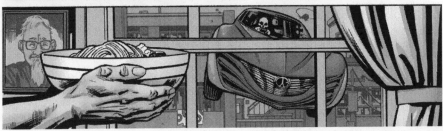

Aquazon says "Don't forget! Everything is hyper-mega! Everybody have fun!" From *Batman, Inc.* Vol. 1 #2 (Feb 2011). Art by Yanick Paquette and Michel Lacombe. Copyright © DC Comics.

Jiro Osamu was Mr. Unknown even though the other Mr. Unknown had died. The continuation of the Mr. Unknown identity was similar to the idea that "Batman and Robin will never die," but due to the viral super-sigil of Batman, the Mr. Unknown identity *did* die and was reborn as the Batman of Japan. Tim Drake's criticized the International Club of Heroes in "the Island of Mr. Mayhew" for being knock-offs of Batman, and Batman reprimanded his partner at that time. But, Jiro's transformation from Mr. Unknown to Batman Japan absolutely is a knock-off. Jiro had his own identity, only to be replaced by the more powerful corporate identity of Batman and the result is a hero that is viewed as a knock-off rather than an original creation.

To compare this with a real-world example in order to show that the corporate sigil isn't regulated to comic books, Legends in Concert is a show that features celebrity look-alikes performing tribute shows in places like Las Vegas, Atlantic City, and Branson, Missouri. The performers of Legends in Concert are only famous for being someone else who is famous and the result is a watered-down rip-off of the original product. Without Legends in Concert, these performers would probably never attain their marginal fame through their own song-writing or performances, but because of Legends in Concert, they get to be idolized for looking and sounding like a pop culture idol.

This is the price of their fame.

If Jiro were to remain Mr. Unknown, he would likely never star in a comic because no one knows the character. But, by adopting the name "Batman Japan," Jiro will star in his own issue of *Batman, Inc.* and will perhaps get his own action figure one day. One path is obscurity and the other is being known for being a rip-off of someone else.

Join or die.

Damned if you do and damned if you don't.

Batman, Inc. Vol. 1 #3

A flashback begins issue #3 as the narrative follows the original Knight and the British super-team, the Victory V's as they attack the super-villain Dr. Dedalus. The name comes from Greek mythology as Daedalus was the creator of the Labyrinth of Crete where the Minotaur was kept in the center. Daedalus also built wings of wax for his son Icarus to fly with, but his son flew too close to the sun, his wings melted, and the boy died. Dr. Dedalus's first appearance is alongside a Metalek scout (first mentioned in *JLA Classified*, first shown in *Batman and Robin*, and explored in depth in Morrison's *Action Comics*) which is a visual cue that Dedalus is also a builder. While Dr. Dedalus appears to be the central threat to Batman, he is, like his namesake, merely the builder of the maze for the real threat.

The leader of the Victory V's, Mr. Albion, has one seemingly throwaway line to the soldiers outside of Dedalus's hideout where he uses the British slang for soldier by calling his men, "Tommies," but the mention recalls the Tommy Gun that Lord Death Man carried in the previous issue. Even in small details like this, the narrative circles back on itself.

It's unclear what happens in the battle between the Victory V's and Dedalus, but Knight is the only survivor of the battle and celebrates by saying, "we locked him in and he'll never get out!" In his hand, he clutches a scrap of paper with the symbol of Dedalus; a spider web with an eye in the center. It's a chilling sigil; one that suggests that Dedalus is an all-seeing, spider-like predator.

In the present day Argentina, a colorful mob boss named Papagayo has captured a spy in his organization named Cimarron of the super-team, Super-Malon (which first appeared in *Flash Annual* #13 during DC's Planet DC annuals in an effort to create more global super-heroes). As Papagayo is about to kill Cimarron, Batman and El Gaucho arrive. The battle goes into the sky as Papagayo takes off in a hot-air balloon, but before he can reveal who he works for, Papagayo is pricked by one of Scorpiana's blue scorpions, and he falls to his death. After the fight, El Gaucho refuses to join Batman Incorporated and Cimarron regrets that they didn't learn who Papagayo was working for. However, the villain's parrot gives away the leader as it shouts, "Oroboro! Boss! Oroboro!"

Ororboro (or Ouroboros) is an ancient symbol of a dragon or a serpent eating its own tail, symbolizing eternity or cyclicality. In *Batman, Inc.*, it will be the symbol of Leviathan and is a visual representation of the narrative cycling back on itself. The death and rebirth aspects also represent the Batman franchise itself and the way Morrison has brought back old ideas from the past and made them new again.

Bruce Wayne visits El Gaucho's alter ego, Don Santiago Vargus. The narration is in Spanish and explains who Don Santiago is. It translates to,

> In Buenos Aires, in the spring, the place where you have to be is the private race track in the splendid villas of Don Santiago Vargas. Provider of miraculous racehorses to princes, sheikhs and potentates, the most eligible bachelor in Buenos Aires plays host to a who's who of beautiful

supermillionaires! Don Santiago Vargas! Extravagant! Irresponsible! Enigmatic!

Notice the mention of "sheikhs" in his description, which recalls Sheikh Farouk from *Batman: The Return.*

Bruce arrives with a woman named Tristessa who will later be revealed as Scorpiana. Don Santiago sheds light on his relationship with Tristessa saying, "You may have seen our names linked in the society columns." This statement recalls the first issue where Bruce and Selina are surrounded by paparazzi as they exit a jet in Japan. So, Tristessa and Don Santiago are not unlike Catwoman and Batman; two people in love and caught on opposite sides of the law. But aside from her contribution to the cyclical narrative, Tristessa is also the second of three raven-haired femme fatales that will appear (the first being Catwoman). During his tango with Tristessa, Bruce took an Ororboro ring from her finger showing that she also works for Leviathan.

As good as El Gaucho is, he isn't as smart as Batman when he asks, "Why the hell is Batman masquerading as Bruce Wayne, anyway? I've met Wayne and you don't fool me." And despite how much he wants to recruit the hero, Batman goes along with the ruse and pretends that he is using Bruce Wayne to get what he wants. This shows that while Batman is ready to expand his brand, he still doesn't trust everyone completely.

El Gaucho and Batman continue working on a case involving three missing blind children and it leads them to a writer named Espartaco Extrano who wrote "a book of short stories about a sinister manipulative figure known as Doctor Dedalus." Batman also reads that Extrano was "killed by three blind assassins" at Casa D'Oro (notice the three letters are the same as Ororboro) even though Extrano wasn't a real person. El Gaucho explains that Extrano was created by a group of writers as part of an elaborate hoax which is an allusion to Jorge Luis Borges' collaborations with Adolfo Casares under the pseudonym "H. Bostos Domecq" used to publish detective and fantasy stories. It's a complex mystery with many twists and dead ends; just like the maze of Daedelus. But, Batman boils it down to the symbolic number three as he says, "Three kids. Three assassins. Three letters."

The issue ends with Batman and El Gaucho investigating the murder site of fictional person Extrano only to discover that it was booby-trapped by El Sombrero, the master of deathtraps, and Scorpiana. When we last saw El Sombrero, he was allegedly killed by the Joker in Arkham Asylum and now he is a crippled villain who has trapped three children and is forcing Batman and El

Gaucho to duel with taser-gauntlets. Note that El Sombrero's calling card is a skull and crossbones wearing a sombrero and that a skull and crossbones sticker is on his wheelchair. The skulls are a subtle visual call back to Lord Death Man from the previous arc.

Finally, the elaborate deathtrap and teaser question motif continue to evoke a 1966 *Batman* TV series feel as the narration asks, "Which kills fastest? The bitter kiss of the scorpion? Or the poison sting of betrayal? Find out next month in *Batman Inc.*"

Batman, Inc. Vol. 1 #4

Kathy Kane was the first Batwoman. First appearing in *Detective Comics* #233 (cover date July 1956), she was created in response to psychiatrist Fredric Wertham's accusations that Batman and Robin were gay. Kathy would be the first character to join the Batman Family and would later be joined by her niece Betty Kane as the first Bat-Girl. The two were successful in expanding the scope of Batman but by 1964, both characters were removed from the Batman family as part of a new initiative by editor Julius Schwartz to take Batman into a more serious tone. Kathy Kane's last appearance in costume would be in *Batman Family* #10 (1979) where she would come out of retirement to help Batgirl (Barbara Gordon) fight Killer Moth and Cavalier. Then, in *Detective Comics* #485 (Aug-Sept 1979), Kathy is stabbed in the stomach and bleeds to death during a fight between Batman and Ra's al Ghul's League of Assassins.

After the mega-event *Crisis on Infinite Earths*, the identity of Batwoman was erased from continuity, but Kathy Kane was still a character that had existed in the DC Universe and had been killed by the League of Assassins. Meanwhile, the first Bat-Girl, Betty Kane, went on to become a member of the Teen Titans under the name "Flamebird" and most recently, and quite ironically, she has been a supporting character in J.H. Williams III's *Batwoman*.

While this historical information is helpful in better understanding the importance of Kathy Kane to the Batman mythology, Morrison gives us everything we need to know about her in *Batman, Inc.* Vol. 1 #4. Batman and El Gaucho may be in the middle of a battle to the death that has continued from issue #3, but the bulk of this issue is the story of Kathy Kane. The main concept that Morrison emphasizes with Batwoman is that she was the first to take the Batman concept and modify it for her own purposes – an exceptionally important idea in a series about the evolution of the Batman brand.

The circular narrative is apparent as the issue begins. The current Batwoman, Kate Kane, holds an Oroboro chain similar to the ring that Scorpiana had in the previous issue. She chases a criminal named Johnny Valentine through a carnival after Valentine had killed three marines. "Johnny Valentine" may seem like a generic villain name, but his appearance in the carnival recalls the first arc of *Batman and Robin* with Professor Pyg (a.k.a. Lazlo Valentin). Kate's father acts as her tech support and reveals that the carnival "used to be Kane's Kolossal Karnival" and the narrative flashes back to Kathy Kane.

Morrison makes some important changes to Kathy's origin including the revelation that she was "Kathy Webb" before she married Nathan Kane. It's an important change because over the years, Bruce Wayne's family history had become entangled with the Kanes which would make his romantic relationship with Kathy awkward given that she is his cousin. Morrison maintains that she was a circus performer, but when Agent-33 attempts to recruit Kathy by saying, "I would give anything I own to work with a legend such as you," we realize that she was an important spy before ever becoming Batwoman. We also learn that she "had directed three award-winning underground films" and also "published poetry" showing that she is more than just a fighter.

Agent-33 hands Kathy a business card for his organization, Spyral. Note that the symbol of Spyral is the eye in a spider web that was seen in the previous issue as being associated with Dr. Dedalus. Spyral wants Kathy to become Batwoman in order to get close to Batman and share his secrets with them. Originally, Kathy became Batwoman simply because she was in love with Batman, so this is a welcome change from her origin story.

Through Kathy, we see that the circular narrative was something that had been occurring before Morrison's tenure on the title. Bruce Wayne recruited circus performer Dick Grayson to be his side-kick, Robin. Kathy Kane was a circus performer who would adopt the identity of Batwoman. She is a dark-haired, mysterious femme fatale like Catwoman, but she is a hero rather than a criminal. But Kathy also continues the motif of the number three in Morrison's *Batman, Inc.* as she is the third of three dark-haired femme fatales after Catwoman and Scorpiana. Catwoman is a reformed villain who teams up with Batman. Scorpiana will always be a villain as she tries to use her love as a weapon against El Gaucho. And Kathy is the spy posing as a hero to learn Batman's secrets.

Later in the issue, we see Kathy practicing martial arts as she battles three men at once. She is looking through a microscope to signify that she is preparing her mind to become a super-hero as well. Finally, we see Kathy looking at different costume designs as she makes her costume. Although the narration reads, "First she figured out exactly how he did what he did... and then she did it better," we are never really shown solid evidence of Kathy expanding the Batman brand and being better than the original.

The first meeting between Batman and Batwoman is shown to be the premiere of a movie as gangster Jimmy the Jackdaw tries robbing an actor. Batwoman arrives and saves Batman's life by shining a spotlight on Jimmy and surprising him long enough for Batman to save the day. Afterward, Bruce and Kathy are at a party and Bruce challenges her saying, "Name one situation where we'd need her and not Batman." Bruce's sexist remarks are similar to the reasoning that had kept Kathy Kane down for so many years. Julius Schwartz had abandoned Kathy Kane in 1964 because he wanted to take Batman in a new direction. In 1979, Denny O'Neil killed Kathy in *Detective Comics* #485 and later said in an interview, "We already had Batgirl, we didn't need Batwoman." For years, writers and editors had been dismissing Kathy as being redundant but Morrison's *Batman, Inc.* is the argument that redundancy is a product of bad writing.

El Gaucho is only a lesser version of Batman if a writer chooses to portray him as such. The International Club of Heroes is a team of knock-offs if they are without personality. Batwoman is redundant when editors don't allow her to be interesting. But, when these characters are viewed as living beings with wants, needs, and histories of their own, they can become interesting characters, and can be viewed as more than just simple redundancy.

Batwoman's relationship with Batman is explored further as we see their first kiss, Robin's frustration with being replaced by Kathy, and the mission where Batman and Batwoman experienced the effects of a powerful hallucinogen. But then we learn that Kathy Kane, formally Kathy Webb, is actually the daughter of the criminal, Dr. Dedalus (a.k.a. Otto Netz, the Spinner of Snares) and that Dedalus is also Agent-Zero, the leader of Spyral. It's an important change to her origin that not only adds more depth to her character but to the mysterious Dr. Dedalus as well.

The final Batwoman flashback shows her teaching Batman the Tango Del Muerte that he danced with Scorpiana in issue #3. Afterward, she breaks

Batman's heart and leaves him saying, "I don't want to feel like mommy at a costume party that has to end sometime. And I don't want Bat-babies, Bruce." In a way, we can interpret Kathy's rejection of Batman's love to be the catalyst for his later rejection of Talia. At one time, he wanted to be part of a crime-fighting family, but after Kathy left, that part of him died. He can no longer love after being heartbroken.

In the midst of Kathy Kane's origin, the current Batwoman, Kate Kane, is still chasing Johnny Valentine through the carnival. She enters a haunted house (note the flaming eye on the ride's car which looks eerily similar to Dr. Dedalus's spider web sigil) and faces off against an assassin dressed in Kathy's old costume. Valentine gets away, but the three marines that he had killed had bullet wounds that matched the braille letters O-R-B which points to oroboro and Leviathan. Kate's father figures out that it has to do with a weapon in the south Atlantic and Kate declares, "right now, I'm reopening the Kathy Kane murder case."

Batman and El Gaucho are barely in the comic, but as they battle for the lives of three blind children, Scorpiana reveals that Gaucho was Agent-33 and he had killed Kathy Kane. Batman is confused because he believed that she was killed by the League of Assassins, but Gaucho has no time to explain. After shorting out Gaucho's gauntlets, Batman is off to find Sombrero.

While the main narrative of *Batman, Inc.* takes a backseat this issue, the story of Kathy Kane is a wonderful departure that revitalizes a silver age character and adds new depth to the current story. Morrison's modus operandi during his *Batman* tenure had been to repurpose old stories and make them relevant again. With Batwoman, he emphasizes her importance to the Batman brand, but changes her to better fit his purposes. The changes to her origin story are welcome, but the changes to her death are more complex in their implications. Having Agent-33 of Spyral kill Kathy adds another twist in the mystery, but doesn't necessary undo her original death of being murdered by the League of Assassins. Batman was sure that she had been killed by "Sensei's men" and that death would add another moment of the al Ghul family taking something from Batman. But, because we are never shown Kathy's death at the hands of Agent-33 or the League of Assassins, we should be suspect of any information regarding her demise.

Batman, Inc. Vol. 1 #5

Kathy Kane was revealed to be Dr. Dedalus's daughter, but Dedalus himself has been a mystery until this issue. Though Otto Netz's story begins when he was a Nazi scientist, we learn that he was using Hitler just as he has used every alliance he has ever made. Dedalus went to England to find a fifth form of matter called oroboro when he was captured and recruited by the British. Oroboro has been hinted at as a weapon before, but calling it the "fifth form of matter" ties it to the elemental motif that began in the first two issues with Lord Death Man's elemental chain of death.

After using his knowledge of Hitler to gain influence with the British, he betrayed them as well. Dedalus explains, "I went solo ... in my cloak of smoke I fought the law *and* the underworld ... I did it only to watch the patterns they made ... the futile attempts to understand or love me, or to defeat me ... when I emerged from seclusion in Argentina to head the United Nations Spyral Agency, I took my new name from an old book. I was Doctor Dedalus." Dedalus is the ultimate spy who has worked for and betrayed nearly everyone imaginable. Now, an old man with Alzheimer's, the villain waits at his lighthouse lair and imagines his nurse dying by poison.

The narrative shifts from Dedalus to a secret agent super-hero known as the Hood and there are a number of reasons why the Hood shouldn't be trusted. First, his narration begins at the end of Dedalus's story which visually connects the Hood with the ultimate spy known for back-stabbing others. Next, the Hood reveals that his real name is "Mr. Cross" which could be a pun for "double cross." Finally, his hood is red effectively making him a "red hood" like Batman's old side-kick Jason Todd. All of these are blatant signs that the Hood is a double agent who has been sent to infiltrate Batman Incorporated.

The Hood says that he was hired by Matron of the organization T.H.E.Y. to stop an international incident between the U.K. and Argentina, and after he lands at the island of Dr. Dedalus, he meets Batwoman, Batman, and El Gaucho. The four battle Scorpiana when Batwoman defeats her and realizes Scorpiana was the one who trained the fake Kathy Kane from the carnival.

When Batman finally meets Dedalus, the old criminal greets him as "the time voyager" showing that he is aware of Batman's transformation. Dedalus's nurse explains that he is "one of a three-man United Nations special intelligence unit" which continues the three motif. While it seemed as if the nurse was there to keep Dedalus trapped but still care for him, he runs in fear from Batman showing that there is more to the nurse than we first expected.

Batwoman asks, "How many twists and turns can one case take?" as Batman chases the nurse up a spiral stair case to the top of the lighthouse. Batman's journey up the stairs is a metaphor for the narrative itself. Readers have certain expectations for how the mystery will reveal itself only to be thrown another twist in the story. For example, the audience expects the fifth form of matter, oroboro, to be at the top of the stairs, but instead, Batman finds the hammer of Mr. Albion from issue #3. The nurse explains that after the British heroes were killed years ago, Dedalus had turned Mr. Albion's hammer into a meta-bomb. The mystery of Dr. Dedalus ends where it began and the reader is left confused by the plot threads with no answers.

After Batman easily disables the meta-bomb by having the Batplane fire missiles at it, we then learn that Dedalus was never really there at all. The man pretending to be Dedalus has been carrying a recorder with the villain's voice. So, both the threat and the villain that Batman were after are nowhere to be found by the end of this arc which is disappointing until we realize that the story was always about the mystery itself.

Something seems to be missing from the mystery of Dr. Dedalus. We know that Dedalus is a man of many names (including Otto Netz, Agent-Zero, Daddy 8-Legs, Sleipnir, the Spinner, and the Master Spy) and that oroboro and Kathy Kane are tied into Dedalus's web. What we don't know, however, is what it all means. It's all a complex web of spies, aliases, and mind games, but it is also the oroboro as the circular narrative turns back in on itself and leaves the reader wondering what was important and what wasn't. Batman best summarizes the mystery saying, "Three blind children, a lighthouse, spiral stairs, an imaginary author and four of us all caught up in the maelstrom. It makes so much sense it hurts…"

The Hood tries explaining it by saying, "Alzheimer's. It all makes some horrible sense, I suppose. The labyrinth of Dr. Dedalus was his own mad, decaying brain." The mystery has the effect of a narrative Alzheimer's. It leaves the reader confused and wondering what had just happened. In this way, Dedalus, or perhaps Alzheimer's disease, is "the hole in things" that has plagued Batman since the night his parents died. The unsolvable mystery.

Dedalus is shown far away in the lair of Leviathan and reveals his true intentions by saying, "While he struggles to prevent his world from falling apart, a new order is rising. Argentina. Japan. Hong Kong. Australia. England. France. A ring around the Earth." The mystery was designed to distract Batman from the real threat of Leviathan, but it also distracted the reader from Leviathan as well.

The issue ends with a sequence set in Africa where Batwing tries liberating children from a Leviathan reeducation school. The scene is labeled a "prologue" showing that the end of this issue returns the narrative to the conflict with Leviathan. The end is the beginning. But, this prologue is also the first appearance of Batwing and though it is very brief, the character will later go on to star in his own series after the New 52 launches. Finally, when a Leviathan teacher says, "Let's go back to the beginning ..." he is reminding readers of the reeducation of youth motif that began in *Batman: The Return* with Omar Farouk killing his father. All of the starting elements of *Batman, Inc.* (recruitment, education, new heroes, terrorism) are back in full swing in this three-page sequence.

Batman, Inc. Vol. 1 #6

The corporate sigil of Batman is the focus of this issue as the narrative bounces around to all corners of the world to show the versatility of the Batman brand. Morrison returns to the idea of class struggle that is inherent between the wealthy Batman battling underprivileged criminals at the beginning of this issue. A new "crime franchise" (note that use of the word "franchise" instead of "organization" has corporate connotations to it) known as the "Average Joes" has moved into Gotham City. Like Joe Chill, these villains are portrayed as "working class" men who are trying to make a living. In order to better understand Bruce Wayne, the Average Joes hire a private investigator named "Nero Nykto." Nykto then explains the information that he has found.

The leader of the Average Joes complains that Bruce Wayne is, "some billionaire with pockets deeper than the Grand Canyon [and] is giving handouts to every half-assed do-gooder in a cape." So, not only does the leader of the Average Joes hate Wayne's wealth, he hates that Wayne hands out money to people who will agree with him. It's basic class warfare where the working class hates the wealthy, but because it's on the comic page, this conflict plays out using colorful costumes and codenames. And because the hero is the billionaire, the reader automatically cheers for the wealthy upper-class rather than the people struggling to survive.

In a television interview, Bruce Wayne explains his reasons for funding Batman Incorporated, but also uses the opportunity to expand the misinformation surrounding Batman. After the reporter tries to solidify the details of who is exactly Batman, Bruce explains, "No one knows who Batman is anymore. Or how many there are." Another criminal franchise known as the Emoticon-Men arrive to kill Bruce when Alfred single-handedly stops them all. Bruce finishes his speech saying, "Batman is everywhere... And if he didn't exist, well... I guess we'd just have to invent him."

The "Batman is everywhere" idea represents more than just the heroes who have joined Batman Incorporated in the comic. In terms of the real world, "Batman is everywhere" means just that. The Batman brand is used to sell everything from toys to bath soap, from cereal to lunch boxes. But, it's the sentiment of "if he didn't exist... we'd just have to invent him" that is really interesting. If Bob Kane and Bill Finger didn't create Batman, some other brand would fill the void to sell products. As consumers, people find corporate brands they like and will purchase anything with that branding on it. Beyond the branding message though, Batman is the opposite of crime. Crime exists, but Bob Kane and Bill Finger created the antithesis of crime in Batman and if they didn't, then some other brand would fulfill that obligation.

Both Batmen (Bruce and Dick) and Robin meet with Commissioner Gordon to prove he is innocent of murder. Gordon shows his Batman badge and asks Bruce, "Does the secret badge make *me* Batman, too?" Bruce replies, "Pretty much." This scene is a reminder that any of us can be Batman. Put on a Batman shirt and suddenly you're Batman. Batman's corporate sigil is powerful because there is nothing like it. Wear a t-shirt from a popular clothing store at the mall and it shows that you support that particular brand which has all sorts of positive and negative connotations based on the image of the brand you're wearing. But, wear a Batman shirt, and you become united with others under the symbol of a hero. Even something as small as Gordon's badge makes you part of the exclusive organization of the big business of Batman.

Red Robin and Batman discuss the structure of the Batman family when Batman introduces his former partner to the Outsiders. Essentially, the Outsiders are proof of the power of the Batman brand. The team was first introduced in *The Brave and the Bold* #200 (the last issue of that series) and then they went on to star in their own series called *Batman and the Outsiders*. They were a team of misfits who could never be taken seriously on their own, but with Batman to lead them (both in the title of the series and in the stories themselves), the Outsiders were able to have their own series.

Bruce Wayne stands over a criminal and says "Batman is everywhere." From *Batman, Inc.* Vol. 1 #6 (June 2011). Art by Chris Burnham. Copyright © DC Comics.

In the Batcave, Bruce is shown at his computer wearing his costume, but with his mask off. This image of Bruce sitting leisurely in his costume shows how comfortable he has become in his identity. Bruce Wayne and Batman aren't two separate people; they are now fully synthesized. He is comfortable as Batman and takes great joy in spreading the misinformation about Batman on the internet. Taking on different identities on a message board, Bruce spreads a number of lies to confuse anyone who would try to find information on him. This is how Bruce Wayne prevents people from discovering that he is Batman – by assuming many identities and becoming the source of lies and misinformation. Bruce Wayne's internet identities give "Batman is everywhere" a whole new meaning.

But not everything is perfect for Bruce. On the way to France, Bruce and Alfred play a game of chess in which Bruce loses. It can be interpreted as a light-hearted commentary on how Alfred is still in control even when Bruce has become a zen-like Bat-God, but it is also a sobering reminder of the game between Batman and Leviathan. Since returning from being trapped in time, Bruce has always been one step behind Leviathan. The Heretic had already been born and killed most of the Kollektiv by the time Batman and Robin arrived in *Batman: The Return*, Mr. Unknown was killed by Lord Death Man before Batman could recruit him, and Dedalus was always ahead of Batman from the start. Bruce Wayne is brilliant, but he isn't infallible.

In France, Batman and Nightrunner save kidnapped children who have murdered their captors in the name of Leviathan. We've seen young killers before in the series, but never with the look of joy that these children have. Surrounded by decapitated bodies and covered in blood with smiles on their faces, these children love to kill. Whether or not they are still brainwashed is less obvious. Omar Farouk had vacant eyes as he shot his father while these children mutilated their victims.

The narrative shifts again to a brief scene in Hong Kong with Cassandra Cain as the new Blackbat as she attacks drug dealers in a helicopter. Cassandra is famous for being the first Batgirl to star in her own series which debuted in 2000. After Stephanie Brown became the new Batgirl (Stephanie had previously been Spoiler and then Robin for a brief time), Cass was without a super-hero name because while there can be many Batmen, there can apparently only be one Batgirl. Here, she has been rebranded as Blackbat – another Batgirl like Betty Kane or Barbara Gordon to be rebranded into something else.

Nero Nykto continues spreading the misinformation of Batman to the Average Joes saying, "Wayne's in Kuala Lumpur, Batman's in Hong Kong. Batman's a girl. Then Batman's in Melbourne, Australia." Here, we see Batman and the new Dark Ranger capturing an actor who works for Leviathan. The previous Dark Ranger had been murdered by Wingman in "The Island of Dr. Mayhew" storyline in Morrison's *Batman*. Now, Dark Ranger is being sworn into Batman Incorporated and the Batman brand continues to spread its influence.

In North Africa, Batwing explains that he and the Kollektiv have broken up a Leviathan training camp. Like the Outsiders before them, the Kollektiv are now indebted to Batman's influence and his brand. But before Batman returns home, he makes one more stop to visit the new Wingman. He tells the mysterious new recruit, "Think of this as your opportunity to salvage a reputation. Welcome to Batman Incorporated, Wingman. Your identity has to remain a mystery no matter what." We won't know who the new Wingman is for quite some time, but it's a great reveal.

Back with Nero Nykto and the Average Joes, Nykto reveals that his name means "dark night" and that he was Batman all along. On television, the internet, and even in disguise as a mobster, Batman is everywhere as he scares criminals into believing that he can be anything they imagine. As Nykto, Batman spreads rumors to the Average Joes saying "Batman is everything you fear" and "Batman died and came back as a kind of god." Not only is Batman everywhere, but he can be any idea. In this way, Morrison is arguing that all Batman stories can exist. Batman can be a detective, a sci-fi hero, a monster, or a god. He's all of these things and that's what gives his brand such power.

The final scene is between Dedalus and Leviathan on a satellite. While Batman travels the globe and recruits his army, they look down from above knowing that they are still ahead of him. Dedalus reports that they have "500 agents [to] form the first battle formation. The youngest and most zealous of these living weapons of Leviathan is barely 18 months old." The effectiveness of an 18 month old killer aside, Leviathan's reach is frightening when 500 soldiers are described as "the first wave."

The two are confident in their victory. Dedalus describes their soldiers as being "trained to imitate the actions of the virus. Infiltrate. Contaminate. Destroy."

While Batman's brand is loud and brash in establishing its sigil across the world, the Leviathan brand acts as viral marketing similar to Jason Todd's own unsuccessful attempts in *Batman and Robin*. It is covert as it settles into the infrastructure, slowly taking control of those who would easily and willingly rebel and throw out the ruling class.

Batman, Inc. Vol. 1 #7

A common motif in *Batman* comics is for villains to reflect some aspect of Batman's personality. The Joker is the most obvious exact opposite to Batman, but a number of other villains were created from the perspective of what Batman would be like if he were a villain. Owlman from the Crime Syndicate of America is the first example of this type of character. From an alternate universe where all of the heroes are villains, Owlman was Batman if he were evil. During Grant Morrison's graphic novel *JLA: Earth 2*, Owlman is revealed to be Thomas Wayne Jr., the son of Thomas and Martha Wayne and brother to Bruce Wayne. On that Earth, Thomas, Martha, and Bruce were killed by a policeman and Thomas Jr. used his family's wealth and influence to become a villain. Other foil villains include Prometheus whose parents were criminals that were killed by a policeman, Deathstroke who is in peak physical condition and, like Batman, trains children, Bane who is a master tactician and born in poor conditions, and of course, Ra's al Ghul.

Villains can be used to act as foils for the hero to emphasize the hero's positive qualities, but other heroes rarely are used in this same way. The International Club of Heroes can all act as foils for Batman, but because they are not villains, they are viewed as cheap knock-offs rather than interesting variations on what could have been. But, in issue #7, Morrison uses the hero Man-of-Bats as a foil for Batman to illustrate what the opposite of Batman could really look like.

Rather than patrolling rooftop to rooftop at night in search of crime, Man-of-Bats goes door to door asking people if they need help. Along with his son (and side-kick) Raven, Man-of-Bats helps people on his reservation kick their drug addictions, battles black mold, provides for single mothers, and rescues kids from their troubled home lives. Meanwhile, at his day job, Man-of-Bats is Dr. Bill Great Eagle and he is on the verge of losing his job due to his political activism.

All of these details are opposite to Batman. Bruce Wayne's father was a doctor, but Bruce chose a life of business. Dr. Great Eagle has no wealth, so he helps people through medicine. Batman strikes fear in criminals while Man-of-Bats lends a helping hand to the people on his reservation. Man-of-Bats has a partner that is his son and Batman struggles with letting his own child be Robin. The red and black motif from "R.I.P." returns in this issue with the Redz Gang led by Sam Black Elk spreading its influence on the reservation. Redz graffiti can be seen marking territory like the words "Zur-En-Arrh."

Raven acts as the voice of dissent as he wishes that he could fight robots or master criminals instead of wife beaters and junkies. Man-of-Bats stands firm in his belief that being a hero is more than just battling colorful villains and in this regard, he makes Bruce Wayne's idea of Batman Incorporated seem shallow. Instead of investing money into communities to make them better, Bruce arms masked heroes in a war on super-terror. And when Man-of-Bats confronts Sam Black Elk about being a drug dealer, Black Elk responds with, "How about what poverty and nobody givin' a damn did for your precious community?"

Black Elk may be a drug dealer, but in terms of the class struggle, he's right. Previous commentary on class struggle through Joe Chill and also the Average Joes came off as pathetic attempts at justifying their illegal actions. Black Elk makes a legitimate case for the concept of Batman being inherently wrong. Instead of lifting people out of a life of crime, Batman beats them down, an act that is symbolically shown through Black Elk kicking a defenseless dog.

Tired of debating Black Elk, Man-of-Bats beats him up and checks his pockets for drugs. When the police arrive, they discover the drugs on Black Elk were mints, and both Man-of-Bats and Black Elk are arrested with the officer saying, "Doc, you just beat the teeth out of a homeless person."

Back at the headquarters of Man-of-Bats and Raven, (which is nothing more than a small house and barn) we see a sign that reads "The Bat's Cave! Secret HQ of Man-of-Bats and Raven! South Dakota's own Dynamic Duo! See the incredible Batsmobile! The Hall of Trophies! The casebook archive! The crime lab! The ghost shirt! Entrance fee $15. All proceeds go to Red Cloud Indian School."

Obviously, there is irony in a secret headquarters that has an entrance fee, but it's also a commentary on branding. In our world, the Batman brand is used to make money for DC Comics, but more importantly for Warner Bros. Entertainment. On the reservation, the Batman logo is used to sell tickets to the HQ of Man-of-Bats to benefit an Indian School. The other implication of this tourist spot is the commodification of reservations. America has destroyed the American Indian way of life and turned it into a tourist destination in some pathetic attempt at cultural preservation. The Man-of-Bats HQ would be more funny if it weren't so damn sad.

Batman visits Raven and enters the Bat's Cave. Inside, we see a smaller budget version of Batman's own Batcave complete with a giant wooden nickel, costumes in cases, bobble head souvenirs, and a drum the color of the Batman of Zur-En-Arrh. Batman admires his surroundings and says, "It doesn't have to take millions, does it? The idea works. Batman on a budget."

It's a statement that's meant to be positive; that the Batman idea can be distilled into something so simple and still helpful and effective. But, there is something hollow and rude about what Batman says here. Bruce Wayne has the wealth and the means to fix the reservation's problems, but instead, he admires what they've done with their poverty. Morrison is arguing that crime can't be beaten through beating down the poverty-stricken criminals of the world, but he's not saying that eliminating poverty will solve the problem of crime either. Just as Batman Incorporated is capitalist altruism, Leviathan is capitalist terrorism. If Batman Incorporated were to fall apart, the corporation of Leviathan would rise up and take the world down a path of ruin. It would be overly simplistic to say that money is the root of all evil or that pulling people out of poverty will automatically make the world better. Even if poverty was eliminated worldwide, the influence of corporate super-sigils can still poison minds and lead people to do horrible things. Money is a weapon that Batman must continue to use in his arsenal and he can't use that tool if he gives up all of his money.

In the backseat of the police car, Sam Black Elk and one of the arresting officers reveal themselves to be agents of Leviathan. As Black Elk breaks from his hand cuffs and stabs Man-of-Bats, the new police officer murders his partner. While it looks like the last stand of Man-of-Bats, Raven and Batman arrive along with other citizens of the reservation to save the day. Raven donates blood to his father and Batman warns that "Leviathan targets communities the law and governments prefer to ignore."

This can be interpreted as an acknowledgment that Batman doesn't do enough for downtrodden communities, but it also shows that Batman understands the methodology of Leviathan. They exist to empower the disenfranchised the way that Batman gives power to all who wear his symbol. Batman is hope in darkness and Leviathan takes control of the darkness.

Batman, Inc. Vol. 1 #8

In 1990, DC Comics produced an original graphic novel by Pepe Moreno called *Batman: Digital Justice*. The comic is notable because all of the art was computer generated meaning that it was completely made via a computer program. The art was a gimmick, and the story is forgettable but because Morrison wants to reuse everything he can from Batman's history, the computer-generated art makes a comeback with this issue. Unfortunately, the computer-generated art lacks detail, making the characters look bland and the headache-inducing coloring lacks any shades of subtlety. Fortunately, there are a few moments where Morrison's script shines to give this issue some substance.

The entire issue takes place in Internet 3.0 which was first mentioned in *Batman: The Return*. Internet 3.0 is a fully-immersive virtual reality world where users can presumably surf the web via avatars. Essentially, Morrison is trying to suggest that if Batman could remake the Internet, then he would make it better. If Batman can remake himself into a powerful, international crime-fighting organization, then he can also clean up the internet and turn it into something more constructive. After all, "Batman is everywhere."

In the middle of Bruce Wayne's meeting with potential investors, a team of zombies bursts into the virtual board room with the leader shouting, "The city of numbers is on fire! All must kneel to the worm captain!" The name of "worm captain" being an allusion to the snake symbol of Leviathan.

As investors panic, Bruce reassures them that "Internet 3.0 access comes installed with free Batman Incorporated anti-viral software." The software is programmed by the computer-savvy Oracle whose Batgirl avatar arrives to save the day.

Aside from the art, the issue is note-worthy because it is the last appearance of Barbara Gordon as Oracle. DC's New 52 initiative will begin the next month and Barbara will return to her roots of being Batgirl much to the chagrin of many fans. In this issue, Oracle shows her superiority in Internet 3.0 as she is able to control multiple avatars at the same time while Batman struggles splitting focus between his Bruce Wayne and Batman avatars.

After returning from the time stream, Bruce Wayne and Batman have become one identity. Batman no longer struggles with this duality and this has given him new focus and purpose in his war on crime. However, in Internet 3.0, Bruce has difficulty in splitting his focus between the Bruce and Batman avatars.

This shows that now that the synthesis is complete, he is having difficulty being of two minds again.

In the previous issue, Batman explained to Raven that "Leviathan agents have infiltrated law enforcement, education, and medical facilities in your area." In this issue, Oracle explains to Batman that the virus is "digging deep into the architecture" of Internet 3.0 which is a metaphor for how Leviathan has been operating in the real world. Leviathan has been infiltrating places ignored places around the world and replacing key members of society. The virus, like Leviathan's agents, has been getting into the structure to dismantle everything.

We know that Leviathan is attacking Internet 3.0, so it's odd when one of the investors suggests that it is the old Internet trying to stop its replacement. It may be out of place, but the statement is a reminder of the youth motif that has run through the series. Most instances of generational conflict cast the new generation as being more dangerous. For instance, the first page of *Batman: The Return* has an old bat fighting younger bats before the old bat goes on to inspire Bruce Wayne. Sheikh Farouk's son Omar kills his father in the name of Leviathan. In the previous issue, the youth on the reservation rise up and battle Man-of-Bats. But, in this issue, the new Internet 3.0 isn't evil at all. It has been remade by Batman and it could be the older generation of Internet that resents the newer generation.

The motif of class warfare returns in full force in this issue as the virus starts attacking the avatars of the investors. Leviathan's virus manifests itself as a tentacle creature reaching out to either kill the investors or take all of their money (the narrative suggests both). It then transforms the avatar of the absurdly named "Belle Bourgeois" into a dog because she "sacrificed her handicapped daughter to a nursing home and her marriage to her career."

Leviathan's virus insists that the attacks on the wealthy are justified because of the sins of the investors and while Belle Bourgeois may have sacrificed her family for her career, the other investors don't seem so bad. Investor Ari Zamaroff's sin is that he is "a self-deluding fraud" and Chun Wei's only crime seems to be his ego. The investors may not be altruistic philanthropists, but they are far from the monsters that Leviathan tries to make them out to be thus making the class war seem incredibly petty and absurd. Yes, the main motivation for Leviathan's attack is to steal money from the investors in order to fund terrorism, but the attacks seem personal as well.

Leviathan is attacking their wealth because they represent the architecture of the world and Leviathan will replace that architecture.

But the class warfare motif gets a twist when it's discovered that one of the investors is the virus. A video game developer named Mr. Tanaka is revealed as the virus and he says, "Real risk is hard to find these days. I thought you'd enjoy a challenge with real repercussions."

The revelation that Tanaka's wealth has led him to boredom and now must create risk within Internet warfare is anticlimactic. If the virus was the old Internet seeking to destroy its predecessor, then it would fit with the motif of generational conflict. If the virus were programmed by poor, down-trodden hackers who worked for Leviathan, then it would connect to class warfare. But because the virus is programmed by a wealthy man, both motifs are out, even though they were suggested in the issue. Tanaka is a villain who fulfills the "bored billionaire" archetype that had been established during the International Club of Heroes arc. As soon after Tanaka reveals himself, he is contained by Oracle and defeated without any more problems.

In the epilogue, Oracle reveals that Tanaka was intending to launder the stolen money through Jezebel Jet's home country, Mtamba. The issue ends with the suggestion that Jet is still alive and that she is the leader of Leviathan.

Batman, Inc.: Leviathan Strikes

The release date for *Batman, Inc.* Vol. 1 #8 was 24 August 2011. In September 2011, DC began their New 52 initiative which relaunched their entire line of comics with new #1 issues and a new continuity. For Batman, this meant that he had been operating as a super-hero for only five years. Obviously, for a comic that draws so heavily upon past Batman continuity, this could be something of a problem. We'll discuss the effect that the New 52 had on Morrison's run in the last chapter of this book but for now, let's just focus on Stephanie Brown.

Over the years, Stephanie Brown (like every other Batgirl) has gone through a number of identity changes. When she first appeared in *Detective Comics* #648 (cover date September 1992) she was the amateur super-hero, Spoiler. Twelve years later, she briefly took up the mantle of Robin and was quickly killed off. Then, in 2008, she was revealed to never have died at all. Finally, she took on the mantle of Batgirl in August 2009.

Stephanie is a fan-favorite character, but the New 52 initiative would replace her with the original Batgirl, Barbara Gordon. Fans were understandably upset with her replacement and then, three months into the New 52, *Batman, Inc.: Leviathan Strikes* was released featuring Stephanie Brown in her last appearance as Batgirl complete with the editor's note that "The events of this issue take place before *Flashpoint* and *The New 52*" reminding readers to not get their hopes up. *Leviathan Strikes* combines what would have been issues #9 and #10 of the first volume of *Batman, Inc.* into one issue. The first chapter of this issue is Stephanie Brown's swan song and it is wonderful.

Chapter one centers around the reeducation motif as Stephanie infiltrates an all-girl school that trains the next generation of terrorists. On the first page, Stephanie is shown with a noose around her neck, surrounded by girls wearing skull masks and dressed in Kathy Kane's Batwoman costume. The girls chant, "We have no fear of death for we are dead! We are dead! We are dead! All hail Leviathan!"

The scene recalls the prologue to issue #5 when Batwing tried liberating a Leviathan school. It will take more than a super-hero crashing the classroom to save the kids being brainwashed by Leviathan and that's where Stephanie comes in. Batman had told her to infiltrate St. Hadrian's school back in *Batman: The Return* and now we're seeing just how dangerous the school is.

Throughout the issue, there are a number of visual jokes as the teachers are drawn to look like pop stars. The narrative flashes back to Stephanie enrolling, and we see her first class features a teacher giving a lesson on how to make a grenade using household items. In this brief scene, the teacher looks similar to Katy Perry and the older teacher, Miss Hexley, resembles Madonna.

Next, Steph is assaulted in the girl's locker room. Four girls pull guns on her and one says, "We've heard your old man is Batman" showing the misinformation that still surrounds the myth of Batman. Stephanie easily defeats the girls but is taken down by another teacher who looks like the pop star Rihanna.

Outside the headmistress's office, Stephanie meets Jolisa Windsor, the daughter of a super-villain named the Highwayman who was mentioned in Morrison's run on *Batman and Robin* #7. The walls have pictures of past graduates of St. Hadrian's including Scorpiana. As Stephanie researches a past graduate of St. Hadrian's named Una Clairmont (who was last seen in issue #4 dressed in a Kathy Kane Batwoman costume), Jolisa notes that "Batwoman got her. And Miss Delicias."

Given that the students of St. Hadrians are female super-villain assassins, one could presume that the three assassins in *Batman* #670 from the "Resurrection of Ra's al Ghul" storyline were graduates of the school.

Stephanie's next class is at the shooting range where a teacher who looks like Lady Gaga instructs the girls to shoot at genitalia. Beyond being a school for terrorists, Stephanie reports that the girls "get hooked up with wealthy middle-aged men like movie directors, actors, or super crooks who can afford a teenage ninja as a bodyguard or an accessory" effectively making it a school for the hired help that every master criminal has in comics and movies.

Once Stephanie is accepted into the elite squad, she has to go through her final transformation at the hands of Professor Pyg's son, Johnny Valentine (who was last seen battling Batwoman in issue #4). The circular narrative has twisted back as the original Pyg transformed people into his Dollotrons and now his son transforms girls into "Death Girls of Leviathan" using the mind-control wafers that we saw in issue #7. Somehow, Pyg has learned that either Stephanie or Jolisa is a traitor and as he moves in for the kill, Stephanie breaks them out using various cosmetic death gadgets like a needle-shooting hairbrush and tear gas perfume.

It turns out that Batgirl isn't alone in her infiltration mission because Batman has also been on the grounds in hiding as the gardener. It isn't as if she needs any help, however, because Batgirl single-handedly takes down the team of Death Girls while Batman confronts Miss Hexley. And in the final pages of the chapter, Batgirl crashes through the window to take down Miss Hexley and save Batman.

There is something perfect about a school that trains side-kick villains but the addition of pop stars teaching the classes makes it even better. But when Stephanie remarks that all she can see is "young girls under the spell of unrealistic and unhealthy role models" we understand that the chapter was a commentary on pop culture icons. Metaphorically, St. Hadrian's returns to the theme of Leviathan's influence getting into the architecture of things, but the metaphor works on two levels: education and popstars.

Batgirl should be idolized. She's a clever hero with strong moral convictions and she doesn't need Batman to save her. Batgirl's mission was difficult, but Stephanie never seemed out of her depth. She was easily able to overcome all obstacles without any real trouble.

Meanwhile, the older, Madonna-like Miss Hexley is overseeing the oversexualized and violent pop star teachers of St. Hadrian's. The next generation of bad influences is being created in a school. Not only is the architecture of education being infiltrated, but pop music is as well. Morrison is no Puritan and he isn't arguing that Rihanna, Katy Perry, and Lady Gaga are evil. His argument is that kids are transformed by their pop culture. If pop music becomes enamored with glorifying violence (as it already has with sex), then a cultural transformation can occur.

But because Batgirl is so perfect in the comic and is so heroic, Morrison is also arguing that if kids read more Batgirl comics, then maybe they could transform the other way as well.

The opening sequence of chapter two returns to the diamond that Batman and Catwoman stole from Dr. Sivana in issue #1. Lucius Fox has been examining the diamond and says, "I don't know exactly what it is, but it has the potential to change the world." Bruce then asks about the Brunnian Ring symbol that he found after investigating Dr. Dedalus and Lucius describes it as a new type of matter like the diamond.

In this way, the diamond and the Brunnian ring are symbols for the Batman franchise. Like the diamond, Batman is unique. He's a creation that can fit into any kind of story. But the diamond is also an opposite symbol because it uses light and Batman uses dark. The Brunnian ring is eternal just as the idea of Batman is. After all, "Batman and Robin will never die." But also, in terms of the narrative itself, the diamond and the Brunnian ring are a clue as to the identity of Leviathan.

Grant Morrison has crafted a number of mysteries that involve identity throughout his tenure on Batman. The Black Glove, Oberon Sexton, El Penitente, the Domino Killer – all were overarching mysteries that kept readers guessing and rereading in order to hunt for clues. But, the identity of Leviathan is a mystery that trumps them all. With Leviathan, it could easily be one of two suspects.

Just as Dr. Hurt's presence could be felt throughout *Batman* and references to the Joker are throughout *Batman and Robin*, Kathy Kane's presence is felt throughout *Batman, Inc.* In a story about heroes who dress as Batman, we are reminded that Kathy was the first person to be like Batman. She is the daughter of Dr. Dedalus and formally worked with El Gaucho as part of Spyral. And given that the Death Girls of St. Hadrian's school are dressed in Batwoman costumes, it would appear that Kathy is connected there too. We are told that she is dead, but we are never shown how, so there is still a good chance that she is alive and the leader of Leviathan.

Jezebel Jet is less of a suspect because she was only briefly mentioned in issue #8. However, her former country of Mtamba is being used to launder money and it is the first place that Leviathan struck, so it is possible. Jet's connection to the Black Glove shows that she has the resources to be a terrorist. Though she was being tracked down by Talia al Ghul's ninja man-bats, we never see her dead body, so there is room for reasonable doubt that she could still be alive (a point that Tim Drake will make in this issue). Finally, the game-like relationship between Batman Incorporated and Leviathan harkens back to the game between Batman and the Black Glove, so a similar methodology is there as well.

After their discussion about the diamond and the Brunnian ring, Bruce and Lucius turn to the Bat-robots first seen in *Batman: The Return*. Lucius explains, "We can build a Bat-robot for around five thousand dollars. That's less than a family hatchback." Bruce responds, "A Batman in every home."

The idea of the "for-profit super-hero" is one that Morrison first explored in his single-issue of *WildC.A.T.s* (Dec 2006) when Hadrian wanted to introduce a Spartan robot in every home saying, "The family Spartan is revolutionizing the personal security industry. Thanks to Halo systems technology everyone can own a superhero. Your own personal man of steel at prices you and your family can afford." Morrison only wrote one issue of *WildC.A.T.s* before other obligations took his time, but the idea of personal, at-home super-heroes is an interesting one and it's good to see it return briefly here.

Then the narrative takes a dramatic shift as Batman, Dick Grayson Batman, Robin, and Red Robin are trapped by Dr. Dedalus. Our heroes must choose one of five doors to save himself and doom the others as every five minutes, another member of Batman Incorporated will die. Dick notes that the colors of the doors correspond to the different elements. The black door represents earth, red is fire, blue is water, and yellow is air. These elements should remind readers of Lord Death Man's murders based on the elements. Batman decides to enter the white door which he realizes is meant to represent the fifth element that Dedalus was trying to create with the Brunnian ring. From here, the narrative resembles an episode of the 60's British television series *The*

Prisoner. The narrative is filled with symbolism and the circular narrative turns in on itself multiple times to show the memory loss that is plaguing Batman.

Batman is wearing a breather when he enters Dedalus's lair and we see a number of henchmen already beaten on the ground showing that the hero has already been here once. Dedalus sits in a chair that is similar to Number 2's chair from *The Prisoner* and explains that the gas in the room is a "powerful mind-eroding agent" that "mimics some of the effects of Alzheimer's disease." The formula was developed by Lazlo Valentin who was transformed into Professor Pyg after enduring Dedalus's Labyrinth.

Dedalus describes his lair as the "belly of the beast" which was also used to describe the Heretic's birth in *Batman: the Return* from inside the belly of a whale. The "belly of the beast" was also part of Joseph Campbell's monomyth and is used to describe the hero's descent into the underworld to return transformed. Usually, this descent occurs in the middle of the story. Morrison has used this narrative device before in his Batman run most notably in *Batman: The Return of Bruce Wayne* where halfway through the series, Bruce enters the cave of the Migani and returns dressed in a costume like he would wear as Batman. Also, in *All-Star Superman*, Superman enters the underworld of Bizarroworld and returns changed and revitalized. Now that the first volume of *Batman, Inc.* is at its end, Batman must enter the underworld created by Dr. Dedalus and a change will occur.

Five minutes have passed for Batman and that means that a member of Batman Incorporated will die. The narrative shifts to Mtamba where it appears that the military has captured Desmond Zavimbi (later named "David Zavimbi") for being the vigilante Batwing. In a classic bait-and-switch plot, "Batwing" breaks in and kidnaps Zavimbi to solidify the hero's alibi. This type of plot is classic Batman and it's a fun twist here. As Zavimbi suits up in his Batwing armor, he begins to explain, "Everything about Jet ... Jezebel Jet ... It's not what he thinks ... I found out who's really in charge here!" Before he is interrupted and he remarks, "My God, is that – bat wings?" which is a blatant clue to the identity of Leviathan.

Back in Dedalus's labyrinth, Batman is helpless as time keeps ticking away. Dedalus says, "We take our memories for granted, never imagining the day must come when they, too, will walk out on us." While it may not be intentional on Morrison's part, Dedalus's words are interesting when compared to the New 52's change in continuity. Readers have taken Batman's continuity for granted and just presumed that it was always there to be mined and used for new stories. With the New 52, much of Batman's history was erased effectively walking out on the reader much like Dedalus's memories.

Five more minutes have passed and now it's the Hood who will suffer the consequences. He accesses Leviathan's files when he is caught by a man only seen in one small panel. Before shooting the Hood, the man says, "We're two of a kind, we double agents, eh? But my true loyalty was always to Spyral, and I answer to the headmistress herself. Deuces high, old chap."

The Hood's role in *Batman, Inc.* is a complex one. He is a super-hero, a member of Batman Incorporated, and a spy who works for Spyral which may be affiliated with Leviathan. The Hood is the culmination of *every* espionage trope possible which makes him an interesting character, but his lack of development until late in the next volume of *Batman, Inc.* is a little disappointing.

Batman relives the death of his mother and laments, "No matter how fast... or strong... or clever I can make myself... I never get there in time." This shows that Batman is nearly broken. Bruce Wayne can invest as much money as he wants into Batman Incorporated, but he can never bring his parents back. Dedalus has stripped away Batman's altruism and revealed it as a selfish excuse to undo the past. As Batman rips a pearl necklace from Pyg's mother of nails, the pearls break and we're reminded of Martha Wayne's death. The pearls then turn into Dedalus's chair showing that the symbol of Batman's beginning has circled back to what appears to be his ending.

Then there is a brief scene as Dick, Damian, and Tim battle Dedalus agents to discover that they are brainwashed members of Batman Incorporated. Ever-impetuous, Damian enters a red door to find his father.

Now, Batman is in a decrepit room where he finds the dead body of Dr. Dedalus. The generational conflict motif returns as Dedalus brags that in his younger days, he would have easily beaten Batman. Just as the next generation is a threat to Batman, Batman is a threat to Dedalus and the previous generation. As Batman investigates the body of Dedalus, he is attacked from behind by El Gaucho and we are reminded that Gaucho once worked as Agent-33 for Spyral under Dedalus.

One last time, the narrative shifts to agents of Batman Incorporated. This time, it is the Outsiders investigating the Leviathan satellite when they meet Lord Death Man. On the next page, we see Oracle taking control of the Bat-robots as the satellite of the Outsiders explodes. Morrison isn't killing the

Outsiders, though. Metamorpho is part of the team and he escaped the Justice League's exploding satellite in the first issue of Morrison's *JLA* making the narrative spiral go beyond Morrison's tenure on Batman.

Dr. Dedalus's own story spirals back to the beginning as he unsheathes a blade from the cane given to him by Adolf Hitler. The recording of Dedalus explains that he has "hung a necklace of deadly meta-bombs around the world like precious pearls." Presumably, the meta-bombs are made from the Brunnian ring. In Batman's eyes, the ring is a renewable energy source, but to Dedalus, it is just another weapon. The imagery of the pearl recalls Martha Wayne's necklace as well making the pearls an object of creation (for Batman) and destruction.

El Gaucho reveals that he was always on Batman's side and after giving Batman the antidote to the mind-eroding gas, he attempts to stop Dedalus. Unfortunately, Dedalus stabs Gaucho in the neck and then returns to torturing Batman. Dedalus has an interesting line of dialogue where he says that he will kill everything that matters to Batman "like you killed my daughter's love for me!" It's an oddly humanizing moment. A Nazi-scientist/international terrorist blames Batman for the loss of love from his daughter.

Batman is only able to stop the meta-bombs because Damian kills Dedalus using the knife from Hitler's cane. The narrative spirals back as Dedalus's end came from his beginning. But the scene is also tragic as we feel Damian's pain. While he was no stranger to killing during "Batman and Son," he had atoned for his sins to become a hero worthy of the mantle of Batman. Now, his only option to save his father was to kill and as we know from the first arc in *Batman, Inc.,* Batman believes, "My people have to be better than that." Damian's first kill was a sign of his immaturity, but this kill is a sign of the tragedy that will always fill his life. Here, after entering the underworld within the belly of the beast, Batman wasn't transformed; it was his relationship with Damian that went through a transformation.

For one panel, the narrative switches to the headmistress whose face is never shown, but judging from her haircut, it appears to be Kathy Kane. She is talking with "matron" on the phone meaning that she couldn't be the leader of Leviathan despite all of the clues that lead to that deduction.

Batman realizes that Dedalus was "misdirection to waste our resources on the eve of war." Just like in issue #5, we realize that the mysteries of Dr. Dedalus are just a smokescreen for the larger mystery of Leviathan.

Finally, Batman discovers that Jezebel Jet had been decapitated as the narrative reaches its climax (or perhaps Morrison is making a rather dark joke with Batman discovering Jezebel as the conflict "comes to a head"). On a red phone that resembles the one Adam West used in the 60s *Batman* TV series, Batman listens as the leader of Leviathan explains her identity, "You thought I'd just forget what you did to me? What you took from me? 'Leviathan!' Give or take four letters, I practically signed my masterpiece. Oh, my darling detective ... I offered you a way out. But now I must destroy you ... completely. You wanted this."

The final page reveals that Talia al Ghul is the leader of Leviathan with the Heretic from *Batman: The Return* standing beside her throne. This revelation is brilliant because it was never obvious before. However, after the reveal, there are a number of red flags that pop up in this issue. Prior to this issue, the two major suspects were Kathy Kane and Jezebel Jet – both former lovers of Batman. However, those were just red herrings for another former lover. Then, the diamond and the Brunnian ring form a "diamond ring" – a joke and a call back to Talia's proposal to Bruce that he joins her and Damian. Of course, Batwing's reference to the sound of "bat wings" is a blatant reference to her ninja man-bats but Metamorpho's observation that Leviathan moves "like nomads" is a more subtle clue to Talia's background.

Also, given the narrative spirals that have occurred through the series, it should come as no surprise that the final villain is the first of Morrison's run, but that's why the mystery was so great. No other mystery in Morrison's tenure on Batman has been crafted as perfectly as this one. With the Black Glove, there weren't enough clues for the reader to guess that the answer was Dr. Hurt. And while Dr. Hurt could have been the devil or Thomas Wayne, the reveal that he was Thomas Wayne from the 1700s mixed with Darkseid was great, but never something readers could solve on their own. Oberon Sexton could only ever have been the Joker or Bruce Wayne. El Penitente could only ever have been Dr. Hurt. But, Leviathan could have been one of two women, and when it is revealed to be a third woman, it is all the more amazing.

Now that Batman Incorporated is in shambles at the hands of Dr. Dedalus, Damian has a half-a-billion dollar bounty on his head, and Leviathan is revealed, the final part of Morrison's Batman drama is ready to begin.

Talia al Ghul, Mother Terrorist

Despite being a mass-murdering terrorist, Talia al Ghul is a sympathetic character when viewed correctly. When reviewing Talia's role in Morrison's *Batman*, one has to remember that she was raised by a nearly immortal terrorist, so everything in her world would be, as Aquazon says in *Batman, Inc.* Vol. 1 #2, "hyper-mega." Talia is relatable because her background is no different than people in our own world. She is a daughter spoiled by her emotionally distant father, a spurned lover by the world's most perfect man, and a betrayed mother by a son that she has done everything for. It just so happens that she is also the leader of a terrorist organization, which means her reactions to not getting what she wants are "hyper-mega." As the spoiled daughter of a terrorist, she didn't get a car when she turned 16, she got a secret lair under London. As a spurned lover, she doesn't key her former lover's car, she creates a terrorist organization to destroy him. As a betrayed mother, she doesn't write her child out of her will, she puts a bounty on his head.

It can be easy to write Talia off as just being evil for the sake of it, but that is disingenuous to the character and oversimplifies her emotions and motivations. She is a woman with her own wants, needs, beliefs, and desires, who happens to have the means to get what she wants. Anything less is unacceptable.

"Batman & Son"

Talia wants her family to be whole and tries to get Bruce's attention by kidnapping him. Her methods may seem extreme, but we can excuse their extremity due to her upbringing (just as we excuse some of Damian's faults). In a world of super-heroes, this is how a spurned lover tries to get her husband back: by stealing a mad scientist's serum and creating ninja man-bats.

After Batman accuses her of carrying on her father's work, Talia asserts her independence saying, "This is my very own little magnum opus." She intends "to hold the whole world hostage to a new kind of terror." Both are hints that Talia will be the primary antagonist later. While Ra's al Ghul was an environmental terrorist, Talia will become a terrorist powered by capitalism. Her father's old ways of terrorism are gone and now she will usher in a new age.

On the first page of *Batman* #658, Talia reveals her motivations as she films a female hostage and tells her, "It's not really about the flying bat-ninjas or the terrorism... not even about the kidnapping. It's not about you at all. This is all about me. And what I want. As a wife and mother, I'm sure you'll understand." Terrorism isn't her motivation – it's a means to end. Ultimately, she wants to be part of a family unit with Bruce and Damian.

And at the end of Morrison's first arc, Talia tries reasoning with her lover. She says, "Reform me. And if you do, I'll combine my vast resources with yours to fight crime at your side... and together we can raise our son to be master of the Earth."

Note that she doesn't say, "Join me." Talia asks to be reformed and vows to "fight crime" and Batman refuses her. She has shown a willingness to change and do good things for the world, but she is denied by the man that she loves and responds by saying, "Then it's war. And you're responsible... for people like us, the world is the gameboard, and nations are pawns" which is the beginning of their war and the first instance of games being part of Morrison's run.

Resurrection of Ra's al Ghul

While this crossover was poorly executed, it is important in showing Talia as a sympathetic and concerned mother. Ra's al Ghul wants to return to the land of the living by possessing Damian's body and despite Talia's loyalty to her father, she still wishes to preserve her son. She values his life not because he is part of a larger plan, but because he is her son. This bond she feels with her child makes his betrayal that much more difficult for her to handle during *Batman and Robin*.

"R.I.P."

Besides "Batman & Son" and "The Resurrection of Ra's al Ghul," Talia had a few brief appearances. In *Batman* #665, she seems jealous of Bruce's romance with Jezebel Jet. In #675, after Damian deduces that someone is out to get Batman, Talia shows concern by saying, "That sensitivity is something else you've inherited from me. Come, we need a plan..." Despite her declaration of war on Batman, she still seems to care for the hero and wants to protect him. She and Damian have minor parts in "R.I.P." but they save Commissioner Gordon and send ninja man-bats after Jezebel Jet to get revenge for Batman.

Batman and Robin

This is the turning point for Talia and pivotal in understanding her motivations for her war with Batman. Damian has become Robin and is fighting crime alongside Dick Grayson. After he is hurt by the assassin Flamingo, Damian returns to his mother to get his spine repaired. While Damian is being repaired, Talia looks on and admires her son. She tells Alfred that Damian will "stride across the 21st century like a new Alexander" and that "he'll accept his destiny as the heir of al Ghul soon enough." She truly believes that despite his time as Robin, he will turn his back on that life and return to her.

During the "Batman vs. Robin" story arc, Talia says that Damian is squandering his potential by playing crimefighter and Damian's response takes away some of our sympathy for Talia. He says, "I saw you rarely during my education and upbringing, mother. I knew you by reputation alone. When we were formally introduced at my 8th birthday party, it was like meeting a movie star."

However, Peter Tomasi's *Batman and Robin* after the launch of the New 52 changes this and shows that Talia had raised him all along. Granted, she was still a ruthless mother, but she is part of his life. Therefore, we can see Damian's speech here as exaggeration.

After replacing Damian's spine, Talia added another enhancement that allowed her to take control of his body. If Damian was going to use his free will against her, then she was going to take his free will away from him. Once the control in his spine was shorted out, Talia gives Damian an ultimatum – give up being Robin or become an enemy of the al Ghul family.

It may seem like she is in the wrong because the audience is on Damian's side, but her perspective is important. Here is a woman who had a child with her "beloved" and has raised him on her own. When she tries to bring the family together, she is spurned by her former lover. Then, her son renounces his name and declares himself an enemy of her family. Whatever part of Talia that was loving and reasonable dies when Damian forsakes the al Ghul name. And, really, who could blame her?

When Kathy Kane rejected Bruce Wayne's love, his ability to live in a Bat-Family died with it. Now, Talia's ability to reconcile with her former lover died with Damian's rejection. From here on, it is all-out war.

Batman, Inc. Vol. 2 #2

The second issue of *Batman, Inc.* Vol. 2 provides a complete history of Talia al Ghul which is essential in understanding her motivations. The issue begins with Ra's al Ghul meeting Talia's mother, Melisande, at a rock concert. Melisande is impressed that the bands have raised $40 million for Africa but Ra's dismisses it by saying, "These wealthy, privileged entertainers could have scraped together that amount in five minutes backstage. Where is the country's aristocracy?"

This is the philosophy that will provide the foundation for Leviathan. Ra's al Ghul wants to use his wealth to empower the poor to become his soldiers just as Talia will later say in issue #6 of the series, "I give them guns and slogans to chant. I put the poor to work building the empire of al Ghul."

In the present, Talia visits her father in his mountain base. A flashback shows Ra's climbing the same mountain with a baby Talia. When he reaches the top of the mountain, Ra's holds his infant daughter above his head and declares "One day. This world will belong to you, my love." Ra's al Ghul is rarely depicted as a caring father and though it's a brief moment, it shows that Talia was promised the world from birth.

Talia confronts her father and explains that the Leviathan flag is "a mix of warlike colors and terrifying female archetypes like Kali Ma, Medusa, Tiamat." Just as Batman is a synthesis of different pulp elements, Talia has become a synthesis of different female archetypes. Kali Ma is the Hindu goddess of time and death, but she also represents change. Morrison has transformed Batman from world's greatest detective to Bat-God businessman and Talia represents the change back to a darker tone for the hero. Medusa is, of course, the snake-haired monster of Greek myth who turned men to stone with a look. Later in

Talia sits on her throne with the Heretic next to her. The final page of *Batman, Inc.: Leviathan Strikes* #1 (Feb 2012). Art by Chris Burnham. Copyright © DC Comics.

this issue, Talia will meet her mother who points to a star called Beta Persei that is part of the Medusa head in the Perseus constellation. Beta Persei is also called "the Demon Star" or "Algol" meaning "al Ghul." Finally, Tiamat is the Mesopotamian chaos monster and goddess of the ocean who mated with the god Abzu to create younger gods, which is clearly a rich metaphor for Bruce and Talia's union to create Damian.

Ra's then tells Talia that he can't allow her to go to war with Batman and declares that she is his prisoner saying, "by answering my summons, by coming here, of your own free will, to my lair — you placed yourself at my mercy and may now consider yourself my prisoner." Note Ra's use of the words "free will" which is an important idea in relation to Talia. She gave Bruce the choice to reform her and he denied her. Talia allowed Damian to choose to be an al Ghul or a Wayne and the boy chose his father. Here, she is choosing to confront her father which has led to her being captured. Perhaps it is these three moments of free will, that led Talia to hate free will and caused her to be so controlling over the Heretic.

Another flashback sequence shows events that shaped Talia's childhood. One panel depicts Talia battling ninjas in the same pose as Damian's own origin story in *Batman* #666. Another shows her studying in the desert. A longer sequence shows the first time Talia witnessed her father being immersed in the Lazarus Pit. Talia kicks a tree down much like Bruce Wayne did in the pages of Frank Miller's *Batman: Year One*. She is given horses and blimps and after Ra's points out that he has given her everything she has ever wanted or needed, Talia responds, "I needed a mother."

In the case of both nature and nurture, Talia was raised to be a terrorist. Without a caring mother, Talia's upbringing was solely influenced by her super-villain father. Therefore, it should come as no surprise that she has raised Damian to be a terrorist as well.

After being captured by ninja man-bats in *Batman* #656, Batman learns that Talia has a secret lair underneath London. We are shown Talia receiving the lair as a gift for her 16th birthday. The scene ends with Talia and Ubu defeating assassins sent by the Sensei. Ra's war with his own father the Sensei continues the generational conflict motif that will pervade *Batman, Inc.*, but it also shows that Talia has known war her whole life, so it should come as no surprise that she is so willing to go to war with Batman.

Then, the issue flashes back to Talia's first appearance in *Detective Comics* #411. She is kidnapped by a Dr. Darrk and a rogue faction of the Assassins League. In that issue, Batman dressed as an old woman to get aboard the train where Talia was being held hostage. The reminder that Batman once had to crossdress as an old woman shows that as absurd as some of Morrison's ideas are, they are no more absurd than some classic stories.

In the present, Talia shows that her love for Batman is completely gone as she blames Ra's for her feelings saying, "You maneuvered me into a one-sided love affair with that cold, driven man." She realizes that she never had feelings for him at all, but that her father manipulated her into loving him. It's an interesting revelation for her because she had always previously been devoted to her "beloved." Now, she is exercising her own free will and rebelling against both her father and her lover by extinguishing her feelings for Batman.

The closing pages show Talia seducing Bruce, nurturing Damian in a test tube, working with the Society of Super-villains from the *Villains United* miniseries that served as a prelude to *Infinite Crisis*, placing a spy in Dr. Hurt's Black Glove organization, and the confrontation between Talia and Batman at the end of the "Batman & Son" story. These scenes show the different sides of Talia: the mother, the villain, and the continuously spurned lover. The issue ends with Talia revealing that Ra's al Ghul's assassins work for her and she is no one's prisoner.

Conclusion

In a 23 March 2013 interview with the Huffington Post, Morrison discusses the overarching idea of family in his time on Batman:

> Well it seemed natural to the genesis of Batman, you know, a way to get to the roots of these characters and to the engine that makes them work. Batman is all about the death of his parents. So I kind of thought that Bruce Wayne, for all that he loves his parents, there must be parts of him that hates his father for not being Batman that night and saving everyone and there must be parts of him that hates his mother for leaving him alone in this bizarre and peculiar life, so what I did was base my entire run on this idea of the bad father, the bad mother, and the bad son.
>
> And the bad father was Dr Hurt. And in the story the bad mother is Talia and the bad son is Damian, and he becomes a good son in the end but it's too late and he dies because really what he represents is this whole twisted loss that's at the heart of the Batman myth. But yeah, it was all based on that original idea about Batman watching his parents die and how that must have affected him and how it affects all his relationships

and all his battles with villains, it's all in there. So we just made it a bit more obvious by playing on, very specifically, is it a bad father, is it a bad mother? And here's a bad little kid who becomes good, which is Batman's story as well.

While Dr. Hurt has no redeeming qualities and Damian becomes a hero, Morrison is more ambiguous with how the audience should feel about Talia. Yes, she is a ruthless leader of a terrorist organization set out to destroy the world, but circumstances have led her to this point. Her father raised her to believe that she would inherit the world one day and after being abandoned by everyone she has ever cared for, one can almost empathize with her rage.

Looking at the issue of free will complicates things further. Batman and Damian were given choices by Talia and when they disagreed with her plans, she wanted revenge. Thus, we can interpret Talia's revenge as an act of her own free will meaning that she is taking ownership over the consequences of her actions. Now that everyone has turned against her, she is embracing her role as super-villain and has no regrets.

From here, Talia will become a much more traditional villain, but that stems from a very complex origin story that makes her the most interesting, complicated villain of Morrison's time on Batman.

The End of an Era

The New 52 initiative caused all sorts of problems for *Batman, Inc.* In terms of publication dates, the New 52 debuted in September 2011, which caused issues #9 and #10 of *Batman, Inc.* Vol. 1 to be collected into one issue, which was released in December 2011. Then, the second volume of *Batman, Inc.* debuted in May 2012.

While most of Batman's history remained intact in the New 52 universe, much of it was condensed into a five year period. All of the male Robins from Dick Grayson to Damian Wayne remained in continuity meaning that Batman had four different side-kicks in the span of five years. However, Barbara Gordon is the only woman to have ever been Batgirl meaning that both Stephanie Brown and Cassandra Cain were written out of continuity. With Barbara back as Batgirl, that leaves Oracle out of Batman Incorporated as well. Then, there is the issue with Damian's age – Batman is the father of 10 year old Damian, but Bruce Wayne has only been Batman for five years.

But, the continuity errors don't end with the Bat-family. The Justice League has only been a team for five years and in that time, they had only let one other member onto the team and that was Martian Manhunter. So, Metamorpho was never a member of the JLA and Morrison's run on *JLA* never occurred – a detail that will be contradicted in the first issue of the New 52 *Batman, Inc.*

The New 52 was meant to restart DC Comics with fresh takes on classic characters which meant that many redundant characters were written out of continuity. Barry Allen was the Flash, so Wally West and Jay Garrick didn't need to exist. Jaime Reyes was Blue Beetle, so Ted Kord wasn't necessary. Cassandra

Sandsmark is Wonder Girl, so no need for Donna Troy. But the Batman franchise (and the Green Lantern franchise) was successful prior to the New 52 so there was no need to change what wasn't broken. Aside from the success of the Batman franchise, Damian Wayne was integral to the story of *Batman, Inc.*, so erasing all of the Robins except for Dick Grayson wasn't really an option.

But instead of viewing the New 52 as the cause of the continuity problems in *Batman, Inc.*, maybe we should see it the other way. If *Batman, Inc.* had concluded before the launch of the New 52, then maybe all of the Robins except for Dick Grayson would have disappeared. Then, the fact that Barbara Gordon was the only woman to ever have been Batgirl wouldn't have been so bad. Or even better, all of the Robins could have been erased except for Dick Grayson and *Batman, Inc.* could have remained in an alternate universe set in pre-New 52 continuity. The idea isn't so far-fetched given that the alternate universe title *Earth 2* debuted the same month as the second volume of *Batman, Inc.*

One could easily pick apart all of the continuity errors that are present in *Batman, Inc.*, but that would undermine the story that Morrison is trying to tell. Instead, it's best to view the series as an example of Morrison's idea of Hypertime.

The easiest way to explain Hypertime is to imagine a river. The river is Batman's continuity and it contains all of the things that will always stay true to Batman's story (the pearls, the theatre, the killer, the parents, the bat). But then, sometimes, the river branches off to form tributaries which might rejoin the river later on. We could view these as the more specific elements of Batman continuity that some writers address but don't have to. For instance, Joe Chill was named the murderer of Thomas and Martha Wayne in *Batman* #47 (cover date June – July 1948), but after the event comic *Zero Hour* rewrote DC's history, the killer was unknown. Then, after Grant Morrison began his run on *Batman* with the mission statement that every Batman story happened, Joe Chill returned to being the murderer of Thomas and Martha Wayne. The tributary known as Joe Chill broke away from the river of Batman continuity and then returned.

We could go on and on with the water metaphor, but let's conclude with streams and creeks which branch off further and end. In terms of the continuity metaphor, these are the dead-end stories that have their uses but are usually never again referred to. In *Detective Comics* #328 (June 1964), Bruce Wayne's faithful butler, Alfred, was killed. Later, in *Detective Comics* #356, Alfred is revealed to have been revived by a mad scientist and transformed into the super-villain, the Outsider. It's a story so ridiculous that even Morrison wouldn't reference it during his tenure on Batman, but Geoff Johns would later rework this idea into his *Forever Evil* storyline with the Alfred of an evil parallel universe going by the name.

Hypertime allows for writers to take old stories and use them for their own narrative ends or it allows for readers to just forget those stories ever existed. With Hypertime, the only relevant parts of continuity are the ones that are immediately relevant to the writer at the time. Joe Chill wasn't Thomas and Martha Wayne's killer unless the writer wanted him to be. Alfred Pennyworth never died and became the Outsider unless someone wanted to revive that plot thread. Hypertime may be an easy narrative out, but considering that comic books allow for *anything* to happen, then Hypertime shouldn't be such a difficult narrative pill to swallow.

Batman, Inc. is an exercise in Hypertime. The details of the New 52 continuity aren't necessary to enjoying *Batman, Inc.* because almost any Pre-New 52 continuity can still be brought up and used. So, it's best to sit back, relax, and consider this story to be set in Morrison Continuity where everything is "Hyper-Mega."

Beyond the issues with continuity are the problems with publication. A lot of the momentum built up in the first volume of the series was lost in the five month gap between *Leviathan Strikes* and the first issue of the new volume. Then, the series suffers a number of starts and stops in the issues themselves. Issue #1 begins the war between Batman and Leviathan. Issue #2 pauses the narrative to tell a flashback story with Talia. On July 20, 2012, a shooter opened fire on the crowd at the premiere of the Batman film *The Dark Knight Rises* and out of respect for the families, DC Comics chose to push back the publication of issue #3. Then, in September 2012, between the cliffhanger in issue #3 and its resolution in issue #4, every comic published by DC was given a #0 issue to tell a backstory of the title. Issue #5 told a future story of Damian as Batman which further interrupted the main narrative. Issues #6 through #10 furthered the narrative, but Morrison takes issue #11 off and is replaced by Chris Burnam.

These interruptions in the narrative made *Batman, Inc.* somewhat difficult to follow as they were being released. But, taken as a whole, Morrison does an excellent job in tying up all the loose ends from his time on *Batman* and hits all the right plot points to finish off a perfect story of magic, corporations, terrorism, generations, and family.

Batman, Inc. Vol. 2 #1

When Bruce returned from his journey through time, he said that he saw a vision of two graves and Gotham in flames. Now, at the start of the second volume of *Batman, Inc.*, Bruce stands before two graves and says, "Tell the others it's over, Alfred. Batman. All of it. This madness is over," just before he is arrested by Commissioner Gordon.

It's a strong teaser that sets a different tone for this volume compared to the previous one. In the first volume, Lord Death Man executed Mr. Unknown in the opening pages, and as dark as that was, there was something fun in the absurdity of the characters. But the gravesite is a reminder that Batman began with the deaths of his parents and now he will end with two more deaths. The spiral narrative has now reached all the way to the beginning of Batman's creation and returns here to the end.

The scene is also symbolic of the end of Morrison's time with Batman as well. Bruce states, "this madness is over" which could be interpreted as the madness that Morrison brought to the character by bringing back the bizarre, sci-fi ideas from the 60s. Alfred asks, "Isn't that exactly what they want, Master Bruce." While he is talking about Leviathan, he is also talking about critics of the first volume of *Batman, Inc.* By setting the scene in a rainy graveyard, Morrison is setting up the reader to believe that the fun days are over and this will mark the return of the dark, brooding, and defeated Batman.

After the opening page, there is a two page spread of Bruce and Damian leaping from the Batmobile dressed as Batman and Robin. A caption notes that it is "one month previously" which tells us that it will be a month of hell to come. Next to Batman's knee is a paper sack for a restaurant called "Dark Tower" which is a reference to Robert Browning's poem "Childe Roland to the Dark Tower Came." The inspiration for Browning's poem comes from a song sung by Edgar when he was pretending to be mad in William Shakespeare's *King Lear.* The word "childe" means "unproven knight," so Roland is an inexperienced knight on a quest for the mysterious Dark Tower. Though Batman is no inexperienced knight, there are a number of similarities between the hero and Roland.

Roland is haunted by the deaths of fallen comrades just as Batman has been before. Both Roland and Batman have dark, gloomy personalities. Also,

Roland's creation was from Edgar in *King Lear* who just appears to be insane – just as the very idea of Batman appears to be insane but is constructed from the zen-like mind of Bruce Wayne. The Dark Tower can be interpreted as a hero's quest that will only end in tragedy just as Batman's own mission can never be won.

The real irony is that the connection between Browning's poem and Batman comes from trash. Browning's poem is a masterpiece and one that has inspired a number of writers over the years and is far from "trash." But, Batman is also a masterpiece in his own way. He's a hero who has had enduring power and provided inspiration as well. Morrison isn't really saying that Browning's poem is trash; he is showing that Batman can be as enduring as a classic piece of literature.

Batman and Robin are chasing a gang of men dressed as goats into a slaughterhouse. Even though the fight scene isn't filled with gratuitous violence, it is still bloody and horrific as cows are murdered, Robin slices a criminal's legs, and a buzz saw slices through a cow's stomach, spilling its contents. As Robin interrogates a criminal, a sniper tries picking off the Boy Wonder, but kills the goat criminal instead. Symbolically, the scene foreshadows Damian's impending death and establishes that this series will be a bloodbath.

Robin's would-be assassin is a man who calls himself "Goatboy" named after the sexual deviant character created by comedian Bill Hicks. Goatboy provides narration for this issue and his story is similar to Thomas and Martha Wayne's killer, Joe Chill. Goatboy's ex-wife had died of cancer and he took up a life of crime to provide for his child. Later in this issue, he acknowledges that he briefly felt guilty for trying to kill a kid that was the same age as his own, but the bounty Leviathan put on Damian's head was too much to resist. Despite being a murderer, Goatboy isn't an evil person. He has a family and wants to provide for that family like most people.

The goat is a multi-faceted symbol that will reappear throughout this volume of *Batman, Inc.* Because goats are anti-social animals, they represent independence, and their natural propensity for climbing makes them symbols of high-achievement as well. Goats are also used as a symbol for lechery, perhaps due to the goat's association with the Greek god of wine and sexuality, Pan. The goat is also the symbol of the demon Baphomet who represents duality. All four of these characteristics (independence, achievement, sexuality, and duality) are aspects associated with Batman as well. So, when Goatboy reveals that the word "Gotham" means "home of goats," we can also interpret this as a home for all of the symbolism that derives from the goat.

In this issue, the assassin Goatboy is being associated with the term "scapegoat" which is a Biblical term associated with people placing their sins upon an animal and releasing it into the wilderness in an act of redemption. Though Talia has placed a bounty on her own son's head, Goatboy acts as the scapegoat for her sin. She isn't guilty for Damian's death because she didn't really kill Damian, Goatboy did. However, Goatboy is also innocent because of his intentions, so by creating a scapegoat and through some leaps in logic, no one is at fault.

Of course, this sort of logical fallacy leads us down a path where murder can easily be justified and is another example of how Leviathan is the opposite of Batman. For Batman, murder is never justified no matter what the circumstance and Leviathan can twist logic to make murder seem acceptable. But Batman's stance on murder becomes much more situational when the murderer in question is Batman's own son. Damian appears to always be the exception to the rule. He is the first part of forgotten continuity that Morrison brought back in his run on *Batman*. Damian has killed three people (the Spook, Dr. Dedalus, and Nobody from Peter Tomasi's *Batman and Robin* run in the New 52), but Batman will keep him around and continue to lecture him about the immorality of murder.

After their battle in the slaughterhouse, Batman notes that the cows are branded with a two-horned star also known as the "demon star" and sign of the al Ghul family. Leviathan replaced people before, and now its influence is getting into food as well. Meanwhile, Robin declares himself a vegetarian and promptly adopts a contaminated cow, naming it "Bat-Cow." While the opening scene foreshadows the dark times ahead, the absurdity of Bat-Cow is a reminder that Morrison will still enjoy some fun, lighthearted moments. Also, with the numbers of the Bat-Family cut down after the New 52, adding Bat-Cow into the family is a sly poke at the corporate mentality that erased members of the Batman family. Stephanie Brown and Cassandra Cain are no longer part of the DC Universe, but they have been replaced by a sacrificial cow – a character that will later be written by the co-publisher of DC Comics, Dan Didio in the *Batman, Inc. Special.*

Morrison then shows a brief moment between father and son. While chasing after Goatboy, Batman lectures Robin on why killing is wrong. Damian threatens to leave the team and insults his father by saying, "I don't know why you bothered to come back from the dead."

Seeing that his conversation with Damian is turning hostile, Bruce changes the subject to compliment Damian on fixing the Waynetech finances. Damian responds, "I was trained to rule the world, father. Mother made sure I was educated to Ph.D. economics standard before my ninth birthday. Yet here I am, jumping around dressed as a super-hero to impress you."

It's a reminder that Damian is more than just Bruce's son or a mere super-hero. He was born and raised to be a warrior-king by his mother, and he turned his back on that empire in order to carry on his father's name. He rejected his al Ghul heritage and so it is more than a little frustrating to him that Bruce should repeatedly bring up his mistakes. Having Batman as a father would be rough, but Damian is up to the challenge.

Across town, Leviathan is meeting with the mob bosses of Gotham City. After Leviathan feeds one of the Brothers Grimm to his own brother, ninja man-bats take the remaining Grimm and drop him near Batman and Robin. Batman looks up to the sky and says, "Looks like your mother's trying to get my attention again," and in the next panel, Batman and Robin look at one another. It's a silent panel, but it's one that shows that despite their bickering, Bruce and Damian are in it together. The dark comedy of the scene masks the levels of metaphor that Morrison is playing with here.

The Brothers Grimm are among the most famous storytellers in the world. Over the years, their fairytales have been distilled into cute, frivolous movies for children, but in their original creation, some were incredibly dark. Forcing one Grimm brother to eat the other is a deeply disturbing act that instantly shows the depths of Leviathan's cruelty and foreshadows the recurring theme of the broken family or the loss of family. By creating the Brothers Grimm, Morrison has stayed within the motif of Gotham City fairytale villains such as Humpty Dumpty, the Mad Hatter, and Mr. Toad. By killing the remaining Brother Grimm in front of Batman, Morrison is signaling that this will be a "grim" story. He is openly challenging his critics and showing that if they want grim, then he will give them grim.

As absurd as Bat-Cow was, this scene in San Francisco is even more bizarre as a hooded man enters a sex shop and asks if his "perv suit" has arrived. The hooded man is British super-hero and super-spy, the Hood who was last seen being triple-crossed by Matron and apparently shot. Underneath the sex shop is the Batcave West complete with display costumes and a giant penny with a picture of Metamorpho's antagonist, Simon Stagg. All of the heroes who had allegedly died in the *Leviathan Strikes* special are revealed to be alive and eating fondue. Wingman reappears and establishes that "Batman put me in charge of this rabble." Batcave West simultaneously reminds readers of the "deaths" in *Leviathan Strikes*, of Wingman's important secret identity, and connects being a super-hero to sexual deviance. This bizarre scene is a far cry from the opening pages at the graveyard.

Back in Gotham, Batman orders Robin to return to the cave after their patrol because of the bounty on his head. When Damian notices that Batman seems happy that the world's most dangerous hired killers are in Gotham City, Batman responds, "It means they're all in Gotham right where we want them." Leviathan was always one step ahead of Batman in the first volume of *Batman, Inc.*, but now, Batman has the upper hand.

Then, Batman and Robin attack a gang that looks much like the mutant gang from Frank Miller's *The Dark Knight Returns*. The gang is loading Demon Star beef onto trucks thereby connecting Leviathan to the gang that will plague Batman in the future. As the issue comes to an end, Goatboy explains to Leviathan that he shot Batman in the head, but Batman is well-shielded and was just blinded. In that moment, Goatboy turned his rifle on Robin and killed him. The last page is a shot from Goatboy's cellphone that shows Batman holding what appears to be a dead Robin in his arms though it should be obvious that he isn't dead for a number of reasons.

Damian clearly isn't dead because the final shot has a hood covering his face showing no bullet hole. Next, the scene before was of the Dead Heroes Club – a team of Batman Incorporated heroes who everyone assumed were dead. Finally, Goatboy is telling the story to Leviathan rather than the reader seeing it occur on the page. All of the panels of Goatboy's story are from his perspective and what he thinks he saw. The bait-and-switch of Damian's death was meant to enrage the audience at the thought of his death so Morrison could trick the audience by showing the hero is alive. Morrison is setting up Damian's real death that will occur later in the run and because of this scene, Damian's actual death will still have readers questioning its validity.

But Damian's "death" here is another kind of circular narrative in a way. At the end of "R.I.P." it was suggested that Batman died battling Dr. Hurt. However, *Final Crisis* was still going on and we are eventually shown that

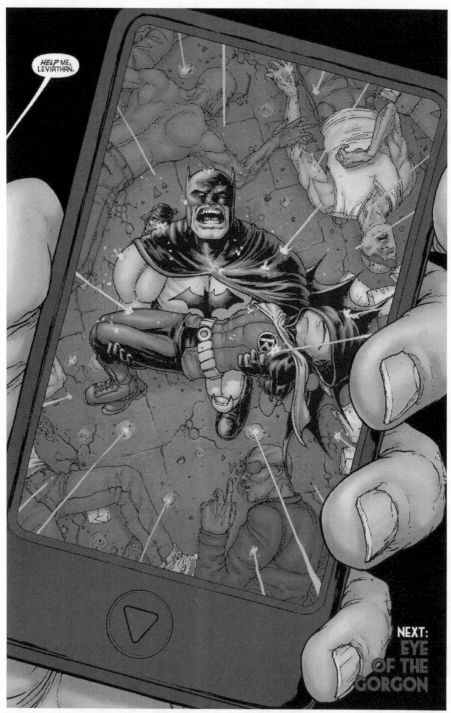

Batman holds a dead Robin's body. The final page of *Batman, Inc.* Vol. 2 #1 (July 2012). Art by Chris Burnham. Copyright © DC Comics.

Batman "dies" after being shot with Darkseid's Omega Effect. "R.I.P." was a bait-and-switch on Batman's death just as Damian's "death" is here. The father and the son both endure the same sort of narrative device.

Batman, Inc. Vol. 2 #3

Leviathan has bragged that its success comes from replacing key people in society and this issue begins with a glimpse at how that would work. It begins with an inner-city teacher being kidnapped and replaced by a representative from Leviathan. She places the Leviathan flag on the chalkboard, pulls a gun on her students, and begins by invoking class warfare, "You're being groomed as slaves, while the rich mock you with the eternal promise of a success you'll never achieve." The narration notes that "the school was in a tough neighborhood where many of the students were more or less neglected by their families."

While socio-economic status had been addressed before in the battle between Batman and crime, this is the first time that Morrison uses the lack of a family as motivation for crime. Leviathan replaces the family that these kids never had and raises them to become terrorists. Batman creates his own family and raises heroes. Even though Bruce Wayne was still missing in the time stream, it's a sense of family obligation that causes Damian to leave his mother and take up the mantle of Robin. Without the honor that comes from family, people are influenced to replace family with whatever sense of belonging they can experience.

But teachers aren't the only ones being replaced. Police officers, social workers, judges and more are replaced so that the whole system changes from one of law to one of Leviathan. Morrison is showing the power of Leviathan's super-sigil and how it differs from standard terrorism. In "Pop Magic!" Morrison discusses how the Nazis operated under old world imperialism, writing,

> The visionary savages still thought world domination meant tramping over the "enemy" and seizing his real estate. If only they'd had the foresight to see that global domination has nothing to do with turf and everything to do with media they would have anticipated corporate stealth-violence methods and combined them with their undoubted design sense; the rejected artists who engineered the Third Reich might have created the 20th century's first global superbrand and spared the lives of many potential consumers.

In *Batman, Inc.*, Morrison is taking the concept of the global superbrand and applying it to terrorism. Al Qaeda uses bombs and guns to kill the enemy, but Leviathan silently invades and changes the enemy from within. Leviathan is what happens when terrorism turns corporate and starts buying out the competition.

Elsewhere, in a night club, Bruce Wayne is dressed in his alter ego of "Matches" Malone to get information about Leviathan from a mob boss named "Fry" (formally known as "Small Fry"). Fry's there to attend the wake for the mob bosses the Brothers Grimm who were killed by Leviathan in issue #1. When Fry asks why Matches won't take off his glasses, the undercover criminal practically admits to being Batman by saying that he has porphyria and his "eyes water in the light," and his "skin burns like a vampire on vacation."

After some goons threaten lounge singer Lumina Lux (whose first and last name both mean "light"), Matches steps in with his crew of thugs who are clearly El Gaucho, the Hood, and Batwing in disguise. But before he can get more information about the deaths of the Brothers Grimm, Batman arrives and breaks up the party. We learn that it was Dick Grayson dressed as Batman, who in turn is imitating Batman dressed as Matches Malone – which is an interesting twist on an old trope. Normally, someone dresses as Batman to make people believe that Bruce and Batman are two different people. This time, it is used to show that Matches and Batman aren't the same.

Back at the Batcave, we learn that Damian somehow survived the assassin's bullet from issue #1, but it is never explained exactly how. Dick asks Damian, "How does it feel to be the new dead Robin?" which is a joke about how clearly *not dead* he is, but also foreshadowing Damian's real death later. Damian will be the next dead Robin and is right now living on borrowed time.

Bruce unveils Talia's web – a visual representation of how every villain from the start of Morrison's time on Batman connects to Leviathan. It's an impressive graph that is fun to study even if it leaves the three ghosts of Batman and Darkseid off of it. Batman insists that Leviathan is at the center of it all, but Damian suggests "we're at the center of all this" which recalls Morrison's first arc "Batman & Son" where Batman's rejection of Talia has led to this war. Damian is willing to see Batman's decisions leading to this war even if Bruce isn't.

Alfred is brushing down Bat-Cow and shares his findings that the cow had been injected with a hormone derived from some of Professor Pyg's experiments. The hamburger made from the Demon Star slaughter house would then be for sale at the Dark Tower restaurants. Again, Leviathan infiltrates by replacing people, but placing mind control agents in the food is even more frightening – the enemy is controlling the population through harmful, addictive fast food.

Damian is also upset at being sidelined from combat and tries to explain to Bruce that Talia's plan is to separate the two of them to leave Bruce unprotected. Batman may work well alone, but ultimately, he *needs* Robin in order to keep himself in check. We can interpret this further as Bruce's need for a family to keep himself sane. In his war on crime, Bruce has never been alone; he has always had Alfred as a father figure or a sidekick as a surrogate child. Without his family, Batman would be consumed by darkness and would die – that's why he needs Damian.

Matches Malone returns to the bar from before (this time, we learn that the bar is named "Three Eyed Jacks" which returns to the significance of the motif of the number three) to meet Robin's would-be killer, Goatboy. Unfortunately, Goatboy doesn't have much information except to spread the fear of Leviathan. He calls them a religion and mentions the symbols of Leviathan including Kali, Lilith, the Dark Mother, and Tiamat. Goatboy's former confidence has been shattered. Instead of being given riches to provide for his child, he's in fear for his life after seeing the Heretic kill a man.

Matches gets into a cab driven by Alfred who notes that the rain is "curious weather for the time of year." It seems like a throwaway line, but it suggests the overall tone of the series. While volume one of *Batman, Inc.* was bright, fun, and bizarre, it always seems to be raining in volume two. There are certainly fun and absurd moments in volume two, but always with the underlying tone that something awful is going to happen.

Lounge singer Lumina Lux calls Matches on his cell phone and begs him for help calling the Brothers Grimm's wake a "masquerade." The alliteration in Lumina Lux's name recalls femme fatale Jezebel Jet and the use of the word masquerade recalls the Black Glove's party during "R.I.P." During that story, Batman's mind was fractured and he had to fall into a backup persona of the Batman of Zur-En-Arrh. This scene is a direct contrast to the masquerade party from "R.I.P." as we see the ultimate example of how in-control Bruce Wayne is of his personality. Halfway dressed as Batman, Bruce takes a phone call and pretends to be Matches Malone – three different personalities working together in one scene.

The door to the party features the goat symbol of Baphomet and upon entering, Matches Malone is beaten by the goons from before. Inside the mansion, Goatboy reveals that he had set Matches up to be the third of three sacrifices that will allow him to buy his way into Leviathan. Damian was the first and the villain Small Fry is the second. Matches is suffocating with a bag over his head and he is surrounded by Jack Ketch, the Hangman and a judge from a Punch and Judy show. Things look bleak for the hero, except that Damian is on the way. The issue ends with Damian dressed as the hero Redbird racing off to save his father.

Batman, Inc. Vol. 2 #0

To celebrate the one year anniversary of the New 52, DC published zero issues of every one of its titles. Each zero issue would tell a story before the first issue which would give the newly relaunched DC Universe a sense of history. Rather than tell the origin of Batman, *Batman, Inc.* Vol. 2 #0 gives a complete history of the organization complete with brief vignettes for all of the key members of the team. Structurally, this issue functions much like *Batman, Inc.* Vol. 1 #6 where various members of the team are featured in action. Issue #0 is also memorable because it is co-written by regular series artist Chris Burnham with Frazer Irving on art.

The issue begins with the ending to "The Island of Mr. Mayhew" arc from *Batman* #667 – 669. Our heroes fly off to safety as Mayhew's Island explodes. Inside the plane, the French hero, the Musketeer says, "If there are any future reunions of the club of heroes … count me out" thereby explaining why he hasn't appeared since that time.

Once again, the narrative flashes back to Frank Miller's *Batman: Year One* with Bruce Wayne bleeding to death in his study as the old bat from *Batman the Return* crashes through the window. On the next page, Batman says, "The first truth of Batman. The saving grace. I was never alone."

When applied to the origin scene, these words are a reminder that even when Batman goes through his darkest moments in life, he is never alone. Even during the days when Batman was without a colorfully dressed partner, he always had Alfred. Without Alfred's medical assistance, Bruce would have died after his first night out as a vigilante. The words "I was never alone" are uplifting and life-affirming, but they also signal a transformation within Batman. He is no longer the dark, brooding, misunderstood avenger of the night; now he is the Bat-God whose mission is to recruit like-minded individuals.

In the Waynetech boardroom, Bruce explains his plan for Batman Incorporated to his stock holders when one investor named Mr. Treadwell seems nervous. Treadwell first appeared in *Batman and Robin* #10 where Damian seemed suspicious of him. Now, it is revealed that Treadwell has been embezzling funds for some unknown purpose, but we can assume he is another agent of Leviathan who has tried to become part of the architecture of Waynetech.

From there, it's a brief stop in England to recruit Knight and Squire and then off to Australia. During "The Island of Mr. Mayhew," the Australian super-hero Dark Ranger was killed by Wingman. Batman has sent Knight to recruit the Ranger's former sidekick, Johnny Riley. Riley doubts himself and cites not being invited to the Club of Heroes as evidence of being unworthy when Squire reveals that Riley was invited, but Dark Ranger's "decision not to bring you along is what got him killed."

The partnership motif has been subtle throughout Morrison's time with Batman, but it is important nonetheless. When Batman was investigating the monstrous, Bane-like Batman from *Batman* #664, he was nearly beaten to death. It wasn't until Robin helped him in #665 that Batman was able to take down the monster. During "R.I.P." it took nearly the entire Bat-Family to save Gotham City from the Black Glove. Morrison's entire *Batman and Robin* run was about the dynamic between Dick and Damian. In *Batman, Inc.* Vol. 1 #7, Man-of-Bats was nearly killed, but his partner Raven arrived just in time to save his life. Dark Ranger's death is a reminder of what Batman's fate could have been if he had truly been alone. Ultimately, Dark Ranger's pride and ego led to his downfall. So, Johnny Riley is left behind to take up his former mentor's role just as Dick Grayson took on the mantle of Batman; the sidekick becomes the hero.

Batman's world tour continues in Russia where he hires a man named Ravil to be the Batman of Moscow. Ravil's life has already ended in the New 52, however. He was killed by the villain Nobody in Peter Tomasi's *Batman and Robin* Vol. 2 #1. In Paris, the Musketeer turns down Batman's offer but vouches for Nightrunner as a suitable replacement. On the Red Prairie Indian reservation, Man-of-Bats and Raven helped put Jeff Moon's life together and now Moon has developed turbines so that the reservation can power itself.

In Japan, Jiro Osamu (formally known as Mr. Unknown) has finished his probationary period as Batman Japan and is now ready to join Batman Incorporated as a full-time member. Within two pages, we are shown four of

Jiro's rogue's gallery including the Spider-Man-like Veiniac, Professor Gorilla (from the pages of *Bat-Manga!*), a giant caterpillar made of cars, and Doubleface whose four eyes "give him unbeatable spatial awareness." Batman advises Jiro on how to beat Doubleface and then requests that he look into reports of "a samurai made of living clay" (also seen in the pages of *Bat-Manga!*). Jiro also reveals that he is interested in dating Lolita Canary of Super Young Team.

Of all the members of Batman Incorporated, Jiro is the most developed. We've seen him at his worst when he tried to kill Lord Death Man. We saw him redeem himself by saving the day. And now that he is a member of the team, we see that he has a rogue's gallery and a love interest. Other characters like Knight and Squire have villains, and we've seen a brief glimpse into Dark Ranger's origin story, but Jiro has all of the necessary prerequisites for a solo story in *Batman, Inc.* Vol. 2 #11.

After admitting his feelings for Lolita Canary, Jiro enquires about possibly using a shrink ray that Batman may have. Earlier in the issue, Knight and Squire also wanted to use a shrink ray for their own purposes. Both instances suggest the members of Batman Incorporated use Batman for his resources. Unfortunately, those are the consequences for using Waynetech money to fund a larger Batman initiative.

The issue concludes with Bruce sitting down to a sandwich that Alfred has brought him; a reminder that Alfred has always been there for Bruce. It's a beautiful character moment in an issue filled with great scenes meant to flesh out the individuals of Batman Incorporated. It's a fun issue and one that acts as a break from the rather dark tone set in the series thus far. Leviathan may have the advantage and something bad looms on the horizon, but for one issue, everything seems so hopeful.

Batman, Inc. Vol. 2 #4

When we last left Batman, he was undercover as Matches Malone and led into a trap by his son's would-be assassin, Goatboy. Now with his head in a plastic bag and a noose around his neck, Batman lights a match and drops it on a trail of gunpowder that he had been leaving behind. Tearing off the plastic bag, Batman shouts, "Call Guinness! I just set a new record for holding breath!" Since Batman had been holding his breath since issue #3, and issue #0 was between these two issues, that means Batman has held his breath for 60 days – a world record, indeed.

The issue is titled "Kill Box" which recalls the kill box from the first issue of the volume when the goat gang led Robin into a slaughter house so that Goatboy could kill him. In this issue, the kill box is the mansion full of assassins. The bounty on Damian's head brought the world's greatest assassins to one location which means that Batman Incorporated won't have to hunt for them. Even when Leviathan has a plan, Batman has a counter move.

The gunpowder goes off and chaos breaks loose as the agents of Batman Incorporated invade the mansion and battle the assassins of Leviathan. Despite being on the same team, El Gaucho and the Hood bicker due to their prejudice of their respective nationalities. Batman Incorporated might be able to spark romantic relationships like the one between Squire and Dark Ranger, but it can't fix every problem that its members have.

In issue #3, singer Lumina Lux was made to appear evil, but in this issue, we see that it was a red herring. Goatboy has now placed a gun next to her head and plans to make her his third sacrifice to Leviathan now that Matches Malone has been revealed to be Batman. The would-be assassin reminds us that he has been doing this to provide for his child and explains the bait-and-switch ending to issue #1 as he tells Batman, "I lied for you — I faked that picture! I put my life on the line for my kid!" and explains that he betrayed Batman because "Leviathan offered more than you." Batman tried buying out Goatboy in the same way that he bought Mirror Master's loyalty during the "Rock of Ages" story arc in the pages of Morrison's *JLA*, but Leviathan pays more for Goatboy's loyalty.

Before Batman can respond, Lumina stabs Goatboy in the neck with a fork, killing him. Batman tells Lumina that he will tell the police that she did it in self-defense and then gives her medication after revealing that he knows that she has multiple sclerosis instead of her non-existent sister.

The scene is a reminder of the destruction that afflicts average people in the midst of the war between Batman Incorporated and Leviathan, but it is also a metaphor for the corruptive influence of the corporation. We sympathize with Goatboy and Lumina because they are two people who are both in need of money to survive and they will do anything to get it. For Goatboy, he was willing to kill a boy the same age as his own son and when that wasn't enough, he was willing to kill more people for Leviathan. The corporation demands more and more of Goatboy's soul in exchange for riches and he is willing to give those things up and justifies his actions by saying it is for his son.

Lumina is no better as she is willing to seduce Matches Malone and lead him to a mansion and his execution in exchange for medication to prevent her MS. She acts out of self-preservation and due to her tough situation, Batman helps her instead of arresting her. This shows that Batman believes in redemption over punishment. Meanwhile, Goatboy becomes the first sacrifice in the war between Batman Incorporated and Leviathan.

Wingman and Damian dressed as Redbird meet and show a natural chemistry in battle together. At the end of the issue, we finally learn Wingman's identity after it had been teased so long ago in *Batman, Inc.* Vol. 1 #6. Throughout the issue, Damian has acknowledged that there is something recognizable about Wingman, but he isn't sure what. Once Wingman reveals that he is actually Jason Todd, Damian is enraged, "He made a fool of us!" he says. "He dishonors our family! Tell me this is a joke!"

Batman recruited Jason Todd because the former Robin had been brought back to life using Ra's al Ghul's Lazarus Pit and Jason had worked with Talia for a time. Also, Bruce believes in redemption for Jason despite his turn as the Red Hood and being the black sheep of the family. This is Jason's chance to make things right and show that he can be a hero, but it is also Batman's chance to make his family whole again. After all, if Bruce can forgive Damian for the three murders he has committed, he has to give Jason a chance for redemption.

Symbolically, Jason is meant to be a reflection of Damian. The two have been rebranded in new, complementary identities of Wingman and Redbird which bonds the two Robins visually in terms of costume design. In terms of personality, both characters are similar because both are petulant, irrationally angry sidekicks who were initially hated by readers. However, Morrison has redeemed Damian over the years and made him a fan-favorite, so this is a small acknowledgment that Jason could be as well. Finally, Jason is meant to foreshadow Damian's death later in the series. Jason is the dead Robin resurrected by the al Ghul family and Damian is the al Ghul family member who will become a dead Robin.

The issue ends with Batman forbidding Damian from being a super-hero any more saying that if he continues, Gotham will be destroyed in the far future. The last panel is of Gotham in flames with Damian as Batman and the numbers "666" in the foreground showing that the narrative will return to the future.

Batman, Inc. Vol. 2 #5

This issue picks up where the last ended. Batman tries reasoning with Damian that he can't continue as Robin. Batman reveals a twist in Damian's future career as Batman saying that Talia "wanted you to join me as Robin. She intends for you to replace me, and that can't happen. Because... if you become Batman... everything falls apart."

The narrative jumps to the future with Damian rescuing a child from a mob of people. We see Damian's hideout in flames along with the rest of Gotham City. The only safe place is Arkham Asylum – a clever dual use of the word "asylum." Inside the asylum, Commissioner Barbara Gordon has rallied her troops and hopes to use the uninfected child to make an antidote to the Joker Serum that has infected the city. In spite of how bleak everything looks, Damian smiles while petting his cat Alfred and says, "I brought you some food."

Batman and Gordon walk through the asylum and Damian says, "I promised I'd protect Gotham City. Down to the last stone. Down to my last breath. I won't stop trying. And if I screw up again ... it proves one thing, at least. Some higher power is aligned against me. And it always has been." These last two sentences are placed on a panel of a Joker-infected eye looking out at the reader to suggest that the "higher power" that is against Damian is the reader.

Damian attempts to enlist the help of the gorilla villain Jackanapes to reverse-engineer the serum from the child but Jackanapes can do nothing to help him. Unlike his father who is able to redeem others, Damian is unable to convince the gorilla to help. Instead, Jackanapes reveals that the child isn't infected with the Joker Serum because the child is the carrier and that Arkham Asylum is now infected as well.

As Damian races to save the asylum, his mind flashes back to how he became Batman. We see Damian lamenting Batman's death in an alley. Then, Dr. Hurt's voice says, "It was all your fault. You let me in. You opened the door to the devil. You exposed the hole in things. Now Batman is dead. Long live the new Batman."

By selling his soul to Dr. Hurt, Damian has corrupted the sigil of Batman. In *Batman: The Return of Bruce Wayne*, we saw that the bat is a symbol of Barbatos which is an aspect of Darkseid. So, while Bruce Wayne used the bat as a symbol of fear to strike the hearts of his enemies, he never gave up his soul in exchange for the sigil. He was still Bruce Wayne underneath the mask. But, Damian gave up his soul to Dr. Hurt (who is also an aspect of Darkseid) to become an invincible symbol of fear. The result makes Damian unkillable unless Gotham dies, but cost Damian his humanity which could be why Damian works alone. Bruce had partners that reminded him of his humanity, but Damian has no such person in his life. All Damian has is a cat and a hostile relationship with Barbara Gordon.

In the infirmary, Barbara has been infected by the Joker Serum and has killed the baby. With a crooked smile, she says, "Joker got what he wanted in the end … He turned us all into monsters" which echoes the Joker's motivations under Morrison's time with Batman. While Batman has always wanted to understand the Joker's mind, the Joker has wanted to break Batman's psyche in order to make Batman more like himself. Now, the Joker's ultimate revenge has been to turn all of Gotham City into the Joker.

But, it's Dr. Hurt who gets the last laugh. As the president of the United States ponders how to solve the situation in Gotham, we see that Dr. Hurt is one of his advisors. Hurt suggests that the only solution is a nuclear weapon that will level the city. The game between the Joker and Dr. Hurt from *Batman and Robin* has extended into the future as the Joker is responsible for the serum that tears Gotham City apart, and Dr. Hurt is responsible for the nuclear bomb that destroys the city.

When the narrative returns to the present, Batman tells Damian, "I had a dream of a future Batman who sold his soul to the devil and destroyed Gotham. Your mother is manipulating events to mold you into that Batman, her agent."

The idea that Damian becomes Robin and then Batman was all part of Talia's plan is an interesting twist, but it also suggests that Bruce refuses to take responsibility for his actions. By suggesting that Talia planned these events, Bruce won't admit to being a cause in the war between Batman Incorporated and Leviathan when he denied Talia. He also continues to make excuses for Damian's actions. After Bruce dies, Damian will sell his soul to the devil and that is an act of Damian's free will, not Talia's plan. But just as Bruce is willing to ignore Damian's actions after he killed three people, he reasons that Damian's choice of selling his soul isn't the problem. Deep down, Bruce is a father who loves his son and believes that he can do no wrong. While this may make him a parent who is blind to his son's faults, it also shows Bruce's unconditional love for his child.

On the last page of the issue, members of Batman Incorporated have discovered Leviathan's Crime Alley base from issue #1 when a bomb suddenly goes off seemingly killing them.

Batman, Inc. Vol. 2 #6

Bruce looks haggard as he races to the scene of the explosion. Inside, Batman discovers that Talia has laid an elaborate trap for him that revolves around the Zen parable of the goatherd and the ten stages of understanding. As Talia notes, the original parable is an ox rather than a goat, but she has changed it due to the symbolism of the goat: independence, achievement, sexuality, and duality.

To summarize the parable to just the parts that are relevant to Batman, a boy searches for an ox and must bring it home. The ox is meant to symbolize our true nature; who we are deep down even if we don't realize it. The boy represents ourselves trying to discover who we are. Despite both of these aspects of ourselves, the boy tries to force the ox to return home with him just as we try to force our own identity.

Identity has been the most important theme through all of Morrison's work with Batman. The hero puts himself through torture to understand who he is. After returning through time, Bruce Wayne became a changed man by synthesizing all of his identities into one. Though he has reached enlightenment, Talia understands that perfection doesn't last and that Bruce must always be evolving and adapting into his next change in identity; and she will usher in his next change through their war.

Batman asks Talia, "Can't we just have a conversation like normal people?"

Talia replies, "Oh, my dear detective. We're not 'normal people.' We're special" showing that this is how a super-villain woman processes her feelings for an ex-boyfriend. As we've seen in issue #2, nothing about Talia's life has ever been normal, so why should the way she processes her feelings be any different? All of Talia's actions come from the pain and loss she felt when her family was torn apart, and she takes revenge because she has the resources to do so.

But the parable of the goatherd is far deeper than Bruce's shifting identity. In a 23 July 2013 interview with Newsarama (a week before the final issue released), Grant Morrison explained:

> Part of what the Batman run has been is recapitulating the years of Batman and the different ways that Batman's been dealt with. So I wanted

to deal with that modern Batman that has started to get bleak again. The stuff that Scott [Snyder] is doing, that John Layman is doing, everyone is starting to get bleak again. You cannot bring Batman into the light, is basically what I've learned.

The parable of the goatherd reflects Morrison's own struggle with creating a new identity for Batman. The ox is the darkness that is inherent in Batman and the goatherd is Grant Morrison trying to shepherd Batman into the light. However, no matter how hard a writer may try to shift Batman's identity to be more lighthearted, Batman will always return to that darkness.

On the rooftop, the members of Batman Incorporated are in dire straits. All of the Outsiders are down (once again showing that they are cannon fodder) and Batwing tries saving their lives while Knight does his best to revive Squire. Batman still tries reasoning with Talia as he asks her to leave them out of their conflict, but because they work for him, they will be caught in the crossfire. After all, her mission is to destroy everything that Bruce Wayne loves.

Talia brings back the motif of class warfare when she says, "This building belongs to Bruce Wayne – one of his patronizing attempts to elevate the poor." When Batman asks what she has done for the poor, she responds, "I give them guns and slogans to chant. I put the poor to work building the empire of al Ghul. I provide purpose."

If Batman is a rich man who spends his nights beating criminals fighting their way out of poverty, then Leviathan is the corporation who hires these poor criminals. If crime is an idea and Batman Incorporated was designed to battle the idea of crime, then Leviathan is the idea of crime as a corporation. Ideas battling other ideas. The two corporate philosophies slug it out on a global scale with their workers caught in the crossfire of two billionaires.

While Batman ascends the metaphorical mountain, all four Robins are present in the Batcave arguing like brothers. Jason plays the part of the forgotten middle child as he taunts Damian by threatening to eat Bat-Cow. Dick acts as the responsible oldest brother as he stands up for the youngest. Tim is frustrated with the others telling them to shut up. Fortunately, Alfred acts as the voice of reason and calms the Robins down. He presents a small animal carrier to Damian and says, "I hope you won't mind a new addition to the menagerie, Master Damian" which refers to Bat-Cow and the dog, Titus, but it also refers to the Bat-Family as a whole.

A kitten leaps out of the carrier and wins Damian's love after hissing at him. Damian names his new pet "Alfred" which recalls his pet cat when he is Batman in the future. Just like in the 50s and 60s, and despite the absence of Oracle, Stephanie, and Cass Cain, the members of Batman's family are numerous.

Continuing his journey up the tower, Batman finds a room of mannequins with pictures of citizens that were replaced with Leviathan agents. A spider web hanging in the corner of the room is a reminder of the complex web that Dr. Dedalus spun and the web of connections to all of the major characters of *Batman, Inc.* linked to Leviathan. Clocks hang around the necks of the mannequins, ticking away, reminding Batman that in his game with Leviathan, he will always be late, always one step behind as he was with the bio-factory in Yemen, Mr. Unknown's death, and Dr. Dedalus's traps.

Batman enters Talia's lair only to discover another dummy. Talia explains her plan and all of the motifs that have persisted throughout the run are laid out again:

> Imagine a world where a new power source replaces oil, gas, and coal. The 'Oroboro' of Otto Netz is exactly that. Imagine what will happen when Gotham's children turn upon their parents. When the global economy shifts. The 21st century will belong to me. To facilitate the birth of this new paradigm, hundreds of my agents have infiltrated your city's infrastructure. At my command, Gotham City will commit suicide. The U.S. economy will stagger and fall.

The Oroboro represents the motif of the new replacing the old. Even though it is a renewable energy source that could replace the more harmful oil, gas, and coal, the Oroboro will throw society into chaos by destroying the economic infrastructure. The snake consuming itself is a symbol showing that renewable energy is ironically still destruction. Leviathan has weaponized both capitalism (not hard to do) and environmentalism (much more difficult).

Batman is then offered a choice: he can either save Gotham City or Damian. Whichever one he chooses, the other will die.

The next scene on the roof is heartbreaking as Knight tries resuscitating Squire saying, "She always told me I could do anything." Just as Robin brings Batman back to humanity, Squire is an inspiration to Knight. But as Squire is revived, the Heretic grabs Knight by the neck and murders him.

Batman arrives and attacks the Heretic, but is beaten and thrown from the roof as Talia insists, "Damian isn't the Batman who destroys Gotham. The 'third Batman' in your nightmare? I made him." Meaning that the Batman of issue #666 isn't Damian at all, but a clone created by Talia.

Things look bleak and get worse from here.

Batman, Inc. Vol. 2 #7

Picking up the action from the previous issue, a ninja man-bat kidnaps Batman before he can fall to his death and the remaining members of Batman Incorporated are left recovering from their last battle. Wingman is off to meet with the Hood and El Gaucho at Batcave East, Red Robin is on the trail of Batman's homing signal, and Nightwing stays behind to comfort Squire. Meanwhile in Yemen, mutant warriors from the Kollektiv, Traktir and Spidra investigate the belly of the whale site from *Batman: The Return* when Leviathan forces are on their way to destroy the site.

In the Batcave, Damian has been monitoring events and insists to Alfred that "none of this would have happened if we'd been together as Batman and Robin."

Damian's statements recall Squire's words to Dark Ranger from *Batman, Inc.* Vol. 2 #0: Dark Ranger died on the Island of Mr. Mayhew because he didn't have his partner there to watch out for him. Likewise, Batman was defeated by the Heretic because Robin wasn't there to help him and all of this is part of Talia's plan. By placing a bounty on Damian's head, she forced Batman to be overprotective. This would cause Damian to rebel against his father thereby dividing their team and making them both vulnerable.

The Heretic's origin is finally revealed as Damian explains his research to Alfred. Talia threatened to replace Damian when he walked out on the al Ghul family in *Batman and Robin* #12. She created a clone and placed it in the bio-factory in Yemen where he was born from a whale. Then, the Heretic trained to become a perfect fighter by killing the other members of the Kollektiv. Now, he is a perfect killing machine and Damian's opposite – an heir to the al Ghul family untainted by Batman's influence.

Wingman tries reconvening with the surviving members of Batman Incorporated, only to be electrocuted and captured by the Hood. This event continues the idea that the Hood is the ultimate spy stereotype. At first, the Hood was an agent of Spyral who had infiltrated Batman Incorporated to learn their secrets. Then he was betrayed by Spyral in the *Leviathan Strikes* special and seemingly left for dead. Now he reveals that his "first loyalty is to Spyral" which makes him a triple-agent. Of course, there is also some irony in Jason Todd (who betrayed Batman by becoming the Red Hood) being betrayed by a man who wears a red hood.

Elsewhere, Talia pulls trigger for Dr. Dedalus's meta-bomb from a safe, and leaves Batman's utility belt for Red Robin to find. She hopes to kill Red Robin as a sacrifice for Kali the Destroyer, but Tim escapes just in time. In the streets of Gotham, the brainwashed children of Leviathan rush Nightwing, Commissioner Gordon, and the police. The children prove to be the perfect army as Gordon says, "They wouldn't use kids. We can't. We can't shoot kids."

While we may judge Talia for using children in her army, her methods are really no different than Batman's. For decades, Batman has been recruiting teens as Robin to fight crime alongside him. Leviathan's influence seems to come from conditioning to the point of brainwashing and Batman seems to offer his sidekicks the choice to join him. Still, both sides rely upon attracting youthful enthusiasm to join their respective causes.

Street kid Ellie from *Batman* #663 and #700 returns in this issue. When Batman first met her, he gave her a job at Waynetech answering phones and now we see her at her desk job as Talia's forces move in to take the tower.

Batman is chained in a safe and thrown into a swimming pool. Talia explains that her tests in the last issue where just to calculate how long it would take for Batman to escape this death trap. Like the room of mannequins in the previous issue, Talia is taking great joy in reminding Batman that he will always be late. He's never fast enough to avoid tragedy.

In the Batcave, for the second time in the series, a frustrated Damian decides to defy his father and leave the sidelines to go save the day. This time, he doesn't have to use knockout gas on Alfred because the old butler knows that sometimes, Bruce is wrong. The issue ends with four panels showing what each Robin is doing: Dick Grayson is battling Leviathan's children, Jason Todd has been captured, Tim Drake is entering Wayne Tower, and Damian is racing off to save them all.

Batman, Inc. Vol. 2 #8

The action in this issue is fast and intense, leaving little room for sentimentality as Damian rushes to save his father. In his armor from *Batman: The Return*, Damian rockets toward Wayne Tower and along the way, he helps Nightwing and Commissioner Gordon by gassing the rioting brainwashed Leviathan children. Meanwhile, Batman regurgitates a lock pick to help him escape Talia's latest death trap. As he struggles to free himself, Talia reveals Batman's issues with romance by asking, "This is how I get your attention?" In her mind, starting a war is the only way he will ever give her attention which is probably truer than Bruce would like to admit.

Inside Wayne Tower, Red Robin protects Ellie from Leviathan agents. The fight scene is interesting for the décor of the Wayne Tower lobby which looks like an inverse to the Batcave. Everything is bright white in contrast to the darkness of the cave. A giant quarter stands proudly as an idol to capitalism. Five suits are displayed in a similar fashion to the Robin costumes in the cave: a suit of armor, a deep sea diving suit, two astronaut suits, and a soldier's uniform. A tank and a small airplane are also on display.

Damian arrives with a horde of Leviathan children. In one action, Damian takes out the children and the Leviathan soldiers by electrocuting them. Before he can celebrate his victory, more soldiers open fire on him when Nightwing also arrives on the scene and saves Damian's life saying, "What would you do without me?" reminding the reader of the partnership motif.

For a brief moment, the battle pauses for a sentimental conversation between Dick and Damian. Seemingly aware of his own mortality, Damian says, "This is our last chance to prevent a catastrophe." Then he boasts, "We were the best, Richard. No matter what anyone thinks." And in order to prove this, for two pages, the story feels like Morrison's run on *Batman and Robin* again.

Dick and Damian leap over a Wayne Enterprises sign as a bomb goes off making a "BOOM" noise. In order to depict the effect, artist Chris Burnham draws the onomatopoeia into the bomb's smoke just as Frank Quitely did in the first arc of *Batman and Robin*. The duo drop blackout bombs, enter the smoke, and onomatopoeia is written on the smoke to show that a dynamic fight is occurring just beyond the veil of the smoke. It's a fun fight scene that captures the energy of the Dick and Damian era of *Batman and Robin*. Then, the Heretic arrives with the Oroboro bomb and everything changes.

During *Batman and Robin*, Dick and Damian would defeat villains by landing their signature move; a double punch to the face. Here, the two try punching the Heretic, but it has no effect. Nightwing is tossed aside and Damian is left to defend himself against his cloned brother. Their fight is brutal and unfair as Leviathan soldiers shoot Damian. Even though Damian pleads with his mother numerous times to call off the Heretic, the fight concludes with the Heretic running a sword through Damian's chest, killing him.

Damian's death is gruesome, and though the death blow is in silhouette, the image is only slightly less graphic as a result. This is the ultimate turning point in Morrison's time on *Batman*; it's the final twist in the circular narrative that brings tragedy back into the heart of Batman. Like Jason Todd before him, Damian is the sacrificial lamb that reminds Batman of his own mortality. The hero can never die, but villains can take all of his loved ones away from him.

On the 1 March 2013 post of the blog *Too Busy Thinking About My Comics*, Colin Smith ponders Damian's death scene and the lack of shock that resulted in the murder of a ten year old. He writes,

> How desensitised, how lacking in empathy, would the reader need to be before the very fact of Damian's death failed to move them? After all, this isn't a panel which increases our understanding of Damian's heroism, or indeed any aspect of his character. It doesn't tell us of anything that we haven't already been told, and it fails to achieve a single thing that a shot with a touch more restraint and respect still might. All this does is shock us, or at least attempt to.

While Smith is certainly correct in his assessment of the scene, he misses an important point in his judgment of the reaction: the impact of Damian's death was lessened due to the nature of comic book marketing.

Released on 27 February 2013, DC Comics had the entire month to tease and promote the issue. DC representatives called retailers to suggest upping orders. Solicitations for the next issue *Batman, Inc.* and most other *Batman*-related titles hinted at a great tragedy that would befall the family. Two days before the release of the issue, the New York Post spoiled Damian's death with the headline "DC killing off Batman's 'Boy Wonder' Damian Wayne in new comic book." And so what should have been the biggest moment in Grant Morrison's run was diminished through the power of marketing.

In promoting the issue, DC undermined the impact of Damian Wayne's death. The outside build-up of this issue could make one forget that a ten year-old boy was murdered in grizzly detail – and that two parents were now childless due to their hatred of one another. Instead, the issue became the next big thing to be sought after, a hot commodity which people would purchase to turn around and auction off to make a quick buck. Instead of talking about the *social* aspects of the depiction, which Smith addresses so well, fans and critics focused on the *commercial* aspects, in which the young character's death became a marketing event.

But that's the nature of capitalism. It's the nature of the corporate sigil. In this way, even this apparent mishandling of the death, Morrison's narrative of a corporatized Batman is capable of absorbing the misstep and commenting upon it. While Damian Wayne is not a living person and therefore cannot be

Batman holds a dead Robin's body. The final page of *Batman, Inc.* Vol. 2 #8 (Apr 2013). Art by Chris Burnham. Copyright © DC Comics.

exploited in the truest sense of the word, the *Batman* franchise demands a sacrifice for corporate profits. In this, Damian is its boy.

Batman breaks free from Talia's death trap, but he is a moment too late and Talia taunts him the whole way. "Our son was a flawed creation. Born from a bottle. A failed experiment. You lost the world that might have been yours. You lost me. You're losing everything. You're losing the game." It's a reminder that Bruce could have prevented all of this had he just joined Talia at the end of "Batman & Son." They would have raised Damian together and built a global empire.

On the final page, we see Bruce holding his dead son and Talia giving into her sadness at the loss of her child. Despite all of her cruelty, she still shows the pain of loss, revealing that while she is the villain, she isn't completely heartless. Regardless, Talia ascribes her reaction as "a moment of weakness, that's all." Meanwhile, former street kid Ellie holds the Ororboro bomb and looks astonished that Damian gave his life to save hers. Two parents grieve for the death of their child, but it could also be a new beginning for Ellie.

Up until this point, the motif of the importance of partnership had always been applied to the hero. Dark Ranger had died because he didn't bring his partner along. Man-of-Bats had nearly been killed when he was separated from his partner, Raven. Knight was killed when Squire was out of commission. While the point had been made many times that Batman needs Robin to survive, this issue shows the inverse – Damian needed Batman to stay alive.

Damian's death in this issue should come as no surprise since Morrison had teased the event since the beginning of the second volume of *Batman, Inc.* In an interview with *The Huffington Post* on 23 March 2013, Morrison talks about how Damian was supposed to die at the end of "Batman & Son" but that

> It wouldn't have worked after four issues because not only did most of the fans hate him, he was too snotty, he was too arrogant, his death wouldn't have mattered a lot. But we've watched him develop for six years and it allowed us to really get into the character and see his willingness to change and I think when you watch someone's willingness to change it allows you to identify with them a little more and it made a little more sense to kill him off once we made everyone love him.

Damian's death is Morrison's ultimate trick. Damian was a character that everyone hated who became a fan-favorite during *Batman and Robin.* By killing the character, Morrison angered fans who had come to love the boy they initially hated. It's an amazing transformation that starts in the first issue of Morrison's run and culminates here.

Later in that same interview, Morrison notes that the sword itself is part of the circular narrative because it "belongs to the very first known ancestor of the Waynes, it was used in Batman: Shadow of the Bat, in the 90s" and that they chose the sword to illustrate "how these things play out over generations and how repetitive patterns play out of destructive patterns and it really never ends."

He also explains that Damian's death was "about resetting Batman's status quo. For a long time Batman's had a dead Robin in the cave and it's always been a glass case with a costume in there and it's the one Robin that Batman couldn't save and it used to be Jason, but he's come back to life but he's still got that case in the Batcave."

Therefore, Damian's death acts as another part of the circular narrative. Batman began with the death of his parents. After years of being Batman, he fell into depression after the second Robin, Jason Todd, had apparently died. But, he came out of that darkness because of Tim Drake. Now Batman has fought his war long enough to see the death of his son. Happiness comes in fleeting moments in Batman's life because of the path he has chosen.

Batman, Inc. Vol. 2 #9

Bruce, Dick, Tim, and Alfred carry a casket containing Damian to a grave. When Bruce returned from time, he saw two graves and the city in flames, and with Damian as the first grave, we can anticipate one more.

The narrative flashes back to the previous issue with Batman battling the Heretic just after Damian had died. Nightwing then joins in the battle and unleashes his rage upon the Heretic. With Robin gone, the original dynamic duo are left to pick up the pieces and avenge his death.

In the present, Damian's funeral is somber and rain pours down as Bruce struggles to find the words to describe his son's death. The scene is contrasted on the next page by Knight's funeral in London. While Damian is laid to rest by the four closest people he has, Knight's funeral is televised as the hero is paraded through the streets. Beryl watches her partner's funeral from her mother's couch and realizes that she has to assume the identity of Knight to continue his legacy. Again, the partner becomes the hero just as Dick Grayson became Batman and Johnny Riley became Dark Ranger. Meanwhile, the British Prime Minister learns of the possibility of a Lazarus Pit thereby giving both Knight and Damian a way out of death.

Bruce seems to have learned nothing from Damian's death, however. Upset that Alfred let Damian leave the cave to get himself killed, Bruce demands that his oldest friend take a vacation. Bruce then rejects the rest of his partners insisting, "This is between Talia and me. No one else." We've seen time and again what happens when Batman is alone, so shutting out his family can't be good for Bruce.

According to a news broadcast, Wayne Tower is still being occupied by Leviathan and children are still rioting in the streets. A family watches the horror unfold and one of their children calls the chaos "cool." Leviathan is violent culture capitalism and when the news sensationalizes real world violence, it leaves children wanting to imitate it.

Flashing back to shortly after Damian's death, we see the Heretic beating Batman more. The Heretic's words echo the narration of the bats from *Batman: The Return* as he describes himself as "Bigger. Faster. Younger. Stronger." Batman is the idea that is opposite of crime and the Heretic believes himself to be a better idea than Batman. Before the Heretic can finish Batman off, Red Robin uses the tank inside Wayne Tower to fire on the monster and the other agents of Leviathan.

Red Robin's rescue perfectly summarizes Tim Drake's role throughout Morrison's time with Batman. Tim had been in Morrison's first issue of *Batman* and played a small, but important part in "The Three Ghosts of Batman," "The Island of Mr. Mayhew," and "R.I.P." storylines. After Damian took the spotlight, however, Tim basically disappeared from Morrison's narrative. However, if it weren't for Tim Drake, Bruce would never have come to his senses after returning from the time stream in *Batman: The Return of Bruce Wayne* #6.

Tim had arrived at Wayne Tower before anyone else and this led to him battling Leviathan agents and saving Ellie. Once Damian arrived on the scene, Tim disappeared from the issue. Now that Damian is dead, Tim resurfaced and is responsible for saving Batman's life once again. In terms of the narrative, Tim's function is similar to Batman's during the days of Morrison's *JLA*; Tim Drake is the forgotten one who always saves the day.

Mayor Hady gives into Leviathan's demands and declares Batman to be an enemy of Gotham City. This echoes the reminder that Man-of-Bats gives on the next page that Leviathan agents declare, "Everywhere the standard of the bat rises, it will be chopped down." No matter what cause Batman Incorporated takes up, Leviathan will be there in opposition. At the heart of this conflict, are two corporations using the power of their magic sigils that are treating the world as their game board with common people caught in the crossfire.

A brief scene between Talia and the Heretic gives some insight into their relationship. When the Heretic addresses her as "Mother," Talia reprimands him and demands that he call her "Lady Talia" because "Leviathan has many children." She had never been a particularly caring mother before, but after Damian had left her, she had completely cut off her emotions when dealing with her other son. The only emotion she can express is anger because the Heretic killed Damian before she gave him the order.

The Heretic is proud that he made a decision on his own, but Talia requires her children to be completely obedient. When she allowed Damian to have free will, her son renounced their family name. While Talia is cruel, Morrison has built her transformation into the Leviathan through logical character development. At her core, Talia is a normal mother who wants the best for her children, but because she is far from ordinary, she dishes out super-villain level punishment for those who disobey or thretean her family. This is what happens when an overbearing mother becomes an international terrorist; the choices are obedience or death.

The agents of Batman Incorporated meet in Batcave East and hash out a plan to stop the Oroboro super-weapon by disarming the bombs around the world. Despite Batman's insistence that the team stay out of the fight, Nightwing is rallying the troops for the final showdown. Of course, Batman's first Robin is the one who knows the importance of partnership. Meanwhile, Batman's second Robin, Jason Todd (a.k.a the Red Hood and Wingman), is shown to have been captured by a mysterious woman. The symbol of spy organization Spyral is in the background and Jason is surrounded by women dressed like Kathy Kane's Batwoman and the girls from St. Hadrian's school in *Leviathan Strikes*. This suggests that the mysterious Kathy Kane may resurface soon.

In the Batcave, Bruce continues to grieve for his son. The final three pages are silent as Bruce embraces his pain and loneliness again.

Batman, Inc. Vol. 2 #10

Jason Todd's redemption was a shock at the end of issue #4, but this issue begins with a bigger shock as Batman meets with the former Third Ghost of Batman, Michael Lane. During Morrison's run on *Batman*, Lane was the Antichrist Batman from *Batman* #666. He was also responsible for causing

Batman's heart attack and nearly killing the hero. Since the end of "R.I.P.," Lane has reformed and taken up the mantle of Azrael to redeem himself, showing that even those who are under the thrall of Dr. Hurt can be saved, redeemed, and put to work for Batman.

Azrael is the title of an assassin created by the Order of St. Dumas. The first Azrael in comics was Jean-Paul Valley who replaced Bruce Wayne as Batman during the "Knightfall" story. Valley's story is similar to Michael Lane's in that he was brainwashed to become an assassin and both are alternate versions of Batman. After the New 52, it became unclear whether Jean-Paul Valley was still in continuity much less Michael Lane, so Lane's appearance here is very important. Lane knows that one day he will be "the devil's herald on Earth" and he prays to avoid that day. Batman deputizes Lane and notes that Lane's Suit of Sorrows "protects its wearer from all harm."

Meanwhile, on the Jungfrau summit, Ra's al Ghul is prisoner of his daughter. The red and black motif and game theory return as the old terrorist plays chess with himself and he uses red and black pieces. Ra's says to Talia, "They tell me you had your son butchered like an animal. Bravo. You have become a monster at last."

The heart of "The Resurrection of Ra's al Ghul" story was a twisted family conflict between father and son. Ra's al Ghul led a war against his own father, Sensei, as he tried to take control of his own grandson, Damian. During that conflict, Talia protected her child out of love and considered her father to be a monster. Everything has come full circle as Talia has become more like her father after the death of her son. Life means nothing for the al Ghul family even the lives of their own family members.

Ra's goes on to praise Talia's plan for being "epic in scope" and "immaculately conceived" but then says that she missed a detail. When Talia asks what detail she missed, Ra's only responds through the deeply symbolic gesture of the black knight taking the red queen on the chessboard. The black knight represents Batman and the red queen signifying the murderous Talia are blatant symbols, but an analysis of their movements is interesting.

A queen is the most powerful piece on the chessboard. She can move any number of spaces connected to her adjacent square. Her movements are a combination of the movements of the rook and the bishop. However, the knight moves like no other piece on the board. He moves in a way that the queen cannot and therefore often catches his opponents by surprise. Talia thinks she has Batman where she wants him, but like the knight of the chessboard, Batman often surprises his opponents.

Bruce Wayne meets with Lucius Fox and the two discuss the financial situation with Batman Incorporated. Bruce is amazed that Waynetech had spent over $100 million on Batman Incorporated – the subtext being that they are losing the war with Leviathan even after spending as much money as they have. Lucius replies that they had spent $2 million on the Ro-Bats and that their potential was wasted when Batman used them as "disposable pawns" (note the chess term). But, Lucius seems most disappointed that the Ro-Bats weren't used for their original intent saying, "These were going to be family robots – a Batman in every home."

Originally, Batman Incorporated was formed to be superhero capitalism, but instead of the symbol of Batman being used to make lives better, it was used to fight a war with Leviathan. We can view this change in mission as a sharp criticism of capitalism; it has the potential to do so much good, but results in petty competition rather than public good. If Morrison's original intent for *Batman, Inc.* was to show the superhero potential for capitalism, then the end of his run shows that capitalism can't achieve greatness. People will always be caught in the middle of corporate giants battling it out.

The scene between Talia, the Heretic and the soldiers who fired on Damian continues this theme of the disposable nature of the worker to capitalism. As the Heretic murders the men, Talia says, "You opened fire on my son. You helped extinguish a life worth hundreds of your own. You, each of you. It will be as if you never existed."

Worth is the key word in this scene. The life of Damian was worth a lot and even though the Heretic is the one who is really responsible for his death, Talia can't kill the Heretic because of his worth. So, the common, nameless workers become the scapegoats to the Heretic's sin and they are murdered. In a corporate sense, the CEO sacrifices the worker because the worker has less worth and can be replaced. Batman's pawns are the Ro-Bats who have cost his company $2 million and replaced the need for some human agents. He spares human lives by using his machines, but he is also replacing the human element of his company which can be seen as replacing human jobs for inefficient machines. Meanwhile, Talia's pawns are human beings who are disposed of for failure. In both cases, capitalism disposes of the worker.

Mayor Hady talks with Talia and begs her to stop issuing demands to which she replies, "I wouldn't be doing my job as the villain if I didn't issue impossible demands. I want Batman to surrender himself to us at exactly 11:00 tonight." Talia's admission of "doing her job" suggests that she is just trying to fulfill a role. She is playing a part instead of taking responsibility. Also, her demand that Batman surrender at 11:00 is a great pun of Batman arriving at the metaphorical "eleventh hour" to save the day.

Batman's agents are positioning themselves on the chessboard as well. Nightwing and Red Robin interrogate a Leviathan agent while Knight and Ranger track down Wingman and the Hood. Knight and Ranger battle the girls from St. Hadrian's and we are still not shown the Headmistress, but her black shoes put her as an opposite to Talia who was shown to be wearing red. If Talia is the red queen, then the Headmistress is the black queen and allied with Batman.

In the Batcave, Bruce sits in Azrael's Suit of Sorrows. The image recalls Frank Miller's *Batman: Year One* and Morrison's own *Batman: The Return* when Bruce sat in his study and decided to become Batman. The narration is reads, "Criminals are a superstitious, cowardly lot. My disguise must be able to strike terror into their hearts. I must be a creature of the night. Black. Terrible. Yes, father. I shall become a bat."

Morrison subverts our expectations once again when the words "I shall become a bat" are now applied to Batman injecting himself with what appears to be the man-bat serum that he stole from Dr. Kirk Langstrom earlier in the issue. Now, Bruce has become a literal "bat-man" and the narrative has returned full circle as the first threat of ninja man-bats from "Batman & Son" will finally be dealt with.

Batman, Inc. Vol. 2 #11

Grant Morrison takes an issue off and series artist Chris Burnham steps into the writer's chair with Jorge Lucas providing art. The beginning of the issue shows Damian's cat, Alfred at his master's grave when the narrative suddenly jumps to a sexy biker gang terrorizing Tokyo. A television announcer says, "We interrupt your regularly scheduled program with an emergency update from downtown Tokyo" providing a fun, in-story reason for the sudden change in narrative. Originally, the biker gang was hired by a Leviathan agent named Lady Tiger Fist (who has... well, tiger heads for fists) to compete in races and become the public face of Leviathan. But when their cybernetic enhancements scarred their faces, the gang was abandoned. Now, Batman Japan and Lolita Canary have teamed up after their date in Internet 3.0 to convince the gang to turn on Lady Tiger Fist.

It's a bizarre digression from the overall narrative, but one that is somewhat necessary after so much darkness. There is one moment of meta-commentary worth mentioning in the issue as well. During their assault on Lady Tiger Fist, it appears that villain has won after she decapitates Batman Japan in a silhouetted panel that resembles Damian's death from issue #8. However, Batman Japan reveals that she had been plugged into Internet 3.0 the whole time. He comments on his own death saying, "Wow! That was violent! I'm glad we rendered it in silhouette!"

Burnham is poking fun at the idea of censorship with this statement. The panel with Batman Japan's decapitated head is still an act of graphic violence and is only slightly dulled by being rendered in silhouette. Likewise, Damian's death was brutal despite being in silhouette. In Burnham's original take on Damian's death, the scene was far more graphic, but it was colored in such a way so as to make it less graphic.

The issue ends with a panel showing Batman as he was at the end of issue #10 with an announcer saying, "We now return you to your regularly scheduled programming."

Batman, Inc. Vol. 2 #12

After spending the past few issues readying himself for combat, Batman finally strikes against Talia. The opening scene recalls the beginning of *Batman: The Return* where an old bat battles through younger ones. Batman is the older bat trying to survive against an enemy that is younger and faster than him. Also, note that it is raining just as it has been for the majority of the series. Most of the issue revolves around Batman unleashing every trick he's got in his fight with the Heretic.

The fight begins with Batman using an antidote to the man-bat serum to remove Talia's ninja man-bat soldiers from the fight. Batman wears into battle Azrael's Suit of Sorrows and the flight suit designed by Lucius Fox. His suit is made of the "meta-material with a negative refractive index" designed from Dr. Sivana's diamond which makes him invisible when he wants to be. Batman's battle with the Heretic takes them across Gotham's skies, from roof top to roof top, on top of a blimp, through an office building, into a Leviathan school bus.

A brief scene with the members of Batman Incorporated breaks up Batman's fight. Now, Nightwing and Red Robin have met up with Wingman, the Hood, and the Headmistress of Spyral to determine if they are all on the same side. Or perhaps a third side that has decided to ally itself with Batman now. The Hood reveals his third side when he explains hat the International Intelligence community would never allow Bruce Wayne to start his own private army. Then, the Headmistress teases that "This is bigger than any of you, including him. It'll be dealt with by a higher power." While the battle between Batman Incorporated and Leviathan seemed to be a two-sided war, this revelation shows how narrow Batman's mindset was from the start.

Obviously, the Headmistress of Spyral is Kathy Kane, but what isn't as obvious is that Kane's Death Girls strike a remarkable resemblance to the 1966 film *The Wild Wild World of Batwoman*. In that famously bad and campy film (which is not at all associated with DC Comics), Batwoman hires a team of girls to act as her agents. The Batgirls are dedicated to their mistress in an almost cult-like way just as the Death Girls of Spyral are to Kathy Kane. Just one more strange 60s Batman given new life in Morrison's series.

During Batman's fight with the Heretic, the Dark Knight humiliates Leviathan's most powerful soldier in front of a bus full of children, showing them that crime doesn't pay. Nightwing and Knight arrive on the scene and simultaneously attack the Heretic in a similar fashion to Dick and Damian's dual-attack in *Batman and Robin*. Once the Heretic's mask is destroyed, it's revealed that he has the head of a baby. The Heretic had been born in an artificial womb and while his body is massive, his head hadn't grown along with it. He's a creepy sight to behold and his lack of physical maturation is a window to his lack of emotional maturation. He's literally an overgrown child.

In issue #9, Bruce says that Damian "struck our lives like a bolt of lightning." Here, Knight swears that she will kill the Heretic, but she is stopped by a lightning bolt that strikes the Wayne Tower "W." Perhaps this is the spirit of Damian trying to prevent Knight from doing something that she might regret later.

When the Heretic confronts Talia about being used by her, she cuts off her son's head; yet another al Ghul betrayed by a parent. His decapitated head, missing the left eye, is reminiscent of Jezebel Jet's own head at the end of the *Leviathan Strikes* special. Talia turns the lights out on Gotham City as a lightning bolt strikes near her. Again, we could interpret this as Damian's spirit trying to prevent the coming events. Then, Talia presses a trigger that activates a bomb embedded in the Heretic's spine which destroys Wayne Tower. The image of Wayne Tower's destruction symbolizes the destruction of Batman Incorporated and the end of Morrison's era.

The last page shows Talia dressed in her own version of the Batman costume. Her garb is a cross between Dr. Hurt's from "R.I.P." and Kathy Kane's Batwoman costume, and the coloring is red and black, continuing that motif. Here, Burnham has made the panels mirror a sequence from *Batman and Robin* #16 in which Batman enters the Batcave to face Dr. Hurt. Talia carries two swords and declares that they will battle "to the death, my detective" showing that she has fully embraced her role as Ra's al Ghul's daughter.

Batman, Inc. Vol. 2 #13

The first issue of Morrison's *Batman* run began from Commissioner Gordon's perspective. Now, the circular narrative concludes with Morrison's last issue narrated by Gordon. While Gordon was present throughout the run, he is one character that Morrison never really explored in depth. Jim Gordon was a companion to "Batman" no matter who was under the mask, but was never more than a minor supporting character until this issue.

After the showdown between Batman and Talia was teased at the end of issue #12, the audience expects the two to battle at the start. Our expectations are subverted again as the issue begins where issue #1 began; with the arrest of Bruce Wayne. Gordon interrogates Bruce over his involvement in the acts of terrorism that have gripped the city and during their conversation, we see the battle between Batman and Talia. The flow of Bruce remembering his battle mirrors the reader's own reflections of Morrison's Batman run.

In the cave, Talia throws aside the cape and mask of Bruce's father and says, " Here we all are, at the grand finale. A flamboyant enemy worthy of Batman. Leviathan – an empty, arbitrary suggestion of vague promises and unformed ideas, like the bat."

Morrison has spent the past seven years establishing exactly what the bat-sigil means and in one line, Talia dismisses it all as "arbitrary." Like Bruce searched for meaning in his life after the deaths of his parents, we search for meaning in the bat.This is meaning that the writer, artist, and audience have placed on a symbol and believed to be real and the villain of the story has proven how evil she can be by crushing that meaning in one line.

Gordon asks Bruce how long they have been friends and Bruce responds, "Since the beginning, Jim. Since it all started." Then the narrative flashes back to moments after Thomas and Martha Wayne were murdered. A young Bruce Wayne is surrounded by Jim Gordon when he was a patrolman and an older woman who could be friend of the Wayne family, Dr. Leslie Thompkins. This one panel is the inverse of the bad Bat-family of Dr. Hurt (the father), Talia al Ghul (the mother), and Damian Wayne (the son). Here, Gordon acts as a surrogate father, Thompkins as mother, and Bruce as the good bat son. It also is evidence of the idea from *Batman, Inc.* Vol. 1 #6 that "Batman is never alone" even at his worst moment.

The idea that "Batman is everywhere" is present as we are shown a montage of Batman Incorporated saving the day all around the world. After a kiss as Gotham burns, Talia says, "Look, I know you like the rules to be cartoonish and the stakes to be clear. My people have orders – if I fail to return, Leviathan will release its hold on Gotham." If their battle seems absurd, that's because it is. Even though Talia has an army with unknown numbers, they are willing to just stop if she dies because that's what happens in fantasy. Cut off the head of the snake and the body is useless. But the catch is that Batman *has* to kill her and Batman doesn't kill. Talia is an enemy that can't be reasoned with or captured. She has to die but Batman is a hero and he can't kill anyone.

Back with Gordon, Bruce revisits his origin explaining, "Two shots killed my father. I was ten years old. The third bullet left a smoking hole in my mother's new fur coat. It left a hole in me. A hole in everything. That's how it felt, anyway. The pain was so terrible, I decided I could never love anyone ever again."

By returning to the "Hole in Things" motif, Morrison is giving us new insight into Batman. Despite the progress that Bruce has made psychologically to become united in his identity, he will always fall back to that moment in his origin. This is Morrison's commentary that no matter how much Batman changes, the story will always return to that moment of loss. Despite the family that Batman has built with Robins, Batgirls, international Batmen, femme fatales, mutated freaks, butlers, cops, and C-list super-heroes, he will always feel alone because that is what the audience is comfortable with.

During their battle, Talia poisons Batman and informs him that he has only minutes to live. Jason Todd arrives and offers to trade the Oroboro trigger with the antidote to the poison. Todd's role in the scene is interesting in its circularity. After Jason Todd was killed by the Joker, Todd was resurrected by Talia al Ghul and he worked for her. Had she not brought him back to life, he wouldn't be here now to bargain with her for Batman's life. After being a villain for so long, Jason Todd's redemption is complete. Symbolically, Todd serves as a reminder that for Damian Wayne, all hope is not lost; dead Robins have their ways of returning.

Talia tries activating the Oroboro ring finding that the bombs around the world have been disarmed by the members of Batman Incorporated. Batman explains that Wayne Industries had created a meta-material before she could, which closes the case on that plot thread. If Batman Incorporated and Leviathan are competing businesses, then Batman Incorporated wins in technological innovation. But, never to be defeated, Talia swears that she will buy Wayne Industries and ruin it. As long as Talia is alive, she will always find a way to ruin Bruce Wayne.

Just before Talia's death, Morrison uses her final words as a commentary on the typical Batman story that the hero is going to return to, "You, with your jokers and riddlers, your evil doctors. All those grotesque mental patients you choose to 'match wits' with. You'll never rise above them. You'll play in the mud for the rest of your life." For a brief time, Batman rose above the criminals of Gotham City and became immersed in a world of spies, terrorism, and international super-heroes. Now that it's over, it's back to the basics again.

Because Batman can't kill Talia, Kathy Kane, former Batwoman and current leader of the spy organization Spyral, kills Talia with a golden gun. Just as Damian was lured into a kill box in issue #1 and the world's greatest assassins were in issue #4, Talia has been led into her own kill box here. Kathy thanks Batman saying, "Some people actually do own the world. We've been closing in on Talia al Ghul for a long time. Thanks for helping us lead her into a trap she couldn't escape."

In terms of the overall story, Spyral's involvement is interesting because it suggests that Batman was never really in control at all. He was just a knight in a game of chess between Kathy and Talia. It's a shocking revelation that the game that has been played across both volumes of *Batman, Inc.* was all a ruse and the central player was Kathy Kane, the first person to steal Batman's style.

But Spyral can also be interpreted as Morrison's frustration with his own lack of control in Batman's fate. As Kathy leaves, she tells Batman, "It all comes

full circle in the end, Bruce... stick to what you do best. And don't try to fir ___.
I don't exist."

Kathy is the voice of critical fans who believe Batman has gone too far and needs to stop being so fun and absurd. She is the symbol of DC Editorial taking Batman back to the status quo before Morrison stepped into the writer's chair on *Batman*. Spyral is the spirit of comics and their nature to always return to the basics after too long in new worlds and ideas.

There's a certain sense of anti-climax at the conclusion to Morrison's time with Batman. Batman doesn't defeat the main villain, he doesn't disarm the bombs around the world, and it's revealed that he was never really in control at all. We've learned that Talia and Damian are the two graves Bruce saw in his visions, but their bodies have been taken which opens the possibility of their return. Bruce Wayne was arrested in issue #1 and interrogated in this issue, but Spyral erases all of the charges brought against him. There are no consequences to the conclusion of Morrison's time on Batman and everything resets to previous continuity once again. But Morrison is an optimistic writer and his conclusion can be interpreted optimistically as well.

Batman may not have directly saved the day, but Batman's influence did. The members of Batman Incorporated saved the world, Kathy Kane stopped Talia, Jason Todd saved Batman – all of these elements are possible because of Batman's influence. Bruce Wayne may not have been responsible for a victory in the end, but Batman is more than Bruce Wayne; Batman is everywhere. Batman is not alone. The bat-sigil is not a meaningless symbol; it inspires individuals to do good and will continue to do so for years to come.

Finally, Commissioner Gordon's final words are both a funeral elegy and a message of hope for the future of Batman, "Batman always comes back, bigger and better, shiny and new. Batman never dies. It never ends. It probably never will." This era of Batman is over, but if Batman is eternal, then something else will come along and be just as wild, bizarre, and beautiful as Morrison's run.

While the issue could have ended there, Morrison ends with a brilliant two-page epilogue. With his daughter dead, Ra's al Ghul has returned to rebuild the League of Assassins. He declares his revenge, as a scientist explains that they will use Lord Death Man's "Lazarus blood" and says that "Talia's nursery is intact." The final page reveals a room of test-tube baby Damians and Ra's al Ghul commanding "Sons of Batman. Rise!"

Ra's al Ghul reveals the Sons of Batman. The final page of *Batman, Inc.* Vol. 2 #13 [Sept 2013]. Art by Chris Burnham. Copyright © DC Comics.

The motif of generational conflict is present in these last pages. Leviathan was a new generation of crime, but it has fallen apart just as the new generation of Batman stories has reverted to the old ways again. The older generation has destroyed the new as Ra's al Ghul has regained power, but his army of the sons of Batman offers a promising future that could result in wild, wonderful stories.

Batman is always being reborn. Gordon is right: Batman's story never ends.

Appendix: A Chronology of Grant Morrison's Batman

All issues written by Grant Morrison unless otherwise noted.

Part 1: Batman

1. "Batman & Son, Part 1: Building a Better Batmobile" (*Batman* Vol. 1 #655, Sept 2006). Art by Andy Kubert.
2. "Batman & Son, Part 2: Man-Bats of London" (*Batman* Vol. 1 #656, Oct 2006). Pencils by Andy Kubert. Inks by Jesse Delperdang.
3. "Batman & Son, Part 3: Wonderboys" (*Batman* Vol. 1 #657, Nov 2006). Pencils by Andy Kubert. Inks by Jesse Delperdang.
4. "Batman & Son, Part 4: Absent Fathers" (*Batman* Vol. 1 #658, Dec 2006). Pencils by Andy Kubert. Inks by Jesse Delperdang.
5. "The Clown at Midnight" (*Batman* Vol. 1 #663, Apr 2007). Art by John Van Fleet.
6. "Three Ghosts of Batman" (*Batman* Vol. 1 #664, May 2007). Pencils by Andy Kubert. Inks by Jesse Delperdang.
7. "The Black Casebook" (*Batman* Vol. 1 #665, June 2007). Pencils by Andy Kubert. Inks by Jesse Delperdang.
8. "Batman in Bethlehem" (*Batman* Vol. 1 #666, July 2007). Pencils by Andy Kubert. Inks by Jesse Delperdang.
9. "The Island of Mister Mayhew" (*Batman* Vol. 1 #667, Aug 2007). Art by J.H. Williams III.
10. "Now We Are Dead!" (*Batman* Vol. 1 #668, Sept 2007). Art by J.H. Williams III.
11. "The Dark Knight Must Die!" (*Batman* Vol. 1 #669, Nov 2007). Art by J.H. Williams III.
12. "A Prelude to the Resurrection of Ra's al Ghul: Lazarus Rising" (*Batman* Vol. 1 #670, Dec 2007). Pencils by Tony S. Daniel. Inks by Jonathan Glapion.

13. **"The Resurrection of Ra's al Ghul, Part 4 of 7"** (*Batman* Vol. 1 #671, Jan 2008). Pencils by Tony S. Daniel. Inks by Jonathan Glapion.

14. **"Space Medicine"** (*Batman* Vol. 1 #672, Feb 2008). Pencils by Tony S. Daniel. Inks by Tony Daniel, Sandu Florea, Jonathan Glapion, and Mark Irwin.

15. **"Joe Chill in Hell"** (*Batman* Vol. 1 #673, Mar 2008). Pencils by Tony S. Daniel. Inks by Jonathan Glapion and Sandu Florea.

16. **"Batman Dies at Dawn"** (*Batman* Vol. 1 #674, Apr 2008). Pencils by Tony S. Daniel. Inks by Sandu Florea.

17. **"The Fiend with Nine Eyes"** (*Batman* Vol. 1 #675, May 2008). Pencils by Ryan Benjamin. Inks by Saleem Crawford.

17.5. **Untitled Sequence** (in *DC Universe* #0, June 2008). Pencils by Tony S. Daniel. A prologue to "R.I.P."

18. **"Midnight in the House of Hurt"** (*Batman* Vol. 1 #676, June 2008). Pencils by Tony S. Daniel. Inks by Sandu Florea.

19. **"Batman in the Underworld"** (*Batman* Vol. 1 #677, July 2008). Pencils by Tony S. Daniel. Inks by Sandu Florea.

20. **"Zur En Arrh"** (*Batman* Vol. 1 #678, Aug 2008). Pencils by Tony S. Daniel. Inks by Sandu Florea.

21. **"Miracle on Crime Alley"** (*Batman* Vol. 1 #679, Sept 2008). Pencils by Tony S. Daniel. Inks by Sandu Florea.

22. **"The Thin White Duke of Death"** (*Batman* Vol. 1 #680, Oct 2008). Pencils by Tony S. Daniel. Inks by Sandu Florea.

23. **"Hearts in Darkness"** (*Batman* Vol. 1 #681, Dec 2008). Pencils by Tony S. Daniel. Inks by Sandu Florea.

24. **"The Butler Did It"** (*Batman* Vol. 1 #682, Early January 2009). Pencils by Lee Garbett. Inks by Trevor Scott.

25. **"What the Butler Saw"** (*Batman* Vol. 1 #683, Late January 2009), Pencils by Lee Garbett. Inks by Trevor Scott.

26. **"R.I.P. The Missing Chapter, Part One: The Hole in Things"** (*Batman* Vol. 1 #701, Sept 2010). Art by Tony Daniel.

27. **"R.I.P. The Missing Chapter, Part Two: Batman's Last Case"** (*Batman* Vol. 1 #702, Oct 2010). Art by Tony Daniel.

Part 2: Batman and Robin

1. **"Batman Reborn, Part One: Domino Effect"** (*Batman and Robin* #1, Aug 2009). Art by Frank Quitely.

2. **"Batman Reborn, Part Two: The Circus of Strange"** (*Batman and Robin* #2, Sept 2009). Art by Frank Quitely.

3. **"Batman Reborn, Part Three: Mommy Made of Nails"** (*Batman and Robin* #3, Oct 2009). Art by Frank Quitely.

4. **"Revenge of the Red Hood, Part One: Red Right Hand"** (*Batman and Robin* #4, Nov 2009). Pencils by Philip Tan. Inks by Jonathan Glapion.

5. **"Revenge of the Red Hood, Part Two: Scarlet"** (*Batman and Robin* #5, Dec 2009). Pencils by Philip Tan. Inks by Jonathan Glapion.

6. **"Revenge of the Red Hood, Part Three: Flamingo is Here"** (*Batman and Robin* #6, Jan 2010). Pencils by Philip Tan. Inks by Jonathan Glapion.

7. **"Blackest Knight, Part One: Pearly and the Pit"** (*Batman and Robin* #7, March 2010). Art by Cameron Stewart.

8. **"Blackest Knight, Part Two: Batman vs. Batman"** (*Batman and Robin* #8, Early Apr 2010). Art by Cameron Stewart.

9. "Blackest Knight, Part Three: Broken" (*Batman and Robin* #9, Late April 2010). Art by Cameron Stewart.

10. "Batman vs. Robin, Part One: The Haunting of Wayne Manor" (*Batman and Robin* #10, May 2010). Pencils by Andy Clarke. Inks by Scott Hanna.

11. "Batman vs. Robin, Part Two: Boneyard" (*Batman and Robin* #11, June 2010). Pencils by Andy Clarke. Inks by Scott Hanna.

12. "Batman vs. Robin, Part Three: Mexican Train" (*Batman and Robin* #12, July 2010). Art by Andy Clarke, and Dustin Nguyen. Inks by Scott Hanna.

13. "Time and the Batman" (*Batman* Vol. 1 #700, Aug 2010). Divided into sections. "Yesterday," art by Tony Daniel. "Today," art by Frank Quitely and Scott Kolins. "Tomorrow," art by Andy Kubert. "And Tomorrow...", pencils by David Finch and inks by Richard Friend. "Batman Gallery," art by Shane Davis, Juan Doe, Guillem March, Dustin Nguyen, Tim Sale, Bill Sienkiewicz, and Philip Tan. "Secrets of the Batcave," designs by Freddie Williams II.

14. "Batman and Robin Must Die! Part One: The Garden of Death" (*Batman and Robin* #13, Aug 2010). Art by Frazier Irving.

15. "Batman and Robin Must Die! Part Two: The Triumph of Death" (*Batman and Robin* #14, Oct 2010). Art by Frazier Irving.

16. "Batman and Robin Must Die! Part Three: The Knight, Death, and the Devil" (*Batman and Robin* #15, Dec 2010). Art by Frazier Irving.

17. "Shadow on Stone" (*Batman: The Return of Bruce Wayne* #1, Early July 2010). Pencils by Chris Sprouse. Inks by Karl Story.

18. "Until the End of Time" (*Batman: The Return of Bruce Wayne* #2, Late July 2010). Art by Frazier Irving.

19. "The Bones of Bristol Bay" (*Batman: The Return of Bruce Wayne* #3, Aug 2010). Pencils by Yanick Paquette. Inks by Michel Lacombe.

20. "Dark Night, Dark Rider" (*Batman: The Return of Bruce Wayne* #4, Sept 2010). Pencils by George Jeanty. Inks by Walden Wong.

21. "Masquerade" (*Batman: The Return of Bruce Wayne* #5, Nov 2010). Pencils by Ryan Sook and Pere Perez. Inks by Mick Gray.

22. "The All-Over" (*Batman: The Return of Bruce Wayne* #6, Dec 2010). Pencils by Lee Garbett and Pere Perez. Inks by Alejandro Sicat and Walden Wong.

23. "Black Mass" (*Batman and Robin* #16, Early Jan 2011). Art by Cameron Stewart, Chris Burnham, and Frazier Irving.

Part 3: Batman, Inc.

1. "Planet Gotham" (*Batman: The Return* #1, January 2011). Pencils by David Finch. Inks by Batt and Ryan Winn.

2. "Mr. Unknown is Dead" (*Batman, Inc.* Vol. 1 #1, Jan 2011). Pencils by Yanick Paquette. Inks by Michel Lacombe.

3. "Resurrector!" (*Batman, Inc.* Vol. 1 #2, Feb 2011). Pencils by Yanick Paquette. Inks by Michel Lacombe.

4. "Scorpion Tango" (*Batman, Inc.* Vol. 1 #3, Mar 2011). Pencils by Yanick Paquette and Pere Perez. Inks by Michel Lacombe.

5. "The Kane Affair" (*Batman, Inc.* Vol. 1 #4, April 2011). Art by Chris Burnham.

6. "Master Spy" (*Batman, Inc.* Vol. 1 #5, May 2011). Pencils by Yanick Paquette. Inks by Michel Lacombe.

7. "Nyktomorph" (*Batman, Inc.* Vol. 1 #6, June 2011). Art by Chris Burnham.

8. "Medicine Soldiers" (*Batman, Inc.* Vol. 1 #7, July 2011). Art by Chris Burnham.

9. **"Nightmares in Numberland"** (*Batman, Inc.* **Vol. 1 #8, Aug 2011**). Art by Scott Clark and Dave Beaty.

10. **"Leviathan Strikes!"** (*Batman, Inc.: Leviathan Strikes!* **#1, Feb 2012**). Chapter one art by Cameron Stewart. Chapter two art by Chris Burnham.

11. **"Batman Incorporated: Leviathan, Part One: Demon Star"** (*Batman, Inc.* **Vol. 2 #1, July 2012**). Art by Chris Burnham.

12. **"Eye of the Gorgon"** (*Batman, Inc.* **Vol. 2 #2, Aug 2012**). Art by Chris Burnham.

13. **"The Hanged Man"** (*Batman, Inc.* **Vol. 2 #3, Sept 2012**). Art by Chris Burnham.

14. **"Brand Building"** (*Batman, Inc.* **Vol. 2 #0, Nov 2012**). Written by Chris Burnham and Grant Morrison. Art by Frazier Irving.

15. **"Kill Box"** (*Batman, Inc.* **Vol. 2 #4, Dec 2012**). Art by Chris Burnham.

16. **"Asylum"** (*Batman, Inc.* **Vol. 2 #5, Jan 2013**). Art by Chris Burnham.

17. **"Garland of Skulls"** (*Batman, Inc.* **Vol. 2 #6, Feb 2013**). Art by Chris Burnham.

18. **"Belly of the Whale"** (*Batman, Inc.* **Vol. 2 #7, Mar 2013**). Art by Chris Burnham and Jason Masters.

19. **"The Boy Wonder Returns"** (*Batman, Inc.* **Vol. 2 #8, Apr 2013**). Art by Chris Burnham and Jason Masters.

20. **"Fallen Son"** (*Batman, Inc.* **Vol. 2 #9, May 2013**). Art by Chris Burnham and Jason Masters.

21. **"Gotham's Most Wanted"** (*Batman, Inc.* **Vol. 2 #10, June 2013**). Art by Chris Burnham, Jason Masters, and Andrei Bressan.

22. **"Interlude: A Bird in the Hand"** (*Batman, Inc.* **Vol. 2 #11, July 2013**). Written by Chris Burnham. Art by Jorge Lucas.

23. **"Fatherless"** (*Batman, Inc.* **Vol. 2 #12, Aug 2013**). Art by Chris Burnham.

24. **"The Dark Knight and the Devil's Daughter"** (*Batman, Inc.* **Vol. 2 #13, Sept 2013**). Art by Chris Burnham.

Grant Morrison Responds

Grant Morrison was kind enough to read this book in manuscript form and answer questions from the author. Because Morrison had already discussed Batman for our 2010 documentary film *Grant Morrison: Talking with Gods*, the author prepared his interview using the relevant portions of those transcripts in order to avoid duplication. This earlier material has been integrated where appropriate and may be clearly distinguished as being in response to the film's director, Patrick Meaney. The publisher wishes to thank all involved, especially Grant and Kristan Morrison.

CODY WALKER: Before your recent seven-year stretch writing Batman stories, you wrote *Arkham Asylum: A Serious House on a Serious Earth* (1989), and he was a member of your '90s *JLA* series. How has your perception of Batman changed over the years?

GRANT MORRISON: I'm not sure how much it's really changed. I see Batman as a character with many faces and facets, and each time I've approached him, I've tried to show a different angle, and one appropriate to the story I want to tell.

Batman in *Arkham Asylum* is more reflective of the '80s paranoid loner portrayal that seemed to arise partly as a response to Frank Miller's work, even though Miller does not write Batman as a paranoid loner but as an operatic larger-than-life hero.

In "Gothic," I was trying to make plain some links between the character and the earliest examples of Gothic fiction, which I was reading a lot of at the time, so this was Batman through the lens of Horace Walpole and Monk Lewis.

The *JLA* stories had Batman on a team of super-heroes, so I wanted to play up the "optimum man" idea of a human being capable of taking his place at the table alongside a modern version of the gods on Olympus. In *JLA*, I played up Batman's super-competence and his ability to work just as well within a larger sci-fi or super-hero context.

The long run I completed last year was my attempt to tell a story featuring all the various portrayals of Batman through the years, while making it seem psychologically believable that one man could have these different "personalities." Even the apparent contradictions between things like the Adam West Batman, say, and the Denny O'Neil Batman simply made him more rounded, complicated, and convincing.

WALKER: Prior to your first issue on *Batman* (or perhaps during it, considering the publication schedule), Bruce Wayne had undergone a change during *52*. How was that change important to your run?

MORRISON: I made it important in the sense that I wanted to build on everything that had gone before, and I was lucky enough to find myself in a position in DC continuity where Batman had decided to take some time off to recharge his batteries and renew his dedication to the fight against crime. I picked up a Batman who seemed ready and willing to change, after being immersed in many years of often quite downbeat stories set in a very real, grubby, violent world of misery and pain.

WALKER: Transformation seems to be a common motif throughout your time with Batman (the Joker's transformation into the Clown at Midnight, Dick Grayson into Batman, Bruce Wayne into Bat-God, etc.). Given how certain elements of super-heroes are static, why do you have such an emphasis on change?

MORRISON: It's more fun. I'm interested in the pliability of super-hero characters, which allows them to survive and still seem relevant through decades of social change. A static character wouldn't survive as long as Batman or Superman, and to imagine a single monolithic approach to Batman seems counter-productive. I like stories that twist and turn, especially when I know everything will be restored to the status quo by the next big retcon.

PATRICK MEANEY: Before "Batman R.I.P." came out, you said that it would be the biggest shock in 70 years of Batman, and I think most people were confused or uncertain about that.

MORRISON: The reason they were sort of confused or uncertain was because I wanted them to be confused and uncertain. And the biggest shock is that Thomas Wayne is trying to kill his son. That's the biggest shock there is: Dad didn't die. Or did he? So "Batman R.I.P." basically leaves you with a proposition that either the Devil has just tested Batman by pretending to be his father or Bruce Wayne's father is still alive and is pretending to be the Devil in order to destroy his son. Either way, it's pretty fucked up, but that's what I wanted people to think. The big shock / reveal that I promised to get people excited about was that his dad was going to be alive and be the villain, but that to me wasn't good enough as a story because it didn't leave those spaces. It didn't leave the chance for debate. It didn't allow people to go online and shout at one another, "It's not the Devil! It can't possibly be the Devil! It can't possibly be Thomas Wayne!" Those are the only two choices, and people can't believe either of them, which makes "Batman R.I.P." quite interesting.

MEANEY: Was the original plan for it to be Thomas Wayne?

MORRISON: No, the original plan was for it always to be Thomas Wayne *or* the Devil; you don't know because Dr. Hurt behaves like the Devil. I said to people at the start that it was the ultimate diabolical mastermind. Well, who is the ultimate diabolical mastermind? The diabolist himself, the Devil. So it was kind of posited upfront as "Here is my idea of the greatest Batman story ever: Batman up against the Devil *and* he beats him." But at the same time, the big shock in this might be that the Devil is his dad. There's your big continuity shock for people who want that kind of stuff. I wanted to give everybody everything with it and then allow them to fight over what they just read in the same way that people fight over the meanings of the gospels.

MEANEY: In *Final Crisis* and particularly in "Batman R.I.P.", a lot of it seemed to be interacting with the internet and people's takes on the material. It was almost as central as the material itself. Is that an evolution of the hyper-sigil idea?

MORRISON: Yeah, the whole idea of the "Batman R.I.P." and the *Final Crisis* stuff and the particular way it was done was really inspired by *The Invisibles* and the kind of culture that grew around *The Invisibles* that existed outside the book and outside my life. Where other people were reading it and taking it on and doing their own things and creating their own artworks that expressed similar kinds of feelings. And what interested me about *The Invisibles* was the way it *had* taken on that life beyond itself. There are websites where people are still discussing it and still talking about it. I got fascinated with the way people interpreted work, and I thought that became the most interesting part of it to me, even though sometimes they interpret it in ways which drive me nuts and seem completely wrong. That's part of the process of putting ideas out. And watching shows like *Lost* and those kinds of things, which have a large extra-narrative participation going on.

So we've got to think, especially with the super-hero comics, there was an element of that that was worth actually bringing into the creation of the comics. It seemed to be really interesting to go for that deliberately; to do a Batman story that implicated Batman's publishing history, so that you would have to go and read up old comics and reintroduce some people to material that maybe they wouldn't have considered before. It's actually quite interesting just because it's from a different time and it's still got something that's worth getting into, and I wanted to bring that in. I wanted to force people to be on Wikipedia looking up obscure tales from Dzogchen Buddhism to understand stories.

In "Batman R.I.P.", the debate around "Who was the Black Glove?" wasn't really an important question at all, but it was made to seem important. And I wanted people to think and to talk and to create stories of their own in their heads and narratives of their own, to the point where – you know those guys on the Mindless Ones website? They're actually writing their own Batman comics based on little snippets that have inspired them. It was to do that and to see how much of that you could play with; how much could you implicate in the creation of the works the people who were reading them and the writer himself and having a kind of dialogue almost. When I would see people's crazy ideas like, "Oh, you think Alfred did it? Okay, I'm going to make you think Alfred did it for an issue." Suddenly, you realize it's *not* Alfred, and everyone's scrabbling about looking for the source of the mystery and talking to one another and debating and getting angry.

You know, with *Final Crisis*, it seemed like the internet practically went to war over it. There were people on one side saying, "This is genius, this is ground-breaking, progressive," and other people just, "This is gibberish. I have no idea what's going on. This is unfair. You shouldn't be allowed to do this." And it was so polarized, you know? It really did the job I wanted it to do but maybe not exactly in the way that I imagined, *(chuckles)* but I think it works. I think it's the way those types of books should be done – to acknowledge that participation and to acknowledge the fact that the comic is an artifact in your hands that is brought to life by being in someone *else's* hands who then applies their consciousness to it and extracts emotions and meanings, or not, depending on who they are.

MEANEY: Do you see the Thogal part of *Batman* as a way of sneaking magic and meditation as a transformative experience into a more accessible narrative for people to consume?

MORRISON: Yeah, definitely. I mean, putting all that stuff in something like *Batman* is a way of forcing people – who wouldn't really care otherwise – to go online and suddenly start reading about Dzogchen Buddhism. And Dzogchen Buddhism is one of the most amazing philosophical systems on the planet. It's so chilly and so rational. I used it as the basis of the Kryptonians in *All Star Superman*, because I figured that a rational enlightenment culture would get to this kind of place. And they're really quite stark; their ideas about death and the afterlife – very stark and almost frightening. But I really think they're onto something that's very scientific and rationalistic. So yeah, to get people to look at that kind of thing, to realize that there's an actual system of thought in our world that deals with stuff that we don't usually like to think about – entire systems of what happens in the last four days of life, every single moment right up until your death and then beyond. And it's so beautifully worked out and so creepily laid out. It's just "This is what happens. You better be ready for it." They seem to know stuff that we kind of avoid, because we don't like to think that closely about death. That stuff is really interesting to draw people's attention to, because it might be useful to them.

MEANEY: Does lacing that into the character's history make it eternal because it'll always be a part of Batman and it'll always exist?

MORRISON: I guess there's always a part of Batman that other writers may not go back to or ever refer to, because it's not an area that *they're* comfortable with. But to me it seemed like, with Batman, we've been told that this guy traveled the world and learned every single martial art and he's mastered all kinds of meditative disciplines. He can slow down his heart, he can do things that only the best yogans on the planet are capable of, so I have to assume that he's also absorbed some of that philosophy while he was learning to do what he can do. For me, it made Batman a bigger character and kind of aligned him more with someone like the King Mob character. But Batman's even cooler because King Mob's got a lot of personal problems. It just seemed to be that's who Batman would be if he were the greatest physical specimen on Earth and the greatest mental specimen on Earth – then you're going to be slightly above and beyond all of us. He has to be more Dalai Lama than the Dalai Lama as well.

MEANEY: Do you feel like "Batman R.I.P." is an attempt to make Batman more like a surreal, Doom Patrol sort of hero?

MORRISON: Nah, not really. That was just more subjecting the ultimate sorted man against the ultimate chaos. No, I wasn't really trying to make him like that. You can *never* make him like that, because Batman isn't flawed like that. He's got his flaws, but ultimately he's a guy that has transcended. Those super characters are more difficult to write on that level, because they don't have the same fuck-ups as us. They don't eat the same biscuits as we do, you know? They don't really get on the bus, but the Doom Patrol did, and Animal Man is kind of the same, I think. People still identify with them because they were all more human. With the Batman and Superman stuff, it's more academic slightly. You're dealing with characters who're not nearly human at all, and you're having to find other ways to make that work.

MEANEY: What would you say to someone who's like "*Final Crisis* might have a hopeful end, but the vast majority of it is awful things," and what does that do to put that out in the culture?

MORRISON: It's basically to rub people's noses in it, I think. When they asked me to do *Final Crisis*, they said, "You're following on this *Countdown* series," and part of *Countdown* was that Mary Marvel turns bad, and that, to me, just seemed ridiculous. This kid's cartoon character turned bad, and suddenly she's got a short skirt on and she's prancing about insulting people. But I thought "OK, if you really want this crap, I'll give it to you. I'll show you what happens when Mary Marvel turns bad." And I took all the worst aspects of Britney Spears's breakdown and, you know, cosmetic surgery, and we just rammed it onto this poor character who didn't deserve any of it. But it was kind of to make people gag and to show them that, behind Mary Marvel in a short black skirt, there are middle-aged men leading. And so that became explicit, and the dark Mary Marvel in *Final Crisis* quite literally was an evil, middle-aged old god behind her eyes leading her enjoyment of this.

So yeah, I wanted to rub people's noses in it, and I wanted to take those elements of comics and boost them up, but at the same time to show that what we've got is super-heroes, and super-heroes will always defeat that. So if Darkseid is a feeling – if Darkseid is, as I saw it, the feeling prevalent in the culture – where there's a judgmental quality to everything, you know? Where you pick up a magazine and every actress is "You're too thin. You're too fat." Or you go online and "You're too stupid. You're too smart. You're too this." Everybody is too *something*, and ultimately it's just too *human*, which is what's sad about it. It's an accusation, you know? It's "This is not done right. This is how it should be. This is this." It's that strange entitlement culture, and I wanted to bring out all that onto the page and kind of make people squirm a little bit. And then show our super-heroes gently unlocking all those dark things and exposing Darkseid as just a horrible bad feeling, a self-loathing, a kind of dying hatred. That was the hope I was giving, because it was written from within a culture that seemed to be on a course of absolute self-destruction. And I had to be showing that "OK this is how it feels to be on the course of absolute self-destruction. Did you want to go there? Do you want to fall ass down?" And ultimately of course, you don't. What you want is President Superman and multiple worlds and hope.

MEANEY: Who's the most toxic character you've encountered? Like the opposite of Superman?

MORRISON: Lex Luthor is a kind of opposite, but he's not. He's quite – Spartacus Hughes in *The Filth*, I think, is my best bad guy. Just the idea of a viral man, and you just swallow him, and you become him, and he's a bastard, you know? He's just everything that's a bastard. But even *he* had some flair about him.

What you notice, I think, in this decade was that I started doing baddies that were badder. Because I used to always do baddies who were kind of absurd, and I always thought of evil as absurd. And then I saw that evil is not absurd. Evil is really bad, *(chuckles)* and evil wants to hurt us. Evil doesn't like us, and there are a lot of people out there who carry that current, and they would be happy to see people sad. They'd be happy to see me broken on my knees and no job. They would love it! They would *actually* love it. And to know that is like *(gasps to illustrate)*.

So people are Darkseid and Dr. Hurt; those were the characters that come out of thinking there are actually people out there who would *really* want to see you fucked up. They would cheer, you know? And I didn't really think they existed before. I thought ultimately you could make friends with everyone and get them to laugh. And somehow *(chuckles)* it doesn't work like that.

WALKER: *Batman: The Return* begins the motif of a generational conflict by telling the story of the bat that inspired Bruce to become Batman battling younger bats. This motif continues throughout *Batman, Inc.*, with Leviathan recruiting youth into its numbers. You previously explored this type of conflict in *Zenith*, but this time there is a sense that the old will always win out. How have your beliefs changed regarding this conflict, and how does *Batman, Inc.* reflect those beliefs?

MORRISON: In the upcoming *Annihilator* book with Frazer Irving, we approach the same conflict from a different angle. So it's not so much that my views have changed but simply that I've tried to see the world through the eyes of many different kinds of characters. When I'm writing about rebellious young firebrands, I try to put myself in their shoes and to see the world as they see it. When I'm writing about a principled, WASP super-billionaire with his own multinational company, then I try my best to view the world from his perspective. In Batman stories, it's old money, sophistication, and the status quo that always wins against derangement and disorder. Having said that, Batman himself is a transgressive, quasi-Satanic figure of the night, so he gets away with being a capitalist because he's cool and sexy and a bit dangerous.

If anything, I feel more comfortable with the Joker – leaving aside his cruelty and homicidal psychosis, I feel very at home writing the Joker's stream-of-consciousness, seemingly non-sequitur but super-meaningful and allusive dialogue.

WALKER: In your relaunch of *Wildcats*, you explored the idea of a grown-up power fantasy where super-heroes create a corporation to save the world, and many of those ideas are fleshed out *Batman, Inc.* Do you think the altruistic corporation is a power fantasy or is that a possibility? In other words, is there any hope for capitalism to be used heroically? After all, Batman may use his wealth to combat crime, but there are moments in your run that the reader is left sympathizing with the downtrodden (Joe Chill, Goatboy) or led to think that his wealth will do no good (Chief Man-of-Bats's reservation).

MORRISON: Batman / Bruce Wayne is the hero of Batman stories, therefore everything he does must be looked at from a heroic angle and considered as part of his war on crime. Do I think there can be such a thing as an ethical, altruistic corporation? In the real world, probably not, but in a universe of super-heroes and villains, a corporation like Wayne Enterprises is simply another weapon in Batman's crime-fighting arsenal.

WALKER: Another motif is the use of corporate logos as sigils. The Bat-symbol is the most obvious sigil (that is meant to be the anti-crime), but along the way, Jason Todd tries his hand at viral marketing to make his Red Hood brand powerful and Talia uses a number of different goddesses to form the Leviathan identity. How do the Red Hood and Leviathan sigils compare to the Bat-sigil, and why are they failures compared to Batman's success?

MORRISON: Leviathan bases its iconography very deliberately on threatening, devouring images of destructive motherhood, so we used as Leviathan's banner a version of the Kali Yantra but with Nazi flag colors. We also used the Ouroboros serpent, the Red Queen, the Wire Mother, and various other images relating to terrifying female archetypes. The Red Hood's attempts to market his crime-busting identity are quite perfunctory and barely thought out. We wanted him to seem a little desperate and ridiculous. They are both failures to the extent that they're trying too hard to replicate what came naturally and organically to Bruce Wayne and Batman.

WALKER: The first chapter of *Batman, Inc.: Leviathan Strikes!* uses pop stars as models for assassins, and it's such an interesting commentary on pop iconography. Why did you address pop stars specifically?

MORRISON: The story was about a school where young girls are trained to become sexy ninja bodyguards for rich men and criminals. Stephanie Brown describes her time there with the words, "All I see are young girls under the spell of unrealistic and unhealthy role models." These were words I'd seen applied in the real world to the young fans of overtly sexualized pop singers like Rihanna and Lady Gaga, so it seemed apposite and amusing to draw the teachers at the "School of Night" to resemble some well-known pop divas.

WALKER: How did the advent of the New 52 change plans for the remainder of *Batman Incorporated*? Due to the reboot, were there characters you wanted to use that you couldn't any longer?

MORRISON: I would have done a bit more with the Stephanie Brown Batgirl character, and I wanted to use Cassandra Cain as Blackbat, but those characters were taken off the table when the New 52 initiative started up and recreated DC history all around me.

WALKER: You've said before that you have an entire history of Knight and Squire mapped out in your head. Would you mind sharing some of that history that we didn't get to see?

MORRISON: I had a story entitled "London's Burning" which was all about Spring-Heeled Jack (a crazed member of the British Royal Family who takes on a villainous identity and functions as a Knight and Squire's "Joker" or "Moriarty" style arch-nemesis). Spring-Heeled Jack murdered the original Knight, of course, and we delved into Cyril Sheldrake's fall from grace after the death of his father. Cyril blows his inheritance on drink, drugs, gambling, and girls and winds up in the gutter, where Beryl Hutchinson finds him. He gets cleaned up and takes on his father's mantle as the Knight of England, with Beryl as his Squire. It was a big, heartwarming adventure story about class and redemption, etc., etc.

WALKER: Were there any characters from *Batman, Inc.* that you wanted to write more about? Who was your favorite?

MORRISON: I liked all of them, especially El Gaucho, who was one of those characters that came to life and developed an energy all his own. I really like Man-of-Bats and Raven too. Having said that, I probably wrote about as much as I'd want to about those characters.

WALKER: I'm interested in the minor characters you introduced in *Batman*, particularly Michael Lane (who started as the Third Ghost of Batman and later became the new Azrael), Ellie (the girl in the Ragged Robin makeup from *The Invisibles*), and the Kollektiv. How do these these characters fit into the Bat-mythos?

MORRISON: They were characters who started out as supporting players and somehow developed a momentum that made them worthwhile revisiting. Ellie was no more than a very minor player, an underage prostitute in an alley. Batman gives her a Wayne Industries card and tells her to get a job. I could have left it there — as a simple demonstration of Batman's attempts to use all his resources to help the victims of crime — but I chose to go back to Ellie, so that we could see how that night in the alley had actually changed her life and how that one small kindness winds up saving the world.

WALKER: Jason Todd was an incredibly strong villain and foil for Dick Grayson in *Batman and Robin*, so it came as a shock when he was revealed as Wingman. Why was his redemption necessary?

MORRISON: It made a lot of sense within the context of my wider story. Whatever else he's been, Jason Todd was once considered worthy of being Robin, so there's a lot more to him than just some ranting, raving super-criminal. As with the other characters, I wanted to take his whole history into account. It seemed to me that Bruce Wayne wouldn't want a rogue agent out there and would, in fact, do everything he could to bring Jason back into the fold where he could keep an eye on him, if nothing else. The restoration of the fallen Robin to active status as one of Batman's allies fit with the themes of my story. Jason is the prodigal son of the Batman family, and eventually the prodigal son has to be welcomed back home.

WALKER: The first issue of your *Batman* run was titled "Building a Better Batmobile," and throughout your run the Batmobile seemed to be a metaphor for the changing nature of Batman. *Batman and Robin* seemed to continue this idea with a new and improved flying Batmobile that reflected the wild, pop adventures of the new dynamic duo. Yet *Batman, Inc.* never featured a new Batmobile. Was this a practical decision, given the global adventures of the hero, or was it reflective of a larger theme?

MORRISON: Actually, I think Chris Burnham did design a new Batmobile which appears first in *Batman, Inc.* #6. We also see another Batmobile under canvas in our final issue, representing the fact that there will always be a "better Batmobile."

WALKER: The week before your run on *Batman, Inc.* ended, Newsarama ran an interview with you in which you said of the final issue: "to a certain extent it destroys the concept of Batman." What did you mean by that? Is it because Spyral is a larger idea than Batman and Kathy Kane saves the day rather than Batman?

MORRISON: There's a bit of that. Spyral is this huge, global, covert organization run by a woman from Batman's past who shouldn't even exist. Ultimately, Batman becomes a pawn in a power game between two strong women, both of whom relegate Batman to a childish world of dress-up, play, and repeat. Next to them, his mission, his world, and his ambitions seem small and somewhat impotent.

WALKER: Looking back over your entire Batman run, what are you most proud of? And what do you wish you could change?

MORRISON: I'm glad I stuck with it and didn't leave after 15 issues as I'd originally intended. It was one of the most creatively-rewarding and engrossing projects I've ever undertaken at DC. I'm glad I was able to introduce Damian, the son of Batman, and make the character stick. I loved writing the adventures of Dick Grayson and Damian as Batman and Robin and felt they deserved a much longer run together. Other than that, there's nothing I'd do differently.

About the Author

Cody Walker graduated from Missouri State University with a Bachelors and a Masters of Science in Education. He is the author of the pop-culture website Popgun Chaos (PopgunChaos.com) and the co-creator of the super-hero crime comic, *Noir City* (NoirCityComicBook.com). He currently teaches high school English in Springfield, Missouri, where he resides with his wife Samantha, their son Duncan, and their two cats Falkor and Meow Meow Kittyface.

ALSO FROM **SEQUART**

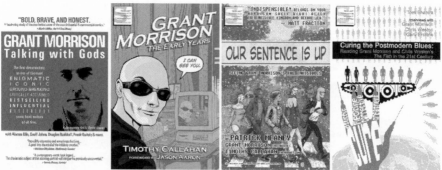

GRANT MORRISON: TALKING WITH GODS

GRANT MORRISON: THE EARLY YEARS

OUR SENTENCE IS UP: SEEING GRANT MORRISON'S *THE INVISIBLES*

CURING THE POSTMODERN BLUES: READING GRANT MORRISON AND CHRIS WESTON'S *THE FILTH* IN THE 21ST CENTURY

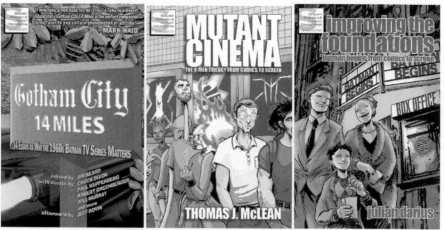

GOTHAM CITY 14 MILES: 14 ESSAYS ON WHY THE 1960s BATMAN TV SERIES MATTERS

MUTANT CINEMA: THE X-MEN TRILOGY FROM COMICS TO SCREEN

IMPROVING THE FOUNDATIONS: *BATMAN BEGINS* FROM COMICS TO SCREEN

WARREN ELLIS: CAPTURED GHOSTS
SHOT IN THE FACE: A SAVAGE JOURNEY TO THE HEART OF *TRANSMETROPOLITAN*
KEEPING THE WORLD STRANGE: A *PLANETARY* GUIDE
VOYAGE IN NOISE: WARREN ELLIS AND THE DEMISE OF WESTERN CIVILIZATION
WARREN ELLIS: THE CAPTURED GHOSTS INTERVIEWS

CLASSICS ON INFINITE EARTHS: THE JUSTICE LEAGUE AND DC CROSSOVER CANON
THE IMAGE REVOLUTION
COMICS IN FOCUS: CHRIS CLAREMONT'S X-MEN
THE WEIRDEST SCI-FI COMIC EVER MADE: UNDERSTANDING JACK KIRBY'S *2001: A SPACE ODYSSEY*

AND THE UNIVERSE SO BIG: UNDERSTANDING *BATMAN: THE KILLING JOKE*
MINUTES TO MIDNIGHT: TWELVE ESSAYS ON *WATCHMEN*
THE DEVIL IS IN THE DETAILS: EXAMINING MATT MURDOCK AND DAREDEVIL
TEENAGERS FROM THE FUTURE: ESSAYS ON THE LEGION OF SUPER-HEROES

For more information and for exclusive content, visit Sequart.org.

33346830R00164

Made in the USA
Lexington, KY
21 June 2014